To Walk the Dog

To Walk the Dog

Dr. Glen Welch

Copyright © 2020 by Dr. Glen F. Welch
All rights reserved

For Dora

You stood beside me through an Army career, a civil service career and even now, you seldom exhibit jealousy over the love I bestow on my characters. I may love them, but I always come home to you.

and for Vickie

Your encouragement and insights made this an easier read. Although you are gone, you are not forgotten but only missed – everyday.

Cast of Critters

Angie – Joe's supervisor

Darnell – A politically correct do-nothing boss

Dave – Joe's friend at GSA

Dr. Joseph O'Flaherty (Joe)

Eldana – Joe's co-worker at GSA, she has a spiritual gift

Felix – Ex-convict, food service worker, spiritual friend

General Smartwell, ("the general") – Joe's right hand in Clearing the swamp

Lorna – Another malevolent character, she is an expert only in Political Correctness and is the bricks and mortar of the swamp

Major Kim – Joe's boss for a while and servant to the ultimate critter

Mara – The malevolent one - she drives Joe away from the fort

Paul – Joe's contact at the rescue mission

Rebecca – Joe's first supervisor at the VA

Reggie – Engineer with few skills except being pleasant

Tibby – Joe's boss at GSA

Top – Joe's Army first sergeant. There is nobody Joe trusts more, enemy to the swamp

Lieutenant Colonel Dick – Joe's last Army supervisor

Foreword

What you are about to experience in the following pages is pure fiction, except for the parts that are not. Many of the incidents described here happened to *somebody*, even if not to the same somebody. Much of the book is the product of a fertile imagination. Other parts are real. The message from God happened just the way it is presented here. The final third part of the book is pure fiction which answers the questions "what if" or "why not." This book is about how your government agencies work. If you don't find it to your liking, it is up to *you* to do something about it.

Chapter One

The Aedes Aegypti, better known as the yellow fever mosquito, is considered the most dangerous animal in the world. By itself, it can pass diseases to anyone or any creature it sips on. Pathogens can range far and wide with its help. In groups it can easily be far more dangerous and is very difficult to fight. However, it is repelled by vitamin B. Since vitamin B is also necessary for intellectual health, could it be that smart people face a lower threat from mosquitoes?

"They hate me – don't they?" Dr. Joseph O'Flaherty was in charge but felt powerless as he watched the scene unfold on the street. It was ugly out there. The car honked as it swerved and then sped down the street. There were dozens of fists in the air – all of the protesters were mad.

The car driver was rattled without knowing why all those people were there. They had been there for days. Now, it was starting to get dangerous. When a protester is almost run over, it will never end well. They were thick out there – as thick as mosquitoes after a good rain – and had the traffic almost stopped on one of the city's busiest streets.

What was that they were holding? It looked like giant pins or nails. What did they plan to do with those? Effigy? Crucifixion? At least that would be something new. Joe saw it all but didn't care. Why should he? Another day that was just like the one before. *I hate this job and I hate this place.* Joe knew he couldn't say the words out loud. Everybody looked to him for leadership, for an example of positivity.

He just smiled though it came out as more of a pained look. Joe had always avoided big cities with their crowding, traffic, pollution, crime, and other problems. So, what was he doing here? He had asked himself this same question for three years now. Of course, he knew the answer but then, it still made no more sense than it had before. There were no rabbits or deer passing by. The air was reeking of car exhaust.

Crime, did I mention that before? He had to always look around to see if anybody was sleeping on or under his car before he could leave. Of course, now he had to check his car out anyway for that other reason.

Glancing up at the overcast sky, Joe realized that the weather matched his mood – gray, and the sun was nowhere to be seen. In the Army, they had called it AWOL – absent without leave. The signs the protesters carried were all about him. He no longer felt anger at the signs. He should feel *something* but there was nothing. Why couldn't he feel something? Anger, sadness, joy – *anything* would do. Maybe this was what depression felt like. Joe had been here now for about three years.

The excitement was long gone. The pay was still good, more than Joe had ever received in his life. It was better than most Americans got, but money had never driven Joe. Lately, he wondered how he got here. Why was he still here? He wanted to leave but how? For an old soldier like Joe, the boss says when the mission is done. Joe knew he would stay until he was released or relieved.

God, please let that be soon. I'm just so tired. Facing the window, Joe noted the increasing rain clouds and prayed they would produce rain – a lot of it. He even saw it in his mind. Maybe he could will it to happen?

A sudden downpour and the protesters were running for their cars. A few lightning strikes and they were moving even faster. The light pole near where they had been standing was struck, causing it to smoke and glow. The security in the federal building would keep the protesters out. Rain would help even more. People never protest when they're wet and miserable.

The general looked at Joe. Ignoring Joe's question, he said "It might rain. I hope it does. We could use some. It sure has been dry. I've had to turn the sprinklers on for my lawn and trees. Even the house foundation has started to crack." The general could always seem to read Joe's thoughts. He hadn't become a general by ignoring body language. Some even called him a psychic when he told them what they were thinking.

Joe wondered how the general always seemed to know what he was thinking. Had he ever been through this himself? Yes, or at least something as bad. If the general could ignore his question, so could Joe.

"Well, it's hard to blame them. This place was created to save money. People came along and decided it was theirs to do with as they pleased. Those people out there don't know that we're trying to give it back to them."

It sounded like Joe was whining. He just had to get it out. "All they know is who the president is and that they've found something to complain about. An election coming, they're like sharks smelling blood. The people that they're so concerned about, were the same ones they complained about when their taxes went up or they heard about five hundred-dollar hammers."

"They're like swamp critters following a lost traveler in

pursuit of their next meal. It's like a swamp and the alligators and crocodiles are natural allies since they understand each other. Still, I hate it. The swamp cleaning, I mean. You already know about the threats but did you know I've taken to putting scotch tape on my car? I check the car out every day when I leave. I hate to sound paranoid."

The general stared a long ten seconds at Joe. He really did sound paranoid. Of course, it's not paranoia when they really *are* out to get you. There was a lot of evidence of that.

The general continued to evade Joe's plea for help. "I know I asked you three years ago but I'm asking again – why *did* you take this job? Why don't you just leave? It's not like you enlisted for this, or have a contract holding you here. The critters are a lot fewer now. Operation Pest Control has gone exceptionally well. Just turn it over to someone else and get your life back." They had both taken on a swamp vernacular over the past few years. It seemed so fitting.

"The president asked me to. That's pretty much it. I've never turned down a service request. Even as a soldier, I always took on the hardest jobs and volunteered for the worst missions. Some thought I had a death wish. Mom always called me a glutton for punishment."

"I wish I could get out of this assignment now, though. I just can't seem to find an exit. I learned early on that quitting can be a bad habit to get into so I always avoided it. Getting shot at is easy. But this ..."

"Hmm. Has it made a difference? Have we made a difference; one that will last?"

"I hope so. Make a difference. That's what drives me, you know. When I was in the Army, I made a difference. I turned more than one mission around. Have I made a difference here, general?"

The general was about to respond, something vague but encouraging. His mouth was open, searching for the right words when they heard "Joe, line 1. It's the president's aide."

Top was nothing if not professional, and his timing – impeccable. Joe always jumped when Top called. Old habits die hard. Top had been Joe's first sergeant, his boss, in the Army. Joe was now the boss but that didn't matter.

Joe reflected on his situation. There was a time that a call from the president would have excited him. That feeling was long past. Now, it was an occasion for dread. Each time, the conversation seemed to be a repeat of the one before. How could he defend himself and his actions yet again? Wasn't he doing what the president had asked him to? The president was such a hard man to work for.

Joe walked past each of the windows, glancing out each one, and completing a circle in the outer office before he entered his own, private office. The general watched this routine. He knew Joe did it, but not why. Still, it had been beneficial, at least once. It probably even saved lives that day.

Seating himself at the big oak desk and slouching down in the chair, Joe took a big drink of the hot tea sitting on his Mr. Coffee cup warmer. Staring at the Star Trek light-up model that his sister had given him, he meditated in pursuit of calm. It still eluded him.

Picking up the phone when he was ready, he said, "Dr. O'Flaherty."

"Joe, great to hear your voice. The boss wants to speak with you. It's pretty urgent. It'll just be a few minutes while I get him on the line."

Here he was, waiting for the president. What was it, dread? Resignation? *Let's just get this over with!* It wasn't getting chewed out or being fired that he feared so much as being asked to stay. He was at the lowest point he could ever remember. He used to be a soldier. That was the best time of his life, if only because he had been young and idealistic.

He didn't feel like this as a soldier. Then, it was a job well done. It wasn't just the uniform or the patriotic music, or even the medals he wore. It was the knowledge that his work was important. It mattered. It was appreciated.

Who appreciated him now? Nobody, least of all himself. A swamp. That's what he called it. After draining the swamp for the past three years, he was becoming just another swamp critter. Even the Prozac wasn't helping anymore.

Twenty years before, Joe had been a soldier, and more than a pretty fair sergeant. Always going the extra mile, he even took heat for it without question. The heat rounds and frequent griping was just part of the deal. Complaints, applause, physical aches – they were just a reminder that he was still alive.

There was also the low pay, hard, even dangerous work and infrequent appreciation. That's what filled the day for most soldiers like him. They knew the value, even if others didn't.

Chapter Two

The shoebill was hungry and almost anything would do. Frogs, lizards, and even young crocodiles were on its menu. Every swamp should have one since they keep the less pleasant critters under control. Sergeants are a lot like the shoebill, keeping critters of all kinds under control.

"Joe, whenever I give you a job to do, you always have to change my directions and do your own thing. Look what you did today. I said to march those five soldiers to the parade ground to cut grass. What did you do? You double-timed them. If I wanted them to run in this heat and humidity, don't you think I would have said so?"

Lieutenant Colonel Dick was irritated but so what? He was always irritated at something or someone.

"You also didn't say I couldn't do that. I got them there in half the time. I was trying to get the job done and make a point. I'll bet they also will remember this the next time they cut grass near your convertible. Their IQs went up by ten points each. How much did it cost you to get all those clippings cleaned out of your car?"

"Humph! Alright, point taken. Now get your ..."

"Goat smelly self out of your office, sir?"

"That's another thing. Stop finishing ..."

"Your sentences, sir?"

Joe did an about-face, glancing around the boss' office as he turned, grinned to himself and left. They understood each other well. Joe did every job one hundred percent. He hated half measures so the lieutenant colonel let him get away with it. The results were worth the aggravation. In the Army, Joe could even be OCD without anyone noticing. Even the chewing-out was almost irrelevant, Joe said to himself.

The Army was home and something Joe understood. After so long in a controlled environment, he was uncomfortable away from the post. It hadn't been that way in the beginning but now he couldn't imagine ever leaving it. He was a soldier, a lifer.

The office where he worked was like the building – old. Built a century before, one could almost hear the voices of the soldiers and generals who had passed through the place. Some even said that they *could* hear them, especially at night.

Now that computers were in use, the old building was showing its age and design problems. Computer wires were in evidence everywhere. But soldiers changed little. Some were professional, and others were gritty with a lot of rough edges.

Joe had been in the Army for twenty-one years. The best compliment he ever received was that he was 'an old soldier.' Not because of his age although there was that, but because his approach was old-school. He was unskilled in office politics and didn't care for anything politically expedient. Leave that to the officers.

Joe just got the job done. He even provided extra security – always did the 360, looked around any room he came into. Old habits die hard if they ever die. Sometimes, they also keep people alive.

People come and go in any organization and that was true of the Army. The Mess Hall was one of Joe's favorite places. Some soldiers complained about the food but it was at least as good as what he had grown up with, though he never would tell Mom that. He always got dessert with each meal. Mom never provided that. Every day at lunchtime, he could be found there.

The boss didn't let Joe get off without any pain. He sent him to check on the guys at the rifle range and make sure they got lunch. Joe was at his beck and call and he couldn't care less if Joe ate or not.

Since he was the last person in before the door was closed, he had time to linger. The best food was already gone, but he managed to get an over-warmed chicken fried steak with the remainder of mashed potatoes and white gravy. It was time for the Mess Hall to get rid of what was left so Joe got extra.

Joe even had some green beans so he could tell Diona that he ate healthy. Joe had always loved her more than life, but sometimes her nagging could take the fun out of things. He also got the last two pieces of cherry pie.

"Better give me a lot of gravy on that dried out steak. Say, I don't believe I've seen you before."

"I just started today."

"Well, I'm Master Sergeant O'Flaherty, but you don't have a uniform on so you can call me Joe."

"Thanks! Glad to know you. I'm Felix." Pushing the tray across to Joe, his sleeve lifted up, revealing a tattoo. Mom and a heart, not uncommon.

"So where did you get the tat? In the Navy?"

"Nah. Never been in the military. I just got out of prison and that's where I got this. But I served my time and got this job as part of my release program."

Joe frowned by reflex. "Did you say you served?" Candor rolled off a sergeant like sweat off a runner and Joe was no exception. Misuse of the language also irritated him.

"Yes."

"Who did you serve? I mean, I know you're serving me today, but who did you serve while you were inside?"

"Huh?"

"Serving is what we do for others. I serve my country in this uniform. You served me my lunch today. Others serve us. But what service did you provide by being in prison?"

"Well, I'm not real sure. That's just the word everybody uses so I use it."

"Maybe we should be more honest, more accurate. I did my time is honest and accurate. Incarcerated, that also works. Service? That doesn't sound like you had a lot of service until you started today."

"I hope this works out for you though. I'll be a regular and if we get the chance, I'd like to get better acquainted. Maybe even help you get started at a good church if you're inclined."

"Thanks! That sounds interesting. Let's talk on my break."

"O'Flaherty, you'd better not be bothering my server." Sergeant Scanlon was in Joe's face with his fat, crooked, wagging finger.

"I was just extending a welcome. The choice is his."

"I'd like to go."

"There, you see?"

"Yeah, yeah."

"You should come with him too."

"Still not giving up on me, huh?"

"Why not come? What can it hurt?"

"Too many hypocrites down there."

"Well, there's always room for one more."

Back at work, Joe sent soldiers here and there, mostly courier stuff. There was that change of command ceremony. As a headquarters unit, Joe had to send half of the soldiers assigned to him. It would be a good experience for Private Jenkins also.

About midmorning the following day, the sergeant major stopped by. Joe wasn't prepared for what the sergeant major had to tell him. No sergeant would have been.

"Great ceremony and Private Jenkins, he's a hoot. I have to tell you this story but don't get on him about it. It had been raining when I got there and the practice was over. Everyone was just waiting for the actual ceremony. I saw all the guys were drenched – except Jenkins. I asked him how he managed that. 'Because, Sergeant Major, I brought one of these.' He raised an umbrella."

"I never thought to tell him about that. It's basic training 101. He should have already known that he can't carry an umbrella in uniform."

"Well, he knows now. But like I said, don't get on him. This is something we can all laugh about."

Joe did laugh. The soldiers in the unit got some fun out of it too. Every time Joe sent someone on a courier run, if it looked like rain, he said, "Better take Jenkins' umbrella." It took Jenkins years to live that down.

The following day was another typical day with more Army stuff. Joe headed up a burial detail and attended one funeral about every week to send off an old soldier in style. Nine soldiers including Joe would do the burial service in Wetmore, about four hours-drive from Fort Prairie. It was going to be a long day.

Colorado is known for its trees but there were none around the cemetery. Barren land, covered with rocks, the occasional Piñon "tree," and a lot of markers. The day's honored old soldier had called this small mountain town his home.

The town itself was small. Except for two churches and a small general store that doubled as a restaurant, there were the homes of a small community. It was one of those blink-and-miss-it places.

March, fire the rifles, fold the flag, and then the short speech – all to perfection as usual. The widow looked to be about seventy-five. Stooped over from a long, hard life and silver, almost white short cut hair, she nodded and smiled.

Then she grabbed Joe's hand and said, "Thank you so much! Bob would have been proud to see you guys today. Thank your team for me and *please* stay for the meal that the church is providing."

Well, they had to eat so why not? The people at the church were glad to have them and peppered them with questions and their own stories from wartime service.

When they got back, Joe reported to the sergeant major.

"So how did it go? Was it a successful burial?"

"Yes, it was a successful burial. We put him in the ground, he stayed in the ground, when we left, he was still in the ground. Very successful!"

"Whatever, O'Flaherty. Now, get out of my office," he said,

shaking his head. What was he supposed to do with guys like Joe?

A few days later, Joe was working on a cleanup detail with his soldiers, when the commanding general passed by. When Joe wasn't deployed or out in the woods for training, there were always details to do.

The work pleased the general but that wasn't what caught his attention. He had been looking for Joe after a visiting general had sent him a message. Joe was responsible for the driver and other support that the general received during his visit. Everything went off, right on schedule, with no problems. That almost never happened.

The general told him about the message and gave him a challenge coin, plus another for the driver that the other general had sent. Then he added, "Master Sergeant O'Flaherty, I hope you never retire. You're an old sergeant and I mean that in the best possible way."

Joe understood. He had limited respect for the newer versions of sergeants, the politically correct type. Joe could be pleasant or unpleasant but he always focused on the mission and getting it done.

About a week later, he experienced the bureaucratic Army in all its finery. *Where am I going to park? I'm running late and all the spaces are taken.* Then Joe remembered the lot behind the building. If he had forgotten it, maybe others did too. It was worth a shot anyway.

Pulling into the lot, he saw it almost too late. The hole was almost big enough to swallow his car. There were no barriers to prevent an accident – just a hole, waiting for a car. Slowly he backed up.

Taking the turn around the building onto the main street, he was again stopped. This time it was for a nice road being repaved. Making it into the office with forty-five seconds to spare and out of breath, he was also out of patience.

"I was beginning to get concerned," the boss said, waiting for Joe's explanation.

"I ran into a large hole in the lot behind the building."

"Oh, yes. I thought you knew about that one. That's why nobody parks back there. It's been like that for about four months now. They have it on the list of repairs though."

"Well, what about the main street in front?"

"What about it?"

"They're repaving it."

"And?"

"Why are they repaving a road that doesn't need it and ignoring a huge hole that does need repair?"

"The main street is more visible. We're competing for installation of the year. We need the visible places to look good." The boss looked at Joe with disdain for even asking the question.

Sergeant O'Flaherty just stared at the lieutenant colonel. At times like this, the Army still made no sense, in spite of twenty-one years of service.

The Army was often strict and regulated. The order made things flow more smoothly but it wasn't for everyone. Private Porteous was the most challenging situation Joe had been through in quite a while. He had been picked up for a DUI. "Driving under the influence, huh? How'd they get you? Did you hit someone or were you speeding?"

"No, none of that. I was just minding my own business

when, well, it's all here in the report." He handed it to Master Sergeant O'Flaherty.

"Hmm. What's ... what's this? It says that the officer was parked and running radar when you passed by.

The subject was within the speed limit when he swerved and drove up on the curb, his vehicle stopping on a residential lawn. I turned on my lights and approached him. He was cooperative so I asked him why he swerved. He stated 'To avoid the possum in the road. You must've seen him. He was seven feet high.' Concerned that the subject might be under the influence of some substance such as alcohol or drugs, I asked him a follow up question. 'How do you know he was a possum?' He responded, 'Because, he turned around and smiled at me.' At that point, I administered the field sobriety test and, when he failed, I administered a breathalyzer which he failed, registering at .11 percent.

"Wow, did you say that? What were you thinking? Were you thinking at all?"

"Sarge, that's not fair."

"I think you stopped thinking just before you took that first sip. After that it was all over. Well, now you have to wait for the commander to do his thing. He'll take at least one stripe and keep you from driving on this fort. Do you have anything to add to what's here?"

"No, I guess not."

"Well then, you'd better just throw yourself on the mercy of the court. Admit responsibility. That will go farther than claiming innocence or persecution. But be prepared to face the music. It's not going to be good for you, no matter how this turns out."

"Alright."

Joe's prediction was spot-on. Private First Class Porteous was now Private Porteous. No First Class. No class at all. He had to pay a huge fine in the local court, high lawyer fees, and was also prohibited from driving on-post for six months which meant his wife had to drive him to work. The Army also took some money, reducing his monthly salary.

Joe had been right. It wasn't good. At home, Porteous caught more heat from his beloved. "How are we going to make it now?" she kept asking him. Life got rough when a soldier messed up.

One day, Joe was standing in front of a building with the sergeant major when Private Porteous drove by. "O'Flaherty, did you see that?"

"Yes. I sure did. Things are never so bad that they can't get worse."

"Well, it's going to get worse for him." The sergeant major was a man of his word. A second punishment was coming. He received another reduction in rank, this time to the lowest rank in the Army. To make sure he didn't drive on post anymore, he was restricted to the barracks for the next two months.

Now, his wife would have to drive to see him every day for dinner or a movie. On the plus side, at least he no longer had any rank to take. He also had limited opportunities to drink since he was always on-call for any job that needed doing.

What is that? The pain was sharp. Then – nothing. The leg wouldn't respond. *That is so weird.* The doctor had a word for it – arthritis. "Me? That's not possible. No way!"

"I'm afraid so. Look Joe, you've led a hard, physical life in the Army. Now the bone spurs are tweaking the nerves and causing the loss of control. Weren't you also wounded once? I thought there was something in the record about a missile or scud."

Joe had been deployed to the Middle East. Now he saw it once again. The loud boom as a scud struck the barracks he was staying in during the war. The huge building shook, and then it was on fire.

Joe was in shock but went on autopilot, the training kicking in as he evacuated the wounded. The first one he picked up over his shoulders using the fireman carry. He carried him down a flight of stairs and outside, at least fifty yards from the building. The adrenaline kept him from noticing the weight of the man. Then, he went back in and grabbed another casualty who couldn't walk.

Every once in a while, he heard a popping sound but paid it no mind. Finally, Jake Mulcahy grabbed him by the arm. "Joe, you're bleeding! You've been hit!"

"Huh?" He looked down and saw the blood trailing down his leg. *Those popping sounds. The fire must've been cooking off all the rounds we've got in here.*

Joe joined the wounded. Surgery fixed the physical damage but the psychological wound never healed. He got the Purple Heart for the bullet and the Soldier's Medal for evacuating six of the wounded.

Later, he heard that a local had left a homing device. The Scud wasn't very precise in its targeting. The homing device helped to pinpoint the area. The Iraqis were just "lucky" in hitting the building. Joe and the others had been unlucky.

Although there were numerous locals employed to clean the building and help with other tasks, they never figured out who had brought the device into the building.

Ever since then, Joe had checked out each room when he entered. Even at home, he had to walk completely around the house before he could sit down, checking it out for things that were out of place. His family knew he had changed but he wasn't violent so they overlooked it. Obsessive-Compulsive Disorder – that was what they called it. Joe just called it being careful.

"Yes, I was wounded. A scud that left me bleeding and stunned, in shock. The pressure of the explosion sent me halfway across a sixty-foot room."

"That had a lot to do with it. Time now to pay the piper."

"So, can't you fix it?"

"Oh yes, I can do surgery but the x-rays show others. We can't do surgery on all of them – and they'll just come back. You'll be getting other twinges. Those aches you described – that's also part of it. It's going to get worse. It's time for you to slow down."

Now, it was time for the surgeon to drop the other shoe. "Joe, we have to do a retention board – unless you retire first. You can't stay on active duty if you're not fit for the work. I don't think the board members would recommend you staying on active duty. Not with all you've got wrong with you. Think about it. You've got the time in and you're not as young as you used to be."

Sean. I'll get his thoughts on it. Stopping at the swimming pool at lunchtime, Joe found his best friend, Master Sergeant Sean Mulvaney at his usual lunch-time haunt. Flattop haircut, stocky build, and a smile that told the world *don't trust this guy*. The high cheekbones told the world that he and Joe were Irish and proud of that heritage.

The sergeant major was there too. African-American, six foot six, three hundred pounds, also with a permanent smile – he was floating in the pool. Mulvaney acted like he was about to dive in when Sergeant Major Brickman saw him. Mulvaney was known by all to be shameless in his antics.

"What you doing Mulvaney?"

"Oh, sorry. I thought it was a beached whale."

"Don't mess with me Mulvaney!"

They found an isolated place to sit and Joe poured it all out to Sean. "Yeah, I noticed you seemed to be slower on our runs. Even saw you fall out the other day. When *you* leave the running formation and start walking, everybody notices."

"I didn't think anybody noticed. I've been aching more than usual. Sean, I'm not sure what to do about it. I've been in the Army so long; I don't know *how* to do anything else. The Army is my home. I live it and I love it."

"Oh, give me a break. Jeez. You *can* do something else. That's the difference between us. You have all that education. You don't have to do this. A rock like me does have to because God made me a great swimmer and gave me a body like Adonis."

"You're not good looking like me but you have all your marbles. Maybe it's time to use them. You can be one of those civilian pukes and sit on your backside drinking coffee all day instead of spending the day in the rain, and the snow, and the mud."

Maybe he *was* a rock, but he was a diamond too. Still...Joe knew he wasn't ready – yet.

A few months later, Joe awoke, realizing that he was an old soldier. He had still been a hard-charging sergeant and tried to ignore the pain. That morning, he had trouble just getting out of bed. He loved the Army. Loved what he did every day.

However, his body didn't like it so much. Arthritis, bad knees, bad back, damaged shoulder – it all spoke to him every day. It said, "What do you think you're doing and do you think I'm going to let you get away with this?" Every day it spoke to him and every day it expanded its already colorful vocabulary. The conversations were not pleasant.

Joe had seen others retire from physical disability. He had always told himself it would be different for him. Well, now it was his turn.

Joe wondered what the future would look like. He would have to become a civilian again. The change would be huge and he didn't feel ready for it. Most of his adult life had been spent in that uniform.

During lunch one day with the sergeant major, Joe told him what was going on. It felt almost like an excuse but an explanation was in order since everybody noticed that old Master Sergeant O'Flaherty wasn't leading the pack anymore. "I also don't know if I'm ready to take the uniform off."

The sergeant major put Joe's fears into words. "It'll be a big change. Everybody's running around out there and nobody's directing traffic." Well, he couldn't continue the soldier's life. A substitute was needed.

The next two months passed without a decision. He was making excuses and finding reasons to miss out on the physical training. At his rank, all he needed was some other place he had to be.

"Joe, you know what the doctor said. You can't run and even walking is hard. What are you going to do? Can you even stay in the Army?" Diona had been with him for, what was it now, 23 years? Her name meant divine and she was certainly that. For Joe, she was there before the Army was. "They aren't going to wait much longer for you to make a decision."

"Yes, I know, and no, I can't stay in. I need a new plan but it's hard. I've done this for so long and I love it, almost as much as I love you. It's who I am. What can I do?"

"Is the Army *all* you are?"

"Well no. At least, I hope not. I don't know. Is it? Is this all I am?"

She laughed. "Not to me, not to the kids. Didn't you tell me there were lots of civilians at the fort so can't you do that? Aren't there some former soldiers there, so maybe it wouldn't be so bad since you would have other retired soldiers to share stories with and others have done it so now, *you* need to retire before you're crippled or they throw you out. Leave on your own terms." Joe had long since gotten over her use of run on sentences. Once she got going, she only stopped occasionally for more air.

"Yeah, that's pretty much what Mulcahy said." As always, she could cut through the fog and shed a bit of light. *Hmm, maybe that would work. It might not be so bad.*

Some of the civilian workers were alright. Of course, there was the other kind that somehow managed to not get fired. Some of them were even in management positions. Old Sergeant McColm had a reason for that too. Years ago, he had said, "Of course, the scum always does rise to the top."

Then he answered his own thought. "But I'm not scum. I've been a good soldier and a great sergeant. Well, I'll show McColm. I'll show them all."

I've got my education, but is that enough? The Army's values are mine. I'm a patriot but a Christian too. Heck, I'm a walking recruiting poster. Joe knew what he was and what he wasn't. It wasn't so much that he bought into the party line or that he had been brainwashed. These values were his and the same as he had been raised to believe in. He was a good match for the Army and it for him.

Joe had worked with civilian employees of the Army and decided that might be a good fit. The civilians always seemed to be smiling. They worked right alongside the soldiers and most had a great work ethic.

If I could just get a job that pays enough so I don't lose any income when I retire. If I can stay right here. If I can find something that I can do. If. So much depending on such a small word.

Fort Prairie, Colorado, was a great duty place. Openings came up, so Joe applied for all of the jobs he felt qualified for. He hated to take the uniform off but it was time – more than time.

His values had been good ones. They should be valuable to the civilians he would be working with. Honesty, integrity, candor, works well with others – this was what employers wanted, wasn't it? In the Army environment, civilians were expected to have these values.

Joe's career had been stellar. He had more medals and ribbons than most soldiers. *About time to get me a sign at the top of the ribbons saying, continued on back side,* he almost laughed.

There were no illusions. The civilian life would be different. It would be more mercenary. Services traded for a salary. Few were the medals awarded to civilians. Twenty-one – that's how many years he had been soldiering. The medals – he had lost count.

****

"Tell me of a time when you made a difference, how you made a difference, and how it felt." Roberta had been interviewing Joe for the job to write contracts and buy things for the Army. It had been going almost an hour but seemed shorter. Stress had a way of doing that. This was the question that stuck out the most.

Joe had limited experience in buying things for the government. Usually, he just went to see the supply sergeant. It was a good thing they had not focused on that. There were other times when he had gotten something creatively to save money. Did they care about that?

"When I was stationed in Italy, I was responsible for security clearances at a NATO base. The Army personnel were arriving without the correct clearance or even starting the needed investigation. I turned that around so that almost all arrived with the clearance. I had to ruffle a few feathers and think outside the box, doing things that were not in the regulation. But it worked and made our country look a lot better since the Army folks could do their job right away. How did it make me feel? Pretty good. Anytime I can make a difference, I feel like I've earned my pay for the day." Roberta laughed. She had that high-pitched laugh that could disarm people.

Her boss came in and introduced himself. "He plans to stay here in the area," she told the lieutenant colonel.

"That's what we need," he agreed. "I'm sorry but my car broke down so I missed the introductions. Could you tell me about yourself again?"

Well, at least he's Army. Joe repeated the speech, glancing at the interviewer to see if she was getting bored. She just stared at her boss, gauging his reactions. What was her name? Oh yeah, she said it was Roberta. Clearly, she was no veteran. Small, slender and well-preserved, she was following her boss' lead. If he liked what he saw, she could hire Joe and not antagonize him.

He seems alright. Not too rigid for a veteran. And that college? Ha! That's more than I have. More than anyone in the office has. How does that happen? I hope we can get this over soon. I need to run by the grocery store. She was all smiles.

Joe knew he was unprepared for a few questions but resolved to do better the next time, if he got an interview, and take this as a lesson learned, the Army approach. He tried to do everything right.

Joe also walked over to her window and complimented her scenic view of the area. He commented on the tree outside. A large branch had been removed and a smiley face burned into the tree where the branch had been.

As he turned around and then left, he remembered to shake her hand and thank her for the interview. It was that OCD thing again. Obsessive-compulsive disorder the shrink had called it. He always had to do a complete circle.

Months later, the expected job offer had not come through. Nobody wanted the old soldier, he suspected. Joe was unprepared when he got the call, offering him the job. He was sure he had not done well and the passage of time confirmed that he wasn't going to get this job. Accepting the job was a no-brainer. He would continue working at the same fort and even see old friends.

Joe would be writing contracts to buy things that the Army needed. Construction was always going on with a lot of old buildings to repair, and that's where he was assigned. He had seen some major waste and he'd stop that.

He remembered the large pothole fiasco – stuff like that made no sense. Master Sergeant O'Flaherty would put a stop to it. No, scratch that. He was going to be Joe, just like he used to be. Still, just like he had done as an old sergeant, he would make things right. Even getting older, he still had a chance to make a difference. It was invigorating.

A new job meant new challenges. *Can I do this? I've been a soldier for so long; I don't remember how to act in public. I have college degrees but so what?*

For the first time since the scud missile, Joe was afraid. He had to learn a whole new trade but he was used to starting over. During the Army career, each assignment was different and he was invigorated by the changes. This would be no different. Lots of changes but that would breathe new life into him.

He fought down the fears. *Get a hold on yourself Joe. You've dodged bullets. Now, all you have to do is sit on your backside and spend money.*

Joe always consulted Dad when he had a big decision to make. "Dad, I won't be able to stay in the Army much longer."

"You haven't done anything wrong have you? No court-martial or anything like that?"

"No, just wearing out. The arthritis, worn down joints from the Army runs, marches, backpack carrying. All the old soldier problems."

"Oh, well then. Welcome to the club. So, what are you planning to do when you get out? Going to come back home?" Home was Lamar, a small town with few jobs.

"Well, I'm thinking about robbing banks," Joe said.

"I guess that would be okay, as long as you aren't working for the government." Dad didn't like the bloated government and despised those who worked for it. It would be quite a while before Joe confessed the awful truth.

****

"What do you mean, you're retiring! What are you – a traitor?" The sergeant major was less than happy. Joe told him as soon as he knew but still ...

"I'm having medical issues; the same ones I told you about. I can't hang on the run anymore. I'm always in pain and it's getting worse." The sergeant major's look softened.

"I know. I just thought I'd give you a hard time for the last time," the sergeant major said. "I think there's a regulation that requires it." Both laughed. "You can't lead from the rear, so this sounds like the right decision. So, where's this new gig of yours?"

"It's in your building, in contracting."

"Yeah, I heard they were hiring. All they have are old women in that section. They need new blood. They need veterans too – and some men to balance it out. You should do well there. But watch your back. I've heard things. I'm not too far behind you.

Save me a seat." Joe shook his hand and they parted on the best of terms.

Joe heard what the sergeant major said but ignored it just as fast. This change was bringing a new sense of purpose to his life. The excitement was building as he thought about what he might be able to do as the one who buys things.

He had seen too much money wasted, too much time and red tape to get the simplest of things done. He could and would fix that. Besides, the sergeant major was old. What did he know?

Chapter Three

The water moccasin looked like the non-poisonous type. That was one of its survival mechanisms. At home in the water and on the ground, it was always hungry. It was also quite deadly. Coiling up at the approach of almost anything, it was ready to strike when least expected. A rattlesnake gave a warning, but not the water moccasin. The water moccasin was like that – sneaky, and deadly. No swamp could be complete without one. This place was no exception.

Man it's cold! Joe had dressed as professionally as an old soldier could, but that dress coat was no replacement for his Army field jacket. February tended to be beyond cold. At least the old building hadn't changed much. It was a lot older than Joe – maybe a hundred years old. He had worked here before but then he wore a uniform. Now, he had no uniform and no rank.

He didn't even know how to address others or even who he was. Twenty-one years in uniform had done that to him. It had left him socially challenged. Everybody was sir or ma'am. But, at least it was an old building and Joe loved old things. That was the historian in him – everything told its own story of the past.

As he walked into the building, the first person he saw was the sergeant major. "I don't even want to talk to you," the old man said. "Abandoned the Army and me too." Joe laughed and said "Good morning to you too Sergeant Major."

"Are you sure you want this? It's a whole new world. I can get your retirement paperwork canceled. Look Joe, I know I've given you a hard time but this is serious. You have to learn a new trade. It's a whole new life. Don't get me started on your new co-workers. You understand the Army but not this. I really think you should reconsider before it's too late."

"Thanks, but no. I have to give this a try. It's been a long time since I was a civilian. I wore myself out as a soldier. It's time to sit on my backside and drink coffee all day." Joe didn't drink coffee but since tea was less respectable and he knew he needed to give up the soda, he chose to minimize the harassment.

"Watch your back." There it was again. Joe knew he should have pumped the sergeant major for more information but now he was out of time and about to be late on his first day if he lingered any more.

Walking down the hall, he saw its old walls and décor in a different way. It was an old building, formerly a hospital, and rumored to have ghosts that were active at night. The sergeant major had been told about them but ignored the warning.

"Ghosts? Yeah, right. Look, it's the live ones you have to worry about, not the dead ones." When he was alone one evening, he saw the light on in the copier room and turned it off. By the time he got down the hall to his own office, the light came back on. The hair on the back of his neck stood up and started slapping him for his bravado. After that, the sergeant major avoided nighttime work.

Entering the Contracting Department, Joe went to the supervisor's office. He had interviewed with her a few months earlier. *Has it been that long?* The government never moves fast. "Good morning. I'm here and ready to work." She stared at him a moment and then recalled who he was.

"Oh, great."

It was as much a question as statement and the cold reception felt as if the air conditioning had just kicked on high. Joe wondered at the reception. *Did she not want him here?* "Where do you want me to sit, Ma'am?"

She laughed. "First things first. I'm Roberta. Let's get rid of that Army stuff right now. Don't call me Ma'am. That's for an old person. Unless you're trying to tell me something?" Joe smiled and shook his head. "I have one vacant office. You'll take that one. See that box of unfiled stuff?"

"Yes."

"Leave it alone. You don't know how we file and I'll take care of it very soon." Her definition of 'soon' would prove to be different from Joe's.

Joe's office was very close to hers. Joe was unsure if that was good or bad but it had been awhile since he had an office with a real door. Soldiers shared space. Since Joe had been working at the same post in the same Army, he already had his security clearance and was able to use the computer that morning.

Roberta ignored him after that first meeting, leaving the computer as Joe's only distraction. She was not more than fifteen feet away but it may as well have been a hundred miles. Joe was untrained, not scheduled for any training, and useless. After a week he wondered, "What am I doing here?"

Joe had been a driving force for many years, wherever he had been. Now he was ignored. Surfing the internet was the only diversion he had for a long time and that got old real fast.

Finally, Jock stopped by his office and welcomed him. Wearing a dress shirt that was too tight against his portly frame, and cradling his favorite coffee cup, he said "Hey, Bub! Welcome to contracting. You're a retired soldier, aren't you?" Balding and eyeglasses, he was the intellectual personification of an old soldier. His gaze said I've been there and done that. His build said that he ate a double cheeseburger everywhere he stopped to do that.

He had served over twenty years in the Army and was now inclined to stay put – no more moving around the world for him. Retirement had given that to him. Coffee was his lifeline and he was never seen without his favorite coffee cup.

Friendly, he had all the answers before the questions were asked. His work ethic was to tell others what to do while finding ways to avoid doing the same. Always addressing those he liked as 'Bub,' he was the office gadfly and grapevine. If he didn't know about it, it hadn't happened. He needed to feel important and other workers coming to him for an answer filled that bill.

He liked the security of government employment but he also liked money. The swamp and he were great allies, giving each other what they wanted most.

"Yes, a master sergeant. Does it show that much?"

"Yeah, plus they told us a retired soldier was coming."

"Aha! So, you're not psychic. Guess what I'm thinking now?"

"I'm not going there. Anyway, I'm a retired warrant officer. Artie is a retired sergeant major. We're the only ones who have been in the military except for the director. He wanted to bump up the military and male presence to balance things out. That's part of how you got the job. The education didn't hurt though. Is it true you have two master's degrees?"

That's where I don't want to go. "Well, yes. Did you say you were a warrant officer? What led you to be here?"

Veterans, when they get together, always seem to have stories to share. Jock had been a warrant officer but he retired when he bumped heads with a superior. His first civilian job hadn't worked out, so he came back to the government, minus the uniform. He wanted stability and was willing to accept lower pay to get it.

"If you need any help, let me know. I'm still new but I've learned a few things." Before leaving, he showed Joe how to get the first courses he would need including one that was online. Roberta hadn't done that. Joe now had something to do, boring as the training was.

The training passed all too quick and Joe again had nothing to do. Surfing the internet filled a few minutes each day but that was tedious. From being the "go-to" guy in the Army to being invisible now was intolerable.

Then, a few weeks later, a meeting was called. It was boring but at least something to do. Joe was listening, trying to interpret the new language he was hearing. Roberta noticed he wasn't talking. "Joe, do you have anything to add?"

"No, I just thought I'd better listen."

"Hmm. We need to get Joe some assertiveness training."

Joe didn't laugh. Nobody did. *She ignores me for weeks and now this. She doesn't want me here. Why did she hire me?* When the meeting was over, Joe stopped by Roberta's office. It was past time to deal with this situation. "Could we talk?"

"Sure. Come on in."

Closing the door, he said, "You may not realize this but you offended me in that meeting."

"I did? How?" Was that fear in her eyes? Guilt?

"You said I needed assertiveness training. I was just trying to listen and learn. Do you think I could have survived an Army career, retiring at the second highest sergeant rank if I couldn't be assertive? For weeks, you've ignored me, never given me an initial briefing or counseling. What do you have against me? Do you want me out of here? What is it?"

Roberta was unaccustomed to such a blunt conversation. She glanced at the closed door. There was no retreat. Laughing, she said "It was just a joke."

"Well, I didn't take it that way. Nobody else did either."

A long gaze followed. Joe was serious and upset. "Okay, I'm sorry. I'll choose my words better in the future. I'm also sorry for ignoring you. I just have a lot of personal issues going on. So, are we good?"

"Yes," Joe nodded as he forced a smile. He stood and again looked out her window. "Still a great view," he said. He glanced at her out of the corner of his eye. *I hope we're good. And that window thing. How long can I get away with that?*

A few days later, Virginia stopped by. "Good morning Joe. Roberta assigned me to work with you. She said you need a mentor."

"More like basic training," Joe said. "I've had almost no training and no work to do. Can you fix that?"

"Oh yes, I sure can. I have enough work for both of us. I'm going to give you some."

"You're going to show me how to do it too?"

"Of course. I don't want my name on it and have it wrong. Come down to my office and we'll get you started."

"Thanks Virginia."

"Call me Ginger. All my friends do."

Ginger was as good as her word and better. She was not so much a mentor as an Army drill sergeant, teaching Joe the most basic parts of the work and demanding perfection. This was fine with Joe. He understood her and strictness was what he needed. It was appreciated.

She was one of those high-stress types. Sometimes she could be unpleasant, but to Joe, that was just a word. In the Army, soldiers were used to challenging conditions. Bad weather, cold coffee, dehydrated food, little sleep – these were just conditions of employment to a soldier. Unpleasant conversations were hardly noticed.

After a few weeks, Roberta called a meeting to let everyone know that a lot of work was coming. She kept emphasizing that. Artie grew frustrated – the old sergeant major in him hated the same thing being repeated. Once was enough so he said, "You keep saying that but I haven't seen it. I say, bring it on!"

Roberta just looked at him, unsure how to respond. They were on different wave lengths. Later, in her office, she asked Joe for help.

"Joe, I don't understand Artie. What's with him? Why is he the way he is? What do I have to do to get through to him?"

Joe shrugged his shoulders. "He's an old sergeant major.

He's used to a straightforward method of communicating. He doesn't see any value in repeating a statement such as that about a lot of work coming.

One time is sufficient for him. He's a simple man. He wants simple talk. That's how all of us old soldiers are. We can be the easiest and best workers you've ever had. We just need things very straight forward."

"Well, thanks. I guess I'll have to learn how to talk to him without repeating. Maybe for you too, huh?"

As the end of the fiscal year approached, stress grew higher. Not for Joe though. He was low-key and seemed immune to stress. Compared to combat, office stress was almost a pleasant way to pass the time. That just irritated the others all the more.

The last day of the year, everybody had to work late – until midnight. Tempers flared, snacks flowed, pizza showed up, and then jokes about the utter insanity of it all.

As midnight approached, a miracle occurred. The clock moved backward two hours. More time to make contract awards since it wasn't midnight yet. Exhausted, everyone went home at one o'clock in the morning – or was it three?

Joe glanced at the still unfiled box that Roberta had said to not touch. It remained as it had been, except for the thick layer of dust on it.

****

"Joe, have you heard?" Jock was always good for the grapevine.

"Heard what?"

"We're merging with the other contracting office."

"I didn't know there was another."

"Yessiree Bub. They do a higher level of contracting and report to other people. Somebody realized they could save money by merging us."

"This is the government – that's not supposed to happen. So, who's going to be in charge?"

"For now, our boss is. But the grapevine says his position is going away. After that, who knows?"

It took almost a year, which was light speed for the government. Then, a few months later, the "Crocodile-In-Charge" from the other office took over. She had few contracting skills, though nobody knew it at the time. Her primary skill set was to be unpleasant. Yet, even calling her that was to do her an injustice. She was so much more.

Mara had managed to move up in the contracting field to the second highest grade – without any college education. Waivers for education were hard to get but Mara managed to get them. Though she made the mid six figures, she had no college and saw no reason why anyone else should either.

Mara Malo Hernandez was vicious to the extreme. Her middle name said it all – vicious and bitter at the world. She took all her frustrations out on one worker at a time and was very skilled at making people want to leave the organization. For her, that was a feeling of power over others and it bumped up her self-image.

The usual government process was counseling and retraining for weak workers. Firing could follow if the process was unsuccessful. Mara ignored all those niceties.

On one occasion, she offered her talents to the garrison commander. "If you want someone to leave, just let me know. I'm very good at getting people to leave." The commander never took her up on her offer but people were still leaving.

Since she had no skills and no education, she used this approach to enhance her own self-image. *Who do I work on today* was her byword.

Old soldiers always compared notes and this place was no exception. The grapevine was useful within the organization and provided Joe an alternate path to find out what was going on. Joe, Jock, and Artie knew what leadership looked like from their Army days and knew how to treat people to get the maximum out of them.

"When we can move up into the supervisory positions, we can take over this place and run it the way it should be run – not like the swamp critters here are doing."

The plan was laid. It wouldn't be a mutiny, but a gradual escalation into management ranks of those who knew leadership. The swamp would be drained. A triad of plumbers was all that was needed.

A month later Joe was walking down the hallway and noticed a dark spot at the end of the hall. "Hey Candi, what's down there?"

"Oh, that, we don't go down there. If you want to last here, never go down there. That's all I can tell you."

As time went by, curiosity got the better of Joe. After resisting the temptation for a few days, when the hall was empty, Joe walked down to explore the mystery. He saw a dim lamplight coming from the desk inside and a dark figure huddled over the desk. He stared a moment and then tapped at the door frame.

The figure jumped. Staring back, he said "Come in. Please come in."

Joe started into the small office when the man yelled, "Back, get back!" Invited in and now he was being ordered out.

"I'm sorry. Not you. It's my dog. I can't get him to stay at home so he comes with me every day." Joe looked but saw no dog.

"I'm Justus. Glad you came by. Nobody ever does. Down, sit, sit! Good boy."

Joe thought about acting the dog part, even the panting. He decided this wasn't the time for it. He did sit, though. *An invisible dog – that's just great.*

"So, what's your name?"

"Joe. Joe O'Flaherty." Justus gripped Joe's hand with a clammy and shaky hand. "I'm on the Construction Team. I didn't even know you were here. I never saw you before that I can recall."

"I don't get around much. I got on Mara's bad side once and she yells at me every time she sees me so I just stay in here. Now, nobody will talk to me. It's as if I'm contagious. Maybe I am. If Mara sees anybody talk to me, they're on her list. You watch out!"

"Have you ever thought about quitting?"

"I can't. I need the job. I need the money. Besides, my wife is just as bad as Mara. So, I just come in here with Rex every day and try to keep from getting yelled at."

"Well, I have to get back to work. Good to meet you though."

"Same here. Please stop by anytime. Rex seems to like you, so it should be okay."

Another day, another victim of Mara. Joe began to realize that he would have to leave this place. Most of those who had been here when he started were already gone. It was not at all what he thought it would be. It was more of a swamp than a workplace. When was he going to get the free time to sit on his back side and spend a day drinking coffee?

I can see my house from here! Sometimes contractors didn't pay the minimum wages to their employees. To make sure they did, people like Joe had to do labor wage surveys with the employees on a government job. Some didn't even speak good English, so communication was hard.

Joe found himself on a tall building that was getting a fresh coat of tar to keep the rain out. Climb the ladder, smell the hot tar, find the boss, then talk to the workers who viewed him as the enemy. "You don't know how much you get paid?"

The worker had a red ball cap, shoes with tar stains, and jeans that had suffered from bleach spots.

"No, I take what I get."

"Where are you from?" It wasn't a required question but Joe was having trouble communicating so he felt like he had a right.

"Ah, I grow up here. I was born here." The look in his eyes was less than convincing as he stared down at the roof.

"In Colorado?"

"Oh, yes." The accent was from somewhere else, somewhere a lot further south. Joe mentioned it to Roberta when he got back to the office.

"Just let it go. We do contracts. ICE does immigration. We need to get this job done so we take the contractor's word that all workers are legal."

"But ..."

"Drop it."

Artie was the first of the triad to feel Mara's wrath. He had been in a three-year intern program and was ready to graduate. A retired sergeant major, he was accustomed to finishing what he started. "I just don't think he's Contract Specialist material. I want him terminated from the program as unsuccessful. Get rid of him!"

"But he's done what we asked. He's learned the job and completed all the course work. He has his certifications. He's completed numerous contracts for us. We have no reason to fire him." Roberta was trying to stand up for him but she was under fire too.

"I just don't care. Do it. Today."

"I'm so sorry Artie. How do I tell you that I know you've done well, but I still have to fire you? I just can't fight this battle."

"That's just fine! But I won't go down without a fight. I know how the Army chain works."

****

"Colonel Blackwood, this is Artie here at Fort Prairie. I'm an intern in contracting."

"Okay. What can I do for you Mr. Artie?"

"Sir, my first name is Artie. I'm a retired Army sergeant major. I'm calling you to tell you about what's going on down here. I'm done with my intern program and now these civilians want to get rid of me. I've done my part. I completed all coursework and all the contracts. I've mentored newer people. I don't deserve this. I need some help here."

"Well, if you've done all that, why would they want to get rid of you? We need good people and a lot of them. This doesn't make any sense."

"I try to do the right thing and don't back down. Like I said,

I'm a retired sergeant major. This director hates people with a backbone. She just wants people who are easy to control. It makes her feel good. It makes her feel powerful."

"I see. Well, just rest easy then, I'll take care of this."

This looked like an opportunity to the colonel. He had been hearing things, lots of bad things. They couldn't all be true. Nobody operated that way. Workers had ways of expressing displeasure. Flat tires after work on a cold, snowy night, complaints to keep the supervisors in meetings with union officials, even unwitnessed threats – they happened to keep supervisors in line. This just couldn't be possible and yet...

"Mara, this is Colonel Blackwood."

"Good morning sir. What can I do for you?" *Did he hear about our great work? Does he want to visit? I wonder if I can get a promotion out of this?*

"I got a call from Artie. I believe you know him?"

"Yes sir. He's not doing so well. I'm afraid we're going to have to drop him from the program."

"Do you have a formal counseling or other documents to back that up? Can you send it to me within the next thirty minutes?"

"Well, I've been trying to work this unofficially. I don't have a lot of paper on him. I didn't want to upset him. He's a large man and a veteran. He seems so violent every time I talk to him."

"That's pretty much what I expected to hear. Drop this. He will complete. He's a decorated veteran and no civilian is going to remove him because she doesn't like veterans and for no other reason than because she can. Do I need to come down there?"

Hanging up, she used her favorite colorful phrase. Brave in the face of little interference, Mara lost her nerve when faced with someone bigger than her.

Artie completed the program, but he knew it was time to pop smoke and get out while he could. What Mara couldn't complete one way, she could do another. She had no respect for military veterans or for anybody. Artie didn't scare easily but knew it would be a good time to leave. He got a job at the Corps of Engineers and stayed there for several years. The triad of plumbers was already breaking up. The swamp breathed a sigh of relief – it was safe.

With Artie gone, Roberta felt the full weight of Mara's talents. It wasn't just the thing with Artie. It was just because she could. "I can't take it! Why is she that way? She belittles me and then expects my best work."

Roberta had missed the point. It wasn't because she was doing a bad job. She was available and Mara needed to have somebody to be hateful to. She hated the world, hated her life, hated herself; but since she couldn't take it out on herself, she needed someone to reflect her hate onto.

Joe just nodded but could offer no advice. This swamp was different from the real Army. In the real Army, it wouldn't have happened or would have been taken care of.

Roberta was developing real insecurities and had trouble just getting out of bed in the morning. After a few months of the harassment, she was unable to come to work. The symptoms were real and it felt like the flu. Apathy accompanied it. She wondered if this was what depression felt like. It was time to get some help.

"Roberta, I'm recommending some sick leave for you." The

doctor was understanding, but this was all he could offer. Of course, there were also the happy pills.

With Roberta missing work during the last two months of the summer, Joe was left to his own devices. As the old sergeant, he focused on the mission to keep things moving.

It was then, his co-worker Mentiroso was put in charge of the section. Menti had more skill than Mara – but not a lot more. What he did have was a disconnection with integrity. He had no problem with the truth since it was not in his vocabulary or set of values. Though Mara valued him both for his sucking up and for the Mexican ancestry they both held in common, it was his truth-irrelevance that made him so valuable.

Menti had been an Army recruiter. So had Joe. However, Joe was unsuccessful while Menti was very successful in that role. Joe remembered what Larry had said so many years before. "If I ever see anyone in the Army with a gold recruiter badge, I'll know that they lost their integrity at some point."

That should have been a warning. Joe overlooked it and wanted to trust Menti. This sense of trusting and expecting others to think like him would be his undoing many more times in the future as he navigated this particular swamp.

"We don't want to work on unfunded projects this summer. If they don't already have committed funding, drop them," Menti said.

"Alright, if you're sure," Joe said. He had his doubts.

"But you do know that is how we do things here. We work unfunded projects and at the end of the year when everybody has money they haven't been able to spend on something, it comes to us and funds the construction projects that maintain this post. That's how it's always been."

"We help others to get rid of their money so they can get the same funding next year and they help us with money for our contracts. Fort Prairie would dry up and blow away without it." Joe was sure Menti didn't understand.

"Mara wants it that way so that's what we're going to do" Menti said.

"Did you explain the process to her? Did you tell her that it's stupid to go this way?" asked Joe.

"No. I'm not going to do that but you can if you want to be fired. Look, you'd better just do it her way."

"Can I get that in writing – maybe an email? I just want a *get out of jail free* card," Joe replied.

"Sure, no problem," Menti was laughing now.

Joe was torn. He knew that the projects he was working on were important and many soldiers depended on him, even if they didn't know it. He wondered, "Well, what do I do now? I know we'll get money at the end of the year and that some of these projects are essential."

As if on cue, a contractor called about a project he wanted to compete for. Joe advised him that they were supposed to drop it but added, "I think this one is important so I'm going to try to continue it in my spare time."

He thought that would calm the contractor. He was wrong. Bad news always travels fast, especially when a contractor is concerned. He called the head engineer who called Joe.

"What's this I hear about this project being canceled? We need that one in a bad way. We spent a lot of time designing this and now you're going to cancel it without even talking to us? Have you lost your mind?"

Arrow Smith was descended from the Apache tribe and could be forceful when he wanted. Right now, he wanted. Arrow was also right to the point, just like Joe. However, Joe was descended from the Southern Cheyenne and, combined with his Irish stubbornness, could also stand his ground.

"The first thing you need to know is that I told that contractor that I would try to keep this one going."

"I know that. He told me. That's not good enough. A maybe is less than what I need. I'm going to talk to your boss about this!"

"That's an excellent idea. You know I didn't come up with this on my own. That came from Menti and Mara."

"Let's talk with them – right now!"

Still out of breath from the walk over, Arrow found Joe and together, they went looking for an answer.

"Aha! There you are. Joe tells me you aren't going to get the contracts we need for our projects. He said that you insist they be funded now. Is that right?"

"Well, we want to make sure we don't waste our time, Menti answered. We need to have money for all our projects. We're short-handed. But we won't stop your projects. We'll work on them. I'm sure that Joe just misunderstood." Menti was lying as coolly as anybody Joe had ever seen.

Glaring, Arrow accepted this explanation. They parted on passable terms, if not great.

"Joe, I'm sorry if I didn't explain well. I hope this doesn't affect our relationship. You know I have the greatest respect for you. How about it, are we okay?" Menti wanted to mend fences and thought Joe was stupid.

"Okay"? Soldiers were honest, honorable, and self-sacrificing. They loved their country more than self. To be caught in a lie was worse than anything. Better to get shot than to lie. Joe was the honorable old soldier, but Menti was not. They were both retired master sergeants but not cut from the same cloth.

The old soldier came out. "You are such a liar," Joe said. "You made me look stupid. Are we okay? What do you think? You know, I think you'd lie if the truth sounded better." Joe realized his response didn't help. He didn't care.

Back in his office, Joe remembered the *Get Out of Jail Card*. He forwarded the email from Menti to Arrow.

"Thanks, Joe," Arrow replied. I thought that was how it was. Good to know who I can and can't trust. I hope you're not going to be leaving there."

"That's hard to say. It's starting to get rough here. Not at all like being a soldier. I feel like I'm in a swamp, surrounded by crocodiles. I may even be on the menu."

"Joe, you *do* sound worried. That's not like you!"

"No, it's not but then I've never been in a place like this before."

Joe had been retired from the Army for two and a half years. He had been in the swamp all of that time. He could deal with an armed enemy. That was easy enough. But the enemy that laughed at him, that lied about him, and even conspired behind closed doors – that was hard to fight or deal with.

Joe knew something was coming but he didn't know what. It was like waiting for the other shoe to drop. He was on pins and needles, straining to hear the latest gossip or whispers, looking for a clue. When it came, it was not what he had been looking for.

Chapter Four

The crocodile was in pursuit. Large for its size, it could move extremely fast in the water and on land. However, it also lacked agility. A zigzag course was effective and escape was thus possible – this time.

Barely successful. Joe could almost hear Mara laughing at him and all his hard work. He had been looking forward to his third evaluation. He knew he had done a lot that year so the evaluation should be a great one. It wasn't signed yet but he couldn't imagine such a rating.

In the Army, he always got the highest ratings. While Roberta was out for the summer, hadn't he run the section pretty much? How did that justify this? Roberta was back now and was also irritated by it. "Joe, I don't think this is right. We're going to ask Personnel if there is anything we can do."

"Do you think they can do anything? Why would Mara do that? What did I do to her?" Joe just walked away. Now it was Joe's turn to not get it. Oh sure, he had done some great work. That wasn't the point. Mara was telling him and Roberta that she was in charge and would make their lives difficult. She had to prove her power over them. There was no way to escape her power except just to get away.

Snakes don't bite because we feed them. They bite because

they're snakes and for no other reason. That's just what they do.

Joe knew but denied the truth to himself. He wanted to work here till he retired. A higher salary was for others. He wanted to take care of soldiers and get the most bangs for the buck. Eliminate waste, provide good leadership to others – show them how it should be done.

However, this job wasn't working out like he had expected. Joe knew that Roberta was already looking for her escape. For the first time, Joe saw things as they were. The picture was not nice – like the barracks looked after the scud hit it.

Roberta and Mara were gone a long time. How long had it been? It felt like hours. Then he saw them. Mara saw Joe before Roberta. She didn't look happy. She had daggers in her eyes and stomped past him, only glancing his way briefly. This wasn't going to be good.

Roberta said, "Joe, come into my office." Joe followed her, not sure what to expect. "You should have been there. On second thought, it was a good thing you weren't there. It was tense. Boy is Mara ticked off." Roberta was actually laughing for the first time in months.

"What happened?"

"The Personnel Director looked at the comments on the evaluation and told Mara she had to upgrade it to the highest rating. She said the comments didn't support a lower rating. Mara's mad. I think she intends to go after you next. I'm getting out of here while I can. You should too."

****

"Jock, what should I do? What would you do?"

"Well Bub," he said, rubbing his belly, "maybe you should

do what Artie did. I know you live close by but maybe you need to commute to another place. Do you want to stay in the Civil Service? You know how Mara can be. It's going to get rough."

"I know but I just want to live a simple life. I'm not looking for a lot of money but I don't want to become fish bait either."

"You've also seen that pay for performance thing. You know how it's working out here. The better workers are supposed to get more money. But Menti is one of Mara's favorites."

"So? What's that got to do with me?"

"Oh, I guess you hadn't heard. Menti gets more money for less work and we get less money for more work. Since Mara gets to decide how the pool of money will be split up, she is giving a lot of it to Menti. She's giving him your money. You should look. It's posted in the hallway."

It was there alright. Right next to Mara's official photo – she seemed to be laughing at Joe. Menti's pay went up by ten percent. Joe's pay didn't go down but it didn't go up either. No annual raise for him. Menti got Joe's raise.

Jock noticed the frown and guessed what Joe was thinking. "There are lots of agencies looking for guys with our training. But you might have to drive an hour to work."

"So, what are you going to do, Jock?"

"I need to leave. Menti is doing too many illegal things. He changed my last award and violated the Anti-Deficiency Act with it. If I stay here, I'm going to have to report it or get caught up with him in it." They both just stared at each other and nodded.

"Yeah, with me it was the Competition in Contract Act that he wanted me to violate for him." *Guess I won't be able to drain this swamp after all. Maybe someday I can come back as a manager or even the director.*

Joe could take a lot of abuse. The Army had taught him to "march on" even when conditions were bad. This pay for non-performance was harder to take. But someday – someday he would get his turn.

Jock had seen the same light as Artie and started applying for jobs. He couldn't work under Mara or Menti so he left and went to work for The General Services Administration. GSA was much more agreeable and treated Jock well.

Roberta saw that and had heard good things for years so she left as well. "Joe," she said at her farewell party, "now we need to get you out of here." Joe just nodded, smiling at the turnaround. She used to ignore him and now...now she liked him. He agreed but was unsure how he would manage it. Just because the others had been successful didn't mean he would be.

The next morning, Joe was working hard to get a contract awarded. Several of the housing buildings had leaky roofs. Soldiers were used to hardships but their families shouldn't have to deal with being rained on while they slept. He was almost done with the work, almost ready to celebrate too when he heard his name.

"Joe! Get out here Joe! Get off that computer; I want to talk to you. You retired soldiers think you're so special. You never do anything and expect the rest of us to carry you. All worn out too. What were you doing in the Army anyway? Drinking and partying every day? There you are. I want you to go with Abbie Lou and do whatever she tells you to do. That's about all a man is good for anyway!"

Joe took a big step toward her, so she wisely backed off.

Joe wanted to tell her – almost did tell her. Would that do any good? He was only three feet away and his eyes wide with twice as much white showing. She was afraid. She knew and he knew too.

Regaining control, he said "I – don't – think – so. Who do you think you're talking to?" She backed up a few more steps, her eyes never leaving Joe. He might do almost anything. Then she turned and hurried back to her office, locking the door behind her. Joe was beginning to feel more and more like Justus. Coming to work here was getting hostile. Escape was in order. It was time to pop smoke.

That night, he discussed his situation and plan with Diona. Her counsel was usually spot-on. Back in high school, she had helped him through more than one dilemma.

Back then, her hair was silky brown, her lips were full. The eyes – they seemed to be laughing all the time. She wasn't so much beautiful as cute. He couldn't believe she saw anything in him. She was a cheerleader. He was from the wrong side of the tracks. Well, her hair was silver now but he hardly saw anything but the silky brown. He saw her with his heart – not with his eyes.

"Joe, you're honest, sometimes too honest. It might have been that thing with Menti that started this stuff. They know what you're made of so they have to get rid of you. You just need to give them what they want. Leaving is probably best. I just worry that you might have a car accident if you commute. Whatever you do is fine with me." Her reassuring smile gave him the encouragement that he needed.

She had meant to have another conversation with him. The doctor said the tests didn't come back with good news. However, Joe had his mind on other things. This could wait. A man can only handle so much at one time. She decided to handle this load by herself for now. There would be another time.

Sometimes, life just stinks. Joe didn't want to leave. He sure didn't want to spend two hours a day on the road. He had done that in Italy and it could be dangerous – so could working in a snake pit.

Even the two-dimensional Joe could see what was coming. It was like a freight train coming with the headlights on and the whistle blowing for all it was worth. It was time to go. He was no longer welcome here. He was an old soldier, but not that old.

These critters hadn't done a day in uniform. Yet, they were infesting the Army – his Army. It wasn't right. It wasn't fair. They should be the ones forced to leave, not him. He resolved to come back and make things right.

****

The moon was full and bright and the sunrise was just coming on. The horizon was more colorful than usual with its hues of red, yellow and amber.

Joe had to admit to himself that he was scared – until he thought of Mara. Combat was easier than working for her. In combat, you can shoot back. Joe wasn't a violent man but that incident with Mara had scared her – and him almost as much. He had almost lost control and he knew it.

Now he was considering leaving the Army for keeps. He had left the Army and become a civilian three short years ago. That was different. At least he still worked for the Army. After a quarter of a century, he was leaving the Army.

Still, that burning orange sunrise was like his attitude. Fresh and full of promise for a new day, it appeared like an omen, providing needed encouragement.

Diona had reminded him to smile a lot. This was a must-do thing. He *just had* to get away from the fort. Failure was not an option. The fort was a swamp, infested by the Maraosaur and similar critters.

Tibby met him in an impressive building – impressive compared with where he had been working. While the offices were modern, the hallways were mid-1950s and very large. A security officer sat at a desk near the entrance, checking identification cards. Balding with a pot belly from too much sitting and too many jelly donuts, he also appeared bored and just ignored Joe.

Tibby was just over five feet and of Mexican ancestry. *Oh great. Here we go again.* Joe had an outstanding batting average – his first impression was almost always wrong and he was counting on this.

Tibby was not Mara. Her voice gruff but a very nice smile, Joe wondered how this would work out. "Let's go to our building. You can drive." It wasn't far. She wanted to see what kind of car he drove and learn what she could on the way over. She knew all the tricks.

Bumper stickers tell a lot about a person. Joe had the retired Army bumper sticker but nothing else. He knew some people hate the military and hoped that wasn't the case here. Still, something like that would be good to learn early on. He had no way to know he had just bumped up his personal stock.

As they drove over, Tibby had not missed the retired sticker. She had a son serving in the Army. She thought, "Well, he seems pleasant enough but very quiet. Maybe that's the Army influence. I'll have to ask Bobby about that the next time he calls. I hope this goes well. Too many applicants and too much other work that I'm not getting done."

The questions were easy. They were too easy. The Army adage "if the attack is going too well, it's probably an ambush" was uppermost in Joe's mind.

Josefina asked the questions and Tibby kept score. Joe glanced at the pad in her hand. Each question generated a checkmark in the same column. *I'm either doing well or bad.* Then, a question that he knew he had nailed left a mark in the same column as the others.

When the interview ended, he wished he had done better. He intended to wow them but now they were done. It felt like a college class he had completed but then wanted to go back and do it right to do it better.

Had it only been an hour? These ladies seemed pleasant. It might be fun working for them. It couldn't be any worse than with Mara. It would also be a promotion which he needed if he was ever to go back to the fort and drain that swamp.

As Tibby walked Joe to the door, she said, "Well, it went very well and that's all I'm going to say." The parting smile was very encouraging but also non-committal. The last interview at Fort Prairie left Joe feeling sure he would not get the job. This interview had the opposite effect. That thought disturbed him.

Weeks went by and ... nothing. It wasn't so much desperation that Joe felt but a need to get out of here. He turned to prayer as he always did when things were rough.

When he had about given up all hope for this job, he got the call. "Would you like to accept the position?"

He pondered it a long time – at least half a second. "Sure!" Two weeks' notice and he was gone.

When he gave his notice, Mara just nodded. "Good luck," she said. The words were there but empty, offered as an obligation and no emotion behind them – it felt tense. Joe couldn't wait to leave her office.

As he started to turn, he saw it. That look of ...what was it anyway? Hatred? Joe had only seen something like that once before. In the war, when they captured that prisoner. That guy's side had lost, it was clear enough. He should have been happy to make it out in one piece. Still, there were diehards. This fellow had been one. Joe gave instructions to secure and watch him closely. There was no telling what he might do. Now he saw it again, or did he? He was so glad to leave the room, he brushed it off.

Mara was not at the farewell dinner. That suited Joe just fine. Menti was there as her representative but said almost nothing. He knew Joe had no respect for him. He wondered what would be said, but he was there to present a report back to Mara. Joe wondered, "Does Menti respect himself?"

Now that Joe could see freedom from this swamp on the horizon, he tried to tell others of the illegal things going on. He talked to Equal Employment Opportunity. He talked to the Garrison Commander. He talked to Criminal Investigative Division. Nobody cared. *Why should I care if they don't?*

As he drove past Fort Prairie on his way to the new job on Monday, he wondered if this was the smart thing to do. A long drive, a little more money, unknown situation. Maybe they would even expect more of him, more than he could deliver. But being chased off – this was such a load of garbage. *I'll be back. You chased me away but I'll be back. Then I'll be in charge!*

Chapter Five

The water was dark, cloudy, and warm. The leech found a new host to secure its livelihood from. Inserting its long feeding tube, the victim felt nothing – the leech had also injected a local anesthetic before feasting on the buffet. The meal continued until the leech had consumed five times its own body weight.

Air conditioning, bright colors, art fit for a king – who paid for all this? From a swamp to a palace? As he walked into his new workplace, Joe found it different, culture shock different.

There were artificial clouds hanging from the ceiling. The lighting and walls were light blue to reduce stress. Offsetting that, the workspaces were cubicles, not offices. There would be no privacy here. New, modern décor instead of the old at the fort. A breakroom with microwaves and refrigerators. No ghost in the copier room. People even smiled at him. What was wrong with these people? *I might have to learn how to do that.*

"Hey, good morning Joe! Great to have you here! Now I want you to take this workstation. We'll get you a computer this morning. We also have a party for you. Now you see how much we wanted you." Tibby was very welcoming – almost like a Mom after a good report card. She had a gruff voice but a big smile and attitude to match. *Hmm. This might not be so bad.* They even left a lot of promotional items on his new desk including a very nice pen with the GSA logo on it. The cheapies that the Army used were hard to find. The only ghosts were those of old airplanes. The building was old but well maintained. The hallways were very wide – the building had been built to construct aircraft decades before.

When the United States had entered World War II, they wanted a fighter plane factory behind the barrier of the Rocky Mountains – the same strategy the Russians used against the invading Germans – so the country had built this one. The expected invasion never came and the building had been used for storage. There were no airplanes in sight but there were offices everywhere.

Joe found a large dining facility too. At the fort, he had to bring his lunch from home. No more. The cafeteria had almost everything an old soldier could want. They even had some better than good cinnamon rolls for morning break.

After a career as a soldier and getting few creature comforts there or at the fort, Joe felt like he had died and gone to the Air Force.

Joe's first assignment was to buy forty-five different tools. "How do we do that? Buy them all at once? Where do we put them?"

Tibby laughed, "No, you get us a Standing Price Quote, an SPQ. Then we can order whenever we need some more. We stock them in warehouses on the east coast and on the west coast. The Army and other agencies order them and we ship them out. It's that simple."

It doesn't sound hard. Maybe I can do this.

A few days later, Tibby asked Joe about them. "Are they done yet?"

"You do know that you gave me forty-five of them and we have to give contractors time to respond, right? Also, the government has the most inefficient and time-consuming processes."

"Oh yes. I just need an update."

"Oh. Well, then, I'm not done but I've got them written up. It takes time to do it right you know."

"Great! That's better than I hoped for. I knew I made the right decision when we selected you. Let me know if you need anything from me."

That was more like it. Joe was used to being given a mission in the Army, backup as needed, and then turned loose on the job. Tibby could have been an old soldier for her approach. She and Joe would work great together.

Not everybody thought the same though. Jeannie had some issues with Tibby but Jeannie had never been a soldier. This was more like a homecoming with turkey and pumpkin pie. Here, Joe was wanted. This didn't *feel* like a swamp at all.

Jeannie was Joe's mentor at GSA. Every new employee got one. She asked for Joe because he already had a lot of skills and would be less work for her. But Tibby rubbed Jeannie the wrong way. Jeannie had been there almost forever and knew the practices better than anyone. She ought to since she had created a lot of them.

When Tibby came into the department, she was in charge and wanted everyone to come to her. They were still coming to Jeannie which made things difficult for both of them. Sometimes there was yelling. Joe didn't see this but there was talk. Jeannie provided some of that talk.

"Don't you see how hard she is to work for? She demands so much and wants everything done her way."

"Well, I'm still new so I'm sure I haven't seen a lot yet." He liked Jeannie but he also liked Tibby. He was going to have to walk a fine line here and not mention Tibby to Jeannie. That would just set her off.

He also never mentioned that Tibby gave him a jar full of Tootsie Roll candy and suckers for his birthday. How did she know that was his favorite? "Tibby, Thanks for the pogey bait!"

"Pogey bait?"

"Yeah, that's what soldiers call candy and other things that we put in the desk."

Most of the people were great. Dave was even older than Joe. He taught Joe a lot about investing too. Dave was one of those 'been there, seen that' guys. "Welcome to the old girls' club" he said. "Glad to see another guy here." It would take Joe some time to understand what Dave meant.

Dave was medium height, stocky build, very white hair with red cheeks and a receded hairline. Close, critical observation was one of Joe's strengths – but people were always harder to analyze. He just took people as they came. That had been helpful in the Army but maybe not so much in a place where people were not as they seemed.

Dave had retired from his previous job as a police officer. One day, Joe asked Dave how he came to be in this line of work.

"Well, it's a hard-luck story. My partner and I got this call. Bill had been going through a lot, stress, that kind of thing. We needed to get evidence from a car wreck that left a man injured and dying. We went to the hospital and Bill asked the nurse for a blood sample from the other driver. We needed to know if he was under the influence. She declined and said her only job was the patient. What I didn't know was that Bill had asked this nurse out a few months earlier and she refused. I think she knew Bill was already married. Anyway, he got mad and started to arrest her for obstruction."

"Then, he demanded that I support him, help him to make the arrest. The nurse was resisting. I said I couldn't do it. I told him this was wrong. He wouldn't listen. I listened to my conscience and grabbed Bill by the arm and put my cuffs on him."

"Our supervisor arrived a little while later but I had already released the nurse with profuse apologies and had the cuffed Bill in the backseat of the squad car."

"Sergeant Rallie said I had done the right thing. But he and I knew my day as a cop was done. Bill got fired and nobody trusted me to be their partner. It was time to find a new line of work so I retired pretty soon after."

As an old cop, Dave was also observant. One day, he asked Joe "Why do you always walk all the way around the room whenever you enter?"

"Do I?"

"Yes. You walk into this huge room and walk the perimeter. When we meet in a conference room, you do it there too. You never sit down until you make the circle. I notice these things. It's an occupational habit. A cop who noticed too little didn't last long."

"I didn't think anyone noticed. I guess we're both damaged goods. In the Army, they didn't notice or, if they did, they didn't say anything. Look, I want this our secret, okay?" Dave nodded.

"When I was young, I grew up on the hard side of town.

Someone was always out to get me. So, I developed the habit of checking things out before I turned my back on anyone or anything. In the Army, I was expected to conduct a regular area survey. Even in an office, I could just do the about-face thing – that means to turn around – which was just as good. Then, there was the Scud attack. That really drove it home."

"Huh?"

Joe gave him that story too. "So, do you think anyone else has noticed?"

"Nah. Everyone here is into their own selves. I bet you could walk around half-naked and nobody would notice."

"Thanks. I'll keep that in mind in case the air conditioning goes out."

Eldana was very welcoming too. "Want a fresh-baked chocolate chip cookie?" African-American, like Jeannie, she was of medium height, smiling and oh-so pleasant. Well, almost like Jeannie except that Jeannie was less than five feet tall.

Joe and Eldana did not work together – each were on different teams. But her kindness was never forgotten. It took Joe a long time to learn her name. For the time being, she was 'the cookie lady.' This place just kept getting better and better. However, Joe knew perfection never lasted. A fall was coming and Joe knew it.

One day, Joe was talking to an item manager, the guy responsible for ordering tools off his contracts and keeping the supply at a good level in the warehouses. Breck was a large yet very pleasant man. He once said, "Back when I was playing football in Los Angeles ..."

"Wait, you played football? Was it in college?"

"I played professional football for Los Angeles," he said, leaning on his cane.

"Wow! So, do you think the football had anything to do with that?" Joe asked, pointing at the cane.

"Oh yes. It had everything to do with it."

Joe heard about government cutbacks one day and asked Bob how secure the job was. "Oh, they never fire any of us. We're ninety percent self-supporting. We buy stuff and resell it to the rest of the government. All the other agencies need us to save them money and most of our budget comes from that profit."

"Wow, that's great! So how much profit do we charge, ten percent?"

"No," Tibby had been passing by and laughed. "Anywhere from fifty to two hundred percent."

Joe almost collapsed right then. *No wonder we always had to do without stuff in the Army.* "How come so much? Nobody would pay that much at a grocery store or a hardware store."

"We're the government. We're the only game in town. For now, the agencies are required to come to us. Also, we can get everything cheaper than the agencies can because we buy in volume. The profit pays for our salaries and other costs. Even the bonuses we get come from that. The more profit we make, the more our bonuses are."

"But such a high markup in the price – how can we justify that?"

"Easy. We're still saving money for everyone who buys from us. We're saving the government and the taxpayers money and saving them from greedy retailers."

"So, who's going to save them from us?"

"Don't you get it? We're saving a lot of money for the government. If we get some rewards for that, what's the problem?"

"Well, we already get a pretty good salary. Why do we need to scrape even more off the top of the cake? Aren't we here to serve the people? Instead of being ninety percent self-supporting, why not try for one hundred?"

She just shook her head and walked away. *If his work wasn't so good ...*

To Joe, this sounded pretty dishonest but a pretty good racket if you can get it. The higher bonuses and the high profit levels? That didn't seem right. *Maybe it'll make more sense later. I wonder if I can affect the profit margins that we charge.*

One day, Joe had a new tool to buy. A socket wrench that was priced at five hundred dollars. *So, this is where the five hundred dollar-toilet seats come from. At a hardware store, they could be bought for a couple of dollars.*

"Ah, I see the problem." Tibby wanted to reassure Joe. "These aren't typical sockets. They can only be used on the Bradley Fighting Vehicle and the Abrams Main Battle Tank. Every time we order them, they have to set up tooling just to make the few that we need. That's why they cost so much." She then ordered one from the warehouse and showed it to Joe. It even looked different from the ones he had seen.

I wonder if those toilet seats were also special purpose. But we all sit on them the same way. Nah!

Most of the people were very pleasant. They were also spoiled. Joe had been through some undesirable work conditions. Fort Prairie topped that list. This place felt like a paradise.

The air conditioning always worked. The computers were the latest and greatest. The cafeteria was open almost all day starting early in the morning for those who had missed breakfast. Many workers were eating breakfast at their desk while working. There were also the trips. It seemed like they took a trip almost at will – and there was a lot of will.

Joe's first trip was to Washington, D.C. It was the *New Associates Orientation*. For one week, they were sent to the headquarters to be indoctrinated into GSA's many missions.

GSA had them staying at the Madison, one of the premier hotels in downtown DC. Each employee had his or her own room, a liberal allowance for meals, and lots of snacks at the morning and afternoon sessions.

The purpose of the training was just to get everyone to understand the mission of GSA. It was a very pleasant trip which introduced Joe to each of the missions that GSA carried out. It was also a huge boondoggle.

Joe was used to the bare minimum necessary. When he had training with the Army, he shared a room at the cheapest lodging available. Not so with GSA. If it was considered good, it had to be had. Joe went along. He also felt embarrassment at such luxurious treatment. *Couldn't they just have given me something to read back at the office and saved the thousands of dollars this must be costing? For all of us here...why, that must be pushing a million dollars.*

"Why were you guys late?" One of Joe's new co-workers went to the Orientation with him. Today, they were meeting with a VIP. These powerful people hated to be kept waiting.

However, Caitlyn wasn't going to move fast for anyone. Embarrassing those with her, she plodded along. Joe was accustomed to being on time and not making people wait for him. Now, the old soldier grew irritated. Soldiers were used to something called formation. It was more than be there or be square. It was more like be there on time or pay the price.

He wanted to tell her "Move with a purpose girl!" He wanted to, but held his tongue. This wasn't the Army. *One more reason why veteran's preference should be practiced in hiring. What's it take to get her moving anyway? No wonder, the office was fine with her going. No way is she going to be missed.*

When he got back to the home office, he mentioned the expensive treatment to Tibby. Her advice was "Accept it and enjoy it. This is the culture."

"But it costs so much. Do we really need to stay in the best hotels? I'd be fine with Motel Six." *Do we need to go anyway?* Joe had seen enough travel with the Army. He knew he was a voice crying alone in the wilderness. He also knew it would be best to just go with the flow. The problem with that was that the flow was taking him into a smelly part of the swamp.

He soon saw more of this 'culture.' Every year, there was competition for Work Unit of the Year. Joe had not been there long but his team was selected. As they stood on the stage and received the award, Joe wondered why he was there. Sure, he was part of the team, but he hadn't been there to do the work that led to this honor. Nobody seemed to mind or care about that.

It felt like the philosophy that all children get an award so nobody feels bad. Joe was the only one on the stage feeling bad. Undeserved merit. The old soldier railed at this treatment. It would soon get more intense. Along with the honor came a thousand dollars in bonus money. GSA even paid the tax so the thousand was what he got. It was a *really* good racket.

When the end of the year came, there was more money. A

complicated formula compared the evaluation of the worker with the profit of GSA, and a few other factors. Out came a dollar amount. It was in the low thousands of dollars. The taxes were again paid so that the bonus was even better. *Profit? How could there be profit if the taxpayer is still paying ten percent of our budget?*

One day, he saw Jock. "Hey Bub, long time no see since the fort. What have you been up to?"

Jock had been working in another department that handled federal buildings. Sometimes they did renovation or remodeling work for other agencies. If they did a good job, the other agency would give the GSA employee a bonus. The result was that Jock got a lot of money for his work beyond his salary. He admitted that it was over ten thousand dollars his first year.

Jock then mentioned that a vacancy occurred in Joe's department and he had applied for it. During the interview, he asked how much the bonuses were. Hearing that it was a lot less than he was getting, he said "Well, I don't know why I'm here."

Without finishing the interview, he got up and left. Jock had embraced GSA and its money. The work and service were secondary. Greed was paramount.

****

Life sure throws a lot of curveballs. Joe was happy with the work but the commute made him get up early. In spite of two decades of Army service, he still hated to get up early. The drivers on the highway in Denver reminded him of the drivers in Italy except that they were even worse. Up at O Dark Hundred, out the door at 6:00 to be there at 7:00 and leave at 4:30. The schedule gave him one day off every two weeks but the cost was high in stress. The ritual was becoming a habit. *I guess I can get used to almost anything.* This went on for several months.

One day, on the drive home, he glanced in the rearview mirror and saw another driver in an old pickup using a cell phone; another distracted driver. Soon, he noticed the slowing down 5:00 P.M. rush hour traffic.

About then came the screeching of brakes. The pickup had crashed into Joe's small Ford Focus, pushing him toward the stalled vehicles in front. Joe flashed back to Italy, where he saw a soldier he had known, crushed between two vehicles. That time, an Italian stopped his vehicle in the middle of the highway in the traffic lane. The soldier stopped in time but the truck behind him didn't. It cost Joe's friend his life.

Joe applied the brakes. Like a gush of wind, Diona came to mind, forcing the strangest thoughts into his confused mind. *What would she do when she found out? Cry of course. Could she handle it? Was she going to be mad at him? Yeah. What did a crushed person look like? Would it be open casket?* He always hoped for a closed casket anyway. Well, his life's race was about over now.

The vehicles in front were getting closer and closer. Holding on for dear life to the wheel, his leg cramping from the extreme pressure on the brakes, the smell of burning rubber, the sounds of screeching tires and breaking glass filling the air, Joe heard nothing else. He didn't see his life pass before his eyes. He saw ... nothing.

Blacking out, after a minute, he came to awareness. There was nothing in front of him. His seat back was broken. The back seat was gone. The trunk – just inches from him. In shock, he just sat there.

After a few minutes, the driver from the pickup asked if he was okay. For a minute, Joe just stared at him. "Huh? What? Where? What happened?"

He turned the key off which was unnecessary since the car wasn't going anywhere. The door still worked, though it took a lot of convincing, so he got out. A stiff neck was now all he felt. Shock was fading and being replaced by anger. Pickup man had almost killed him. He just had to be on his cell phone while he was driving. Now the police were there.

"I guess traffic just stopped and I didn't notice," pickup man said.

"It didn't stop – just slowed to about ten miles an hour. It always slows here this time of day." Joe didn't like the way pickup man was trying to evade responsibility. How about an apology? No, not even that.

The next day, Joe called Tibby and let her know he wouldn't be in for a few days. He told her about the accident. The car was a total loss.

"Are you alright? Take whatever time you need." Mara wouldn't have said that. A new, used car, same model and color were what Joe needed to try to forget the wreck.

Insurance paid most – but not all of the replacement. He thought about a lawsuit for the rest of the costs. Prayer helped but he was still unsure. He asked Jeannie who advised against it.

"Joe, we're Christians. We just need to forget and move on." That was what he wanted, just move on and try to forget. She was a good mentor, and she was right.

Chapter Six

In the swamp, carnivorous plants also have their way. The King Monkey Cup is the largest of the carnivorous plants and has been known to capture scorpions, mice, rats, birds – and maybe even honest civil servants, digesting them in enzymatic fluid.

"What do you mean, I don't work for you anymore? Am I fired? What did I do?" Joe liked working under Tibby, so the news was a big surprise.

"Joe, I thought you knew. We never fire anybody. Not only are you Civil Service, you're also in a shortage field. People in your field are hard to come by. People in your field like you who know the job, are *really* hard to come by."

"Why is that? Why are we so hard to come by?"

"Corporations pay a lot more than the government. I don't usually tell people that. I might lose them."

After a year, supervisors were being changed. The performance of the organization had declined and Darnell's plan was to move people around. Maybe a shakeup would freshen and invigorate everyone. Darnell was the top boss in the department and had worked for GSA her entire career. She was a desk sitter with the backside to prove it. If GSA had become bloated over the years, so had many of the leaders. This idea – it was more of the same.

The teams stayed the same except for the supervisor. Joe was assigned to Rachel. As good as Tibby had been with Joe, Rachel was just as good – maybe better. Was that even possible? They were different but both had been easy for Joe to work with. They assigned him the work, backed him up when he needed it, helped when he needed it, and otherwise just let him do his work. For an old soldier, it just didn't get any better.

Before long, Joe was called into Rachel's office. *I hope I'm not in trouble. Let this not be bad.* He kept praying as he approached her office. He had been doing this since he was a kid. If he thought he was in trouble, then he wasn't. It was a great psychological tool that almost always worked.

"Joe, come on in. I've got something I need to discuss with you. For years now, GSA has been working with a process that had people throughout the government sending money to buy stuff. It's called a Military Interdepartmental Purchase Request or MIPR. The military sends money and GSA buys what they ask us to buy. However, a lot of the time, they sent extra money and it just sat on the books."

"They did this on purpose to hide money. They also used it to keep the same budget from year to year. A lot of it was even forgotten. We've had an Inspector General audit and the IG told us to get rid of those MIPRs. There's millions of dollars there. If we can, we buy what they want. If not, we return the funds."

"We have to cancel these out, whatever it takes. A lot of the contact people on the documents are no longer available, so this requires research and investigation. That's why we want you to help on this special team. You told us that you used to do some investigations in the Army."

"Yes, I guess I did."

"Also, a lot of the people who sent this money won't be happy. This was like money in the bank for them. You were military, Army I believe?"

"Yes."

"So, you should talk their language. Talk to them; make them understand why we are doing this."

Great, so not in trouble. Hmm, sounds like a lot of extra work. That's not so great.

"This program probably also enabled these people to get their reputations for being miracle workers – getting stuff when there was no money, or so it seemed."

"Okay, glad to help," Joe was less than truthful. "How do we do this? Who's in charge of the team?"

"See Magda. She's in charge. Thanks for taking this on. Joe?"

"Yes?"

"Don't mess this up. That would be bad. It could even be grounds for getting fired."

"No problem." The words were easier than the reality. Why did she have to say that? It was almost like a warning. Had he ever messed things up badly? Joe had no illusions of what this would do to his workload. But he also couldn't see an easy way out of it.

Sometimes the best way out of something was to go through it. It was like combat, being surrounded and going on the offensive to punch a hole through the bad guys' lines. It wasn't so much what one wanted to do as what they *had* to do, so it should be done with enthusiasm.

Joe was not getting fired, but this was also not going to be productive work. Worse than that, it felt like he was being told to help hide some bad things. It felt like when he promised his brother that he wouldn't tell Mom who the girl was he had been out with.

GSA had been caught in an audit and was now told to get rid of those hidden funds. Return them if possible. Everybody knew it wasn't possible. The money was from previous years. If not obligated, the funds were lost. Returning them meant wiping them away – just as if they had never been.

This was why Dad hated the government. It was why most of the people in the country didn't trust it. Joe had come here to write contracts and save money for the taxpayer. He hadn't come here to re-hide hidden money.

It needed to be resolved but not by him. Use lower paid people to do it. At his level, it was just going to be another waste. Taking out a foxhole with a nuke made no sense. He also knew there was no way he could get out of it.

"Joe, when can we meet? When can you start?" Magda was anxious. She was responsible for a good result and wanted a promotion too.

"How about never? Is never good for you?" Joe was flippant. It had worked in the Army to lighten the mood but Magda had never been in the Army and had never met someone like him.

"Dave, what's with Joe? Do you know what he said to me? He said he would never work on that project."

"Oh, don't worry about him. He's alright. Just let him know what you need. He'll do it. He's just being funny, pulling your leg. Hold onto your leg and it'll work out."

The work was long, hard, and tedious. Most of the contact

people were gone. The military was like that. People here for a few years and then reassigned somewhere else. Maybe even retired.

The slow progress was taking its toll. Eventually, Joe talked with Rachel about it. She needed to know what the cost was going to be.

"I'm having trouble doing this work and keeping up with all my contracts. Since our bills are being paid by those contracts and not from resolving these MIPRs, I just want you to know I'm not being very effective. I'm not making much money for GSA."

"Joe, you're my best worker. I need you to keep working on your contracts. If you want, I can get you off the team. Do you want me to do that?"

Really? Why did you put me on it in the first place?

"Yes, I think so. I hate to just quit but this is a real snafu and I think it's more profitable for GSA to have me write contracts than resolve all these old actions. I really do want to make a difference."

Leaving her office, he felt a huge weight drop from his shoulders; almost like dropping a forty-pound rucksack after a twenty-mile road-march. The contracts to buy tools were where GSA made money.

The project needed to be done. He had no doubts about that. But using his skills this way was a great waste. Better to get someone like Jose or Mickey to do it. They weren't very effective in writing contracts. Maybe they could handle this. It was time for them to earn their high government salaries.

Jose and Mickey were birds of a feather. They had been here for years. Never fired because GSA didn't fire anyone, they were also almost useless. They had risen to the top journeyman grade, and received the top pay. However, their best skills were in operating the copier or other simple tasks. Poster examples of government bureaucracy, they existed in the swamp.

Like the leeches that exist off other critters or the unwary visitor to the swamp, they were not vicious like Mara had been. They might even know more about contracting than she did, which was still not saying a lot. Eligible for retirement, they refused to leave. Why didn't they just retire and get out of the way?

Bob was another leech. An engineer by job title, he was as useful as a square tire. If something was assigned to him, Joe could count on it being very late. One day, he asked Breck about Bob. "Has he always been this way or is this the 'getting older' effect?"

Breck laughed, "No, this is pretty much how he's always been."

"Then why is he still here?"

"GSA doesn't fire anyone. Once someone is here, GSA just makes the best of the situation."

"Wow, even in the Army, they fired people." The next day, Joe walked by Bob's desk and saw him concentrating on something on his computer. *Well, at least he does do something some of the time.* When Joe passed back by, he saw the reason for the lack of movement. Bob was asleep. A posterchild for the government – or a swamp leech. Is there a difference?

Joe fell to his knees, yelling out "Augh!" *Better make it look good.*

Bob jumped from his chair, falling on the floor. "What? What happened?"

"Oh, sorry, I just tripped over my own clumsy feet," Joe said standing up. "Are you alright? Looked like I woke you up."

"Nah, just thinking. Deep thinking."

The following day, Bob was excited. "They found my car! I'm going down to see my car!"

"How did you lose it? Was it stolen?"

"I used to think so. It wasn't where I remembered leaving it. So, I reported it to the police as stolen. But, they never found it. I had about given up hope. I even collected on the insurance."

"So, how long has it been anyway – six months?"

"No, it's been twenty years."

"What! I know I didn't hear you right. Did you say *twenty* years?"

"Yeah. That's why I gave up and the insurance company gave up too and paid my claim."

"Well, where did they find it?"

"You know that old warehouse they're tearing down on Wabash?"

"Sure. An eyesore. Been abandoned for years."

"My car was in there. They found it during the demolition and said that they need for me to remove it so they can blow the building up – or is it down? Anyway, I guess I had parked it in there and forgotten."

"Were you drinking that day?"

"Back then, I was drinking every day. Smoked pot too. I was drinking like a fish and smoking like a dragon. I even put on shows. I would show how many cigarettes or joints I could handle at one time. In between drinks, I had one in every viewable body hole – the nostrils, ears, several in the mouth. Others in the bar would be stomping and clapping to whatever tune was on the jukebox while I did my show."

"I only quit when my liver gave out. I had to have a transplant - haven't drank or smoked since."

No, just sleep all day. "So, how's the car? Did they tell you? Maybe it's worth a lot now as an antique?"

"It's all rusted out. It'll have to be scrapped for junk. But I still want to see it."

This explained a lot about Bob. Pot, alcohol, wild times that caused a car to be misplaced for twenty years. Nobody even asked to have it towed off before now. It was a crazy world and Bob was a huge part of it.

In spite of all the swamp critters, Joe found GSA a vast improvement over the fort. After about a year, Jeannie asked him how it compared.

"Joe, why did you leave the fort to come here? I mean, don't get me wrong, it's great working with you. But after that terrible car wreck, is it worth it?"

Looking up at his six foot three, the sub-five feet Christian empathy in her came flowing out. That smile would disarm a desperate felon. The dark brown eyes glowed with...what was it? Empathy? Compassion? She was a Christian yet also a mystery.

"Well, yes it is. There are some things worse than death. I served in the Army for twenty-one years. I was used to a standard of ethics and behavior, to say nothing of how I was treated. But when I retired, I became a civilian at the fort and I saw things that made no sense."

"Like what?"

"Well, after decades under some outstanding leaders, I

started out with a supervisor who used the "F" word, yelling it. She was going through a bad time and shared her misery with her workers. She also ignored me for a long time when she should have been training and developing me. Those things she pushed off to another worker. After a time, she came to see my value. But then, she was replaced by far worse critters."

Jeannie laughed at the use of that word. "Okay, tell me. Why were they 'critters' and what made them even worse? Sounds like that would be hard to do."

"But not impossible. I call them critters because that's the nicest thing I can think of. They didn't behave very human ... or humane."

"The Army command brought our office under a woman who was prejudiced against almost everybody not of Mexican descent. She disliked education and intelligent people. She knew almost nothing about contracting. Worst of all was her hatefulness. She may have had a bad self-image of herself and needed others to brutalize in order to feel better about herself.

She abused my supervisor and then showed us that she intended to make me her next target. She even bragged about how mean she could be. The lawyer for our office showed me where we had almost one hundred percent turnover of our people over the previous year. Discretion being the better part of valor, I decided to pop smoke and get out of there."

"Pop smoke?"

"It's an Army thing. What you do to cover your escape."

"So, I guess this place is a bit better?"

"A bit? It's like day and night."

"Do we have any faults that you've seen? I mean, compared with the fort?"

"Well, I hate to say anything bad. This place and the people have been great to me."

"So, there is something. Now you have to say it. Spit it out."

"It's just the money."

"Aren't you getting enough? You get the same as the rest of us."

"That's just it. I spent twenty-one years in the Army accepting whatever I got and glad to get it. I came here and I'm getting bonuses that I never signed on for. They were never part of the deal."

"That bothers you? Give the money to me. I'll spend it for you."

Joe laughed. "It's not just that. We charge profit from others including the Army. That's where most of our budget comes from. But don't you see? It comes from somewhere. The taxpayer pays taxes to support the Army. The Army pays our prices, including the profit, to get what they need. Every extra dollar we charge is that much less for the soldier in the Army and of course, for the taxpayer too."

"Those bonuses come from the taxpayer and we brag about how much we save the government. Then the trips for training we could get locally or online and staying at the best places. It all adds up to millions of dollars."

"Why, we could generate *all* of our budget, instead of most of our budget, if we cut out those things."

"As a soldier I got by with what was available. The building I worked in at the fort was nowhere near as nice as this one. We should be ashamed every time they hand us a bonus!"

"Then they start with the patriotic talk. They say things

like we're doing a great job serving our country. It's starting to make me sick."

"I never looked at it that way. My school, even the project where I grew up was government funded."

"I never told you about the small town in Colorado where I grew up. My Dad still lives there. There's no way I can tell him about the bonuses. He already views the government and its programs as a national welfare program. He says it takes the wages he gets and gives them away to others. He's never received a government dollar in his life. He might have to take Social Security but he views that as something he's earned after paying into it for years. He thinks I rob banks for a living. That would be more honorable to him. So, do you see my dilemma?"

"Yes. But I still like the money and I won't be turning it down."

"I guess I won't either. I'll just have to learn to deal with it."

****

Two weeks later, it was evaluation time and Joe had hoped for the best. Of course, at the fort, he had also hoped for the best and he saw where that got him. Remembering that, he walked into the supervisor's office, prepared for the worst. Rachel asked him to sit as she noticed his lack of a smile.

"Joe, I am so happy with your work. I'm giving you the highest rating this year. Your work is always on time or early. When you have a problem, you research it first and even bring me a solution. If half my workers were like you, I wouldn't need the other half. Don't ever leave here. I need you. We need you."

Ah, if Diona would say that. "Thanks. I like the work and working under you. It's great to feel like I'm making a difference." The frown was replaced by a smile that he couldn't avoid. Being appreciated was a new and hard to deal with situation. That last place – there sure wasn't a lot of appreciation there. The Army? If they liked and appreciated you, they showed it by messing with you. This warm fuzzy stuff would take a lot of getting used to.

Joe did like the work and the place too. Even without the bonuses, he was making more money than he ever thought he would when he was a soldier. He had doubted the wisdom of his decision to leave Fort Prairie. That seemed like a lifetime ago.

Now, he couldn't imagine working anywhere else. That's the problem with imagination. It distracts you when you have work to do and abandons you when you need to be more creative.

Joe hadn't forgotten the swamp at the fort. It was a goal delayed. Get more experience and advancement, then he would be in a position to go back with his plunger.

****

"What! You told him what? I just heard from her. You've got to change it." Josefina was going ballistic.

"I can't. He already knows what he's getting. He's earned it too."

"I'm not arguing about that. His work is great. But you let him off the hook on that project. You could've used it to resolve this problem. Don't you see? You've got to think about what *she's* going to do. She's not playing games. She doesn't care if I am of Mexican descent like her. That adds up to exactly nothing. Now I have to hide. Maybe I can take leave – a lot of it." They were both scared.

Chapter Seven

The slippery elm was everywhere. Named for its slippery inner bark, it was prolific and grew everywhere in the swamp. Native Americans used the inner bark as a medicine. Even now, it is taken for coughs, constipation, and well, just about anything else.

"Oh Danny Boy, the pipes, the pipes are calling." Joe was feeling great and the tune came from nowhere, just like the mood. He had come in early to work on an important project that he wanted to complete ahead of schedule. Avoiding the big city traffic that early in the morning was just an added bonus.

He had learned most of the ropes, even helping others who had been there longer. They saw him as an expert and came to him, stroking his ego. He saw his mentor, Jeannie and said, "Good Morning." The tune came on again "from glen to glen and down the mountainside." He should have kept quiet because Jeannie pounced on him.

"Stop right there. Joe, we need your help. Bob's Tools has done it this time. They're *so* done!" Jeannie had formed a special team to develop a new approach.

Bob's Cut-rate Tools knew the government playbook and was out-swamping the government swamp. They always bid low on a contract and got the contract. They manufactured their own tools and the quality was always fine. However, their facility was small so their speed was terrible.

GSA made money by buying and reselling tools. But the tools from Bob's were now running very late; more than a year late. That meant the Army did without those needed tools for a year.

That couldn't continue – not if GSA wanted to survive. Jeannie decided to create a mathematical formula to evaluate bids. Joe was new to this part of the process. He didn't know that her approach was frowned on by almost everybody in their field. He just saluted and moved out to the attack.

For a while, the approach worked well. New contracts went to other companies. Bob's was not getting anything new and there was talk of terminating the existing contracts.

Then, Bob the tool man called and had a great story about Joe. "Joe is being unfair! He told us our tools are garbage and he'll make sure we never get another contract. We're going to sue GSA!"

Rachel and Josefina asked Joe for his side of it. "Joe, did you say that?"

"No. I never even had a conversation and never sent them an email or a letter. I just followed the new approach and they usually come in low because of their terrible past performance."

"That's pretty much what we thought."

"So, am I in trouble? Do I need a lawyer?"

"Joe, you kill me." Rachel was laughing. Rachel dismissed Bob's complaint while Josefina just stared at the floor. Mara would never have done that.

Josefina watched Joe leave. Her lips were slightly parted but no words came out. "Rachel, why did you do that? You could have made *her* happy. You could have gotten both of us off the hot seat." Josefina knew Rachel had lost an opportunity. She was getting desperate.

"I couldn't. I just couldn't. We've complained about some of these bad workers we have. Then we get someone like Joe who lives to serve. How can we trump something up?"

"I know what you're saying but..."

Some of the good guys also complained. One of them – Jim's Quality Tools wasn't taking it. "I don't understand why we lost this contract. We've been providing it for twenty years. We think we should get the contract."

Jim was a very unusual supplier. He did all that was possible to provide American-made tools to the government. When a manufacturer went out of business, Jim bought their stock to continue selling American products as long as possible. Since they went above and beyond, Joe wanted to make things right. He told Jim why the contract went to another company.

Jim wasn't buying it. He protested the contract. This was Joe's first protest and it got ugly. After copying thousands of pages of documents and sending them to the Government Accounting Office, Joe thought the protest was simple and he would come out on top. He did not. More questions came up and again the GAO ruled against GSA.

The back and forth went on several times. Each time, there was a fine point that Josefina said was worth fighting for. Each time, they lost. Joe thought Josefina was just being stubborn. He didn't know about her other motive. She needed something, almost anything to resolve her own personal dilemma.

Finally, Joe told Rachel and Josefina, "Maybe we just need to end this. Every time we fight, we lose, and when we lose, we have to pay Jim's legal costs which are very high with their expensive Washington DC lawyer. We need to cut our losses and move on."

Josefina wasn't buying it. Sooner or later she would have enough on Joe and then she could get off that hot seat. "I think there's a point to be made," Josefina said. The battle and the costs continued.

One day, on a restroom break, Joe considered the situation. Like a lot of men, he seemed to do his best thinking in there. "Time to think outside the box. We need to avoid the bad suppliers like Bob's. But we also need to get good prices. But we also need to avoid protests. If we could write everything we need into the solicitation. Then we could just make price the only factor."

"Wait, why can't we? We know how fast companies can get the tools to us. Our records show us the performance record of all those companies. If we just make that part of the standard, we can make price the determining factor. We'll get what we need!"

It was so simple; it was probably wrong. Some lawyer would say "You can't do that." Then they would explain in legal gibberish the *why*, and Joe would just have to nod in feigned agreement. It would be like in the Army when he replied "hooah" but his voice said "I don't have a clue."

Excited and out of breath, Joe went to see Rachel. "We just need to change our process to specify a low price, technically acceptable mode and make delivery and performance part of the requirement. We already have all the information we need. Let's do this as an LPTA!"

"I don't see why we can't but then again, I'm not a lawyer. I sure don't want either of us to go to jail for this."

Chanephe was the lawyer. She was uncertain. She also had better things to do and was already late for lunch. Why can't you just do what you've always done? Why do you have to make this so hard?"

Rachel told her why. "It's not working. We're getting bad contractors. Now we have an unwinnable protest. The old way is broke."

Chanephe kept watching the door. Her lunch date would be here any minute. She could keep arguing but then she would miss that date – and he was more than good looking. She was even hoping for a ring. She gave in. "I don't think it's ever been done before. But there's also no reason we can't do it. Let's try it."

"Great!" they all agreed.

"Now, not to be rude, though I really don't care, but get out of my office. I'm expecting someone good-looking and that sure isn't either of you."

The new approach was new to the government but also to the contractors. Joe reassured them. "If you have good performance and can meet the delivery period, you will qualify. If you have no performance history, you still qualify. However, bad performers will not qualify."

The results were spectacular. No protest, no bad supplier, and a low price. Everything that was good. Soon, all of the other workers were using it. Joe had recreated GSA, or at least his corner of it. Money was saved for GSA and for the taxpayer. Joe had that warm feeling all over. It was almost like being back in the Army. This would save lots of money for the government and make him look good. He had made a difference. Those big holes in the parking lot were getting just a bit smaller.

****

GSA had been great but Joe wanted to find a way to get back to that swamp at the fort. Rachel and Josefina had also been cold lately. What was that about? "Have I done anything wrong?" he asked.

"No, not at all." As the phone rang, he was still confused. "Excuse me. I have to take this call." Well, first time for everything. Always before, she had just told him to wait. Now, what was it? She really seemed to be getting rid of him. So odd.

"No, I haven't been avoiding you. What do you want me to do? Look, I told you before; we're working this as fast as we can. Do you want us to get fired? Yes, I know you don't care but what good would we be to you then?"

Joe overheard the near end of the conversation but it made no sense. The door slamming shut behind him was another story. Josefina and Rachel were under pressure – a lot of it.

Joe knew it was going to be a great week. Like always, he was wrong. The next day was a Tuesday but it behaved like a Monday – and what a Monday. Joe came in all primed to do great things. He was moving so fast, he failed to see the sign "Wet Floor."

The floor was more than wet. It had been waxed – and then some. The custodial crew was in such a hurry that they waxed the wet floor before it had dried. Then the next shift came in, saw where the previous shift forgot to note they had waxed the floor. They waxed it again. They usually used slip-resistant polish on the concrete floor. However, they ran out of it, so the new crew used the other stuff.

Joe never saw it. He was feeling great and singing "I Believe I Can Fly." Then, he really was flying. When he woke up, he was on a gurney in an ambulance. His face was covered with blood. It felt cold. *Why is it so cold?* He tried to ask "What happened? Where am I?" However, it just came out as, "Wha' hakken?"

"Slow down, your nose is broken. You took a bad spill."

"No. I don' use drugs." His ears were ringing. *Can't somebody shut off that alarm?*

"Not pills." She was yelling now. "You took a bad spill. Take it easy. We'll get you to the hospital. Your boss and your wife already know. They'll meet us there."

It was the first time Joe had ever been in an ambulance. That time in the Army with the explosion, the hospital had been next door so they just helped him walk over there. This time it was the full treatment including the flashing lights. Joe felt special for the first time in a long time – and guilty too.

Dr. Torres had a terrible bedside manner. However, he knew his stuff. "Joe, you have a concussion, a badly broken nose, and this will probably add to your arthritis as you age."

"You're lucky. What were you thinking, leaping in the air like that? Were you trying to metamorphose into a bird? No, no, don't talk right now. I just do this from time to time since you can't answer back – it makes me feel like the king. Thank you. Thank you verra much." The world's worst Elvis impersonator and he was Joe's jailer.

Rachel was in the room about three hours later. "How are you feeling? Do you know what happened?"

"I fall dow." The nose was definitely affecting Joe as were the drugs.

She let out a deep breath, so Rachel-like. "Yes, you fell

down. That floor was really slick. They took care of it after you fell so nobody else got hurt. You might have a lawsuit here."

"Nah. I've never sued in my life. Besides, I hear a broken nose gives a man more character. But I do expect lots of ice cream."

"You'll get it. Oh, by the way, a lot of your co-workers are pulling for you."

"Oh yeah? Well if they're pulling for me, why aren't they here? They should be here with magazines and chocolate and dancing girls."

"They are – well most of that anyway. They're just outside. The nurse wouldn't let them in. She said, one at a time."

"Oh, well then, let them in with their tribute. Thanks for stopping by." He grinned at her that usual Irish grin – so hideous now with the nose bandaged up.

After a few days to fix the nose and make sure Joe wasn't going to die from the concussion, he was out on probation. The only good thing about the hospital stay had been the ice cream. There was no house limit.

Two weeks from the accident, he was going back to work. He was getting stir-crazy and the house felt more like a prison than a refuge. Things would get better now – it would take a year to fully recover but at least he could sit at a desk.

As he entered the building, he was careful of the floor, looking everywhere for signs to beware of the sneaky floor. When he got to the office, he immediately went to his computer. However, there was no computer, nor even a desk for it to sit on. The telephone was still there but sitting
on the floor.

"What are you doing here?" Rachel yelled.

"I work here. I didn't expect a welcome back party but I didn't expect to be yelled at either."

"We were told you would be out two months. They thought you might have a blood clot in your head from that concussion."

"No, I always act this intellectually challenged."

"Very funny. Did the doctor discharge you or did you just make a break for it?"

"I'm on probation. Where is my desk?"

"We're getting new furniture and since you weren't expected back for a while, we thought your stuff would be a good place to start. The new one should be delivered in ninety minutes. Why don't you just go down to the cafeteria and take a break? I bet the doctor told you to take it easy. That's probably one of the terms of your probation."

Joe grinned. Being found out always brought out the guilty look.

"Before you go though, come into my office. I have something to talk over with you." Now she was serious. This looked bad. Here he was, jumping to conclusions again. *It's probably nothing serious. Maybe a safety talk. She'll tell me to quit skating on the floor. Yeah, that's it.*

"Joe, I heard about an opening here in another department. It's a promotion and I think you should apply for it."

"Huh?"

"Look, I'm not trying to get rid of you, but I think you need to move up. We love you here but ... don't give me that look!"

"What look?" Was she feeling guilty about something?

"Those puppy eyes again. You always do that and then I feel

bad. Put in for that job. I can't tell you everything that's going on, but this will be a good thing for you."

There it was again. Something under the surface but a secret too. What Joe wouldn't give to be a mind reader right now.

"Well, if you're sure."

"Yes. I'll send you a link to the job. Use me as a reference. You'll get the job. I'm sure of that."

She had found a way out of the dilemma. She couldn't tell Joe what was going on but she knew, that he knew, something wasn't right.

A month later he got the job. He was happy, but Rachel was ecstatic. "That must be what she looked like as a High School Cheerleader," Joe thought.

When she stopped jumping around and caught her breath, she said, "See, I told you that you could get it. Your pay is going up, so your wife should be happy too. Go call her and give her the good news. Take the rest of the day off and take Diona to dinner to celebrate."

What Joe didn't know, what he couldn't know, was that her excitement was more than for him. It was also for herself. She was free. It was this alone that caused her to prove she still *could* jump. A feeling of ecstasy that only the pursued or the prisoner can easily relate to – that was what motivated her now.

The following week, as Joe started to turn over projects to others, Rachel decided it was time for the goodbye talk. "You've been more than awesome here. Your work was always early. And that new approach? It's already catching on and saving us thousands of dollars. It'll probably wind up saving us millions over the long haul. I hate it that you're leaving but I'm sure glad you were here."

"Well, thanks. I just tried to do my part."

"Your part? Don't you know? If everyone worked like you, I could get by with a lot fewer overpaid employees. If you ever want to come back, just say the word."

"Well, thanks. That means a lot to me – more than medals or money." She never saw the tear in his eye as he walked away.

Well, that gets me off the hot seat. How can she fault me now? Maybe he'll be free of her in that other office. She was crying now too.

Dave was the second one he had to find a way to say goodbye to. Work partners, sharing their knowledge and encouragement on a daily basis – how does one say thank you for all that? How can one say goodbye?

He was thinking of what to say when Dave beat him to it. "Well old man, I hear you're leaving. We need to go fishing. I have a great boat. Just name the place. We have a lot to talk about. Things we can't talk about here."

He was older than Joe and had never served a day in the military. However, his respect for soldiers and his values left Joe seeing Dave just like an old soldier.

"How about Julesburg Reservoir? They have some walleye." The date was set and Dave would bring his boat. Joe hadn't been boat fishing since his teenage years when cousin Darrel had taken him. The results were about the same. One fish caught.

"Well, I guess they'd call it catching instead of fishing if that's how it worked out." Dave was trying to lighten the mood. The silver lining in a slow fishing day was that they had lots of free time to talk.

"Joe, I might be interested in coming over there if another opening comes up."

"But why? Don't you like it where you are?"

"Oh, it's alright but it's mostly women there. With you leaving I'm thinking about a change too. I don't see things getting a whole lot better and maybe a change is what I need. I've still got at least five years before I can go and…"

Beep. Beep. Dave's work cellphone was ringing. He grabbed for it, felt it slip, and almost caught it as it bounced in the air. The splash as it went in the water was sickening. A five hundred-dollar cell phone with government access systems and codes on it and now it was gone, in the deepest part of the lake. "Joe, did you see…"

"Yes, I sure did. Man, that's terrible. What are you going to do?"

"What can I do? It's gone. There's no way to get it back. I'll just have to report it on Monday."

"Wow! If I hadn't seen it, I might not believe it. It would just be another big fish story. You won't get in trouble for this will you?"

"Well, I'm supposed to have it with me since I'm on call. Of course, I'm also not supposed to wash it. I might have to pay for a replacement." They both laughed at the tragedy. It wasn't exactly funny but what else was there to do?

At work Dave reported it. Rachel was sympathetic but she had a process to follow. "First you have to report it to the security office. Were there any other witnesses?"

"Yeah, Joe saw it happen."

"Good. But he'll have to do a statement too. The phone is one thing but the information on it is another."

"It should be password locked against access and nobody should be able to open it. Since it went in the deepest part of the lake it should be rusted out before anyone finds it, if ever."

"Yes, you're right about that. It'll come up at staff meeting. You know you'll be getting a lot of laughs."

****

"Dave, this is the security office. Could you come down here please?"

"Sure. Can you tell me what it's about?"

"It's about that phone you reported losing two weeks ago."

"What now? I did everything you told me to do."

"It's been found."

"Found? How? I saw it go in the lake. So did Joe."

"Well, it looks like you've got an additional witness to that. We got a call a few hours ago from Jack Roehm. Do you know him?"

"No."

"Well, anyway he said he caught a five-pound walleye at Julesburg Reservoir yesterday. Took it home to clean and found the phone inside. He brought it by an hour ago and we were able to track the serial number."

"You've got to be kidding. No way. "What a fish story!

Since it was time to start handing off work projects, Joe saved his best project for Lorna. He had been working with her for two and a half years. She was very young, about twenty-five and pleasant, if somewhat plain looking and unable to get together a great wardrobe. Long, straight, stringy hair completed her dull look. That was part of her charm – simple and down to earth.

Many times, she had come to Joe for advice and the relationship had been good. He liked her so why not give this to her so she could shine? He also hated to just drop something that looked so promising.

"This is a folder about reverse auctioning. It's another way to get our prices down. If you're interested in looking into it, you might be able to get some kudos for it."

She snatched it out of his hands eagerly, even greedily. "How's it work? I've never heard of it."

"Well, instead of bidding prices higher, you get the suppliers to keep bidding lower. Ultimately, the government gets to the lowest possible price. It might save us millions of dollars if it works like they say it will."

Contractors hated the approach but Joe worked for the people – not for the contractors. During his Army days he often had time to kill; long days without end, punctuated by an emergency. Reading western novels by Louis L'Amour helped with that. Nothing spoke to him louder than the phrase 'Riding for the Brand.' Loyalty had to go to your current boss – that was above almost all else.

"I'll look at it later today. Thanks! I'm your friend for life."

There was still that nagging voice "You failed!"

"No, I didn't. I improved the methods here and saved a lot of money."

"So what? You're still leaving. Like a whipped dog with its tail between its legs. You're a failure."

"Shut up. I'm just going to go get more experience in another job. I'm going to make it. This isn't a retreat. It's a strategic repositioning."

"Quitter!"

I'll show you. I'll show them all.

Chapter Eight

The spider-eating assassin bug found what he was looking for. A spider web advertised the presence of a spider. Touching the web to simulate a trapped insect, he enticed the spider to come to him. As it approached, the spider found that it had been tricked and was itself, to be the lunch.

Joe had entered another corner of the swamp. "This time it's going to be different." He told himself that but he wasn't sure. Of course, this time it came with a promotion. GS-13. *Wow! I never thought I'd reach this level. When I retired, I just wanted a livable wage and to be left alone to do my job.*

But that nagging doubt remained. Why did this keep happening? He kept leaving jobs. It was like when he was in the Army and got reassigned every few years.

Diona didn't understand either. She had put up with the Army moves. Now, she didn't have to move but he kept on doing it. "Why do you keep changing jobs? Every two or three years you have to change jobs. Why?"

"You just don't understand."

"You sure got that right."

"Something came up each time, so I left. Rachel told me to take this job. I'm not sure why, but I trust her judgment." He looked into her usually soft brown eyes. He needed some encouragement, some support. The look was different. Hard, compassionless – there was also no support, no partnership. This wasn't the Diona he had depended on for so many years.

"Joe, things don't just happen. Are you doing something wrong? Do you make your bosses mad at you? Maybe you have a self-destructive need." Now the psychology was coming out. Joe hated it when she did that. It was like mind games.

The conversation was over. Nothing he could say would satisfy her. He didn't know why things happened. She was right though. It did seem to be more than coincidence.

Didn't he have more college than any of his peers? His ratings were always good. It was just so frustrating. To know that something is wrong but not know what it is was so frustrating. The unsolvable mystery – that was what it was. This didn't happen in the Army. Why did it happen as a civilian?

Just one more promotion and Joe could go back to Fort Prairie as the boss. New clothes from an upscale men's clothing store advertised that he was a professional. He was determined to do more than succeed. Dress for success – wasn't that what they said? He was going to outshine all the others. All he needed was a chance, an opportunity.

Back in a cubicle, this one was different. Walls six feet high, a locking door, three times the floor space of a typical cubicle, this looked like the Taj Mahal of cubicles. Joe wasn't sure what to expect but this wasn't it. All of the other workers were slumming with typical cubicles while he got the best.

"Good morning Ma'am. I'm here and ready for duty. Is that my cubicle? It looks like it's for a Senior Executive."

"Good morning to you too," Angie laughed. "Glad to have you aboard, as my Navy husband would say. Yes, that's your cubicle. You're my only contracting officer so I can afford to give you the best. I've also got a reserved parking space for you. If it seems like I'm trying to buy your loyalty, you're right. But I know you've got a lot of questions for me and I have a lot for you. For now, just spend some time in the contract files."

Joe found the files, but what a mess. They had been left incomplete by others in the rush out the door as the organization reduced its size. At times, he thought of himself as the janitor. This was no exception. Joe was the janitor with a mess to clean up.

Expecting more of the high-quality leadership he had gotten from Tibby and Rachel, Joe found some differences. Angie had been around a long time. She needed a contracting officer for her branch to provide telephone services to all federal customers in the four-state region.

"Joe, in addition to the ongoing contracts, we have a new requirement. We're bringing internet phone service to all federal buildings. We call it "voice over internet protocol," but since that is a mouthful, just use VOIP."

"However, this is the future so we need to get it right. Since we have to have high speed internet anyway, it just makes sense to save money by using internet-based telephone service. It's a whole lot cheaper."

"This is your opportunity to shine since you have the national pilot and after you get this done, we'll share it around the country. Ultimately, it will be worth billions of dollars. You're on the hot seat now."

Okay, no pressure. Just focus on this one. It's only six million dollars. Only six million dollars? When had he started thinking like that?

"Got it. No problem."

"Are you sure?"

"No, but what else can I say?" Both were laughing now.

Joe spent the next month reviewing his contracts and the new one. "Angie, I just reviewed the contract we want to award this against. It doesn't look like it covers this type of work. That means we can't do this."

"No problem."

"No problem? Maybe you don't understand. What I mean is we can't do this. It would be illegal."

"No, I understood just fine. However, Headquarters wrote the contract and said they would modify it to cover this."

"I'm not sure that they can do it. It looks illegal to me, modifying the contract now. Although I'm sure that the contractor will be willing since it means extra money for them."

"So, if HQ does modify it, will that be okay? I mean, you can use it and won't be responsible if someone else modifies it, right?"

"Well, yeah. I guess so." It didn't smell right but the responsibility was with someone else. Joe knew the huge pressure that everyone was under. He was also unwilling to do the illegal thing, but if someone else did it and took responsibility... The people at HQ were above Joe's paygrade and they were supposed to be a lot smarter. Lawyers would be reviewing it too. How could he say no?

Fired. Joe didn't see it coming. Almost nobody did. Angie was removed from the supervisor's position. Joe got along well with her. He thought everyone did. But there were rumors, complaints, creaks under the floorboards that only those in the know or with their ear pressed to the floor were aware of. Lee was placed in charge. He had been Angie's second. Now, he was first. Did he cause the replacement? Only those in the know, knew for sure. Joe was not political so he just did his work.

A few months later, the first contract was awarded – six million dollars and billions more to come. Joe had created the template and approach. Without him it wouldn't have happened.

It should have gotten Joe that coveted GS-14 that he needed to go back and clean the swamp at the fort. There were cake and lots of celebration. Backslapping too. That was when the speeches were made, recognizing everyone for their role – everyone except Joe.

Well, I guess I should just be happy to have had a role in this. Happy in a job well done. Joe kept telling himself that it was okay but he knew it wasn't. Even an old Christian soldier likes a pat on the back. When it's stolen, that just doesn't set well. Joe smiled but even that was a lie.

Lee was like a catfish, a total bottom feeder. Scooping whatever falls from the hunters and going in for the kill if it sees a defenseless or sick fish. Even when things didn't need to be said, he said them. He was rather like the catfish that can't keep its mouth shut.

"Hey Joe, how's it going?" Dave had met him for lunch and they walked the enormous hallways of the old aircraft factory.

"Okay, I guess. Just a lot of work. I guess that's probably why I feel tired."

"Are you sure that's all?"

"No. I feel like my corvette was stolen before I even got to drive it."

"Huh?"

Joe laid it out for Dave.

"Man, that stinks. I see what you mean. Hey, did you hear that they're talking about making the supervisor jobs in our section GS-14s? Maybe you should apply. We have a supervisor opening coming up. You used to work there so you know what we do. You've only been away a year so you don't have to learn a lot. You're even well-liked and respected. You'd just have the twins to worry about. But you're more tactful than I am so you should do well."

The 'twins' were not twins at all, nor even related. However, they were both female, both about the same twenty-something, and very close friends. They thought alike and behaved alike. They supported each other and all the workers knew if you riled one, you riled the other as well. They were an unbreakable alliance.

"Hmm." Joe wanted to get promoted so he could qualify for the director's job at the fort. If he could get the supervisor job, and then it was upgraded to GS-14, that would help him to reach that goal. Except for a supervisor that ignored his accomplishments, his current job wasn't so bad. But, maybe…His mind turning and scheming, Joe was already warming up to the idea.

"So, what about the twins? What are they up to nowadays?"

"Well, they're both branch supervisors. One would be your boss if you got the job."

"Which one?"

"Lorna. Rachel is retiring and took a non-supervisory job for her last few months. You would be applying for her job. Oh, and Rachel would work under you. How's that for a kick in the head? But both of the twins are a piece of work."

"How so?"

"Well, Lorna wants everything exactly her way. She doesn't like Christians and is oh, so politically correct. I wouldn't trust her very far. Traci is so unapproachable. She keeps her door locked all the time. She won't talk to her workers except when she has to. She won't even say good morning to anyone. Everybody knows that she hates her job but loves the money. There's no problem with leadership since neither of them have any. Oh, and there's that new approach you invented."

"Yes?"

"They're claiming they created it. Just like your current boss, they took credit for what you did."

"Well then, they owe me – big time. I've worked under difficult people before. If it gets bad, I guess I could just do the one year with Lorna and then look for another position. I can handle that much. They can't fire me for my religion, can they?"

Dave just shrugged his shoulders. He knew what the twins were like more than anyone else. Joe would find out.

Joe rationalized it, convincing himself that it would be a good move. *I worked well with her the last time I was there. I did her a favor when I left and gave her the 'fedbid' thing to look into to increase her personal stock. I think it should be okay. Dave probably exaggerates things.*

A few days later, he saw Lorna also walking the enormous hallways, getting exercise, just like Joe. 'Hey, Joe. How's it going?"

"Great. Just trying to clear the cobwebs on my break. And you?" He looked closely at Lorna. The past few years had been great for her career but not for her. The hair was graying and stringier than Joe remembered.

Facial hair was pronounced. Was that there before? He was

almost envious since she had more facial hair than he did. Sometimes he hated the Cheyenne genes he carried that had cost him the hairy manliness of others. For a moment he wondered if she also had more hair on her chest than he did. Getting the shivers from that thought, he quickly dropped it.

"Same. Good seeing you."

Well, maybe my stock is higher than I realized. Maybe I should apply for that job. I can always turn it down if I change my mind. Don't stare at the hair!

****

The interview was over almost as soon as it started. At least, that's how it felt. One hour – that was the standard interview. One hour to make or break. One hour to sell oneself. It was also a telephonic interview to make it a level playing field for those who lived far away and couldn't attend an interview in person. In theory, it also eliminated biases and prejudices.

The following days turned into weeks. Joe prayed about it as he did about almost everything. The Almighty can see farther than anybody, so Joe passed the decision to him.

"Lorna, if you hire Joe, you won't be able to control him. You know that don't you?" Magda remembered Joe's flippant way when they were on that special team a few years earlier and read into it a whole personality.

She also knew Joe was a retired Army sergeant which carried its own stereotyping. Of course, she also wasn't wrong.

Lorna remembered how they had worked well together before. She remembered he had mentored her and even given her that special project that gained her a lot of upper management notice, so she ignored the warning. Why any worker at that level needed to be controlled, neither of them even considered.

Leadership was a foreign word so, just like Mara, they exercised control, sometimes management, but never leadership.

"I need him. We need him. He's worked for the Army which is one of our biggest customers. He knows how they operate. He's worked for other departments here at GSA. He has done other types of contracts – the same ones we're talking about using. He has an enormous amount of knowledge and I intend to tap into it. Also, all the supervisors here are women. That looks bad. Any questions?"

****

"Great news, Joe!" The person on the other end of the call didn't even bother to identify herself. It had the same prefix as Joe had on the caller ID, but that could be any of five hundred people at GSA.

"Huh? Ah, who is this please?"

"Oh, sorry. This is Tami in Human Resources. I thought everybody knew my number by heart," she laughed. "Anyhow, I'm calling to offer you the supervisor job you applied for. Do you still want it?"

Thank you, Father. "Yes. Yes, I do."

"Great! I'll close this out and let them know you accepted. Be on the lookout for my emails. That will be from Tami with an 'I'."

Joe owed his supervisor a heads up. He was a little surprised when Lee didn't say any of the usual things. 'You're leaving? No, say it isn't so. We're going to miss you but good luck to you.' No, none of those things were said.

Instead, "Okay. Just let me know when. I guess we should start looking for a replacement." Leadership was not his strength either – and he had been in the Air Force.

One last surprise awaited Joe as he prepared to leave. Lee prepared his performance evaluation. It wasn't bad but not top notch either. He gave Joe top marks in all areas but one. That one was a no-brainer since it only required a few networking meetings. There were also the millions of dollars in profits that GSA would be getting after Joe's VOIP project.

"Why aren't I getting the top score in this area?"

"I just don't feel comfortable giving you the top score. That would give you a top score overall. If I do it for you, others will want it."

"So? You won't be giving it to me. I earned it didn't I? Aren't these evaluation criteria, yours? I just followed the game plan during the past year. If others have earned it, they should get it. If not, then they should get what they did earn. You made the rules. I just played the game by them." Lee just shrugged his shoulders.

Not right. It's just not right. But what are the choices? Are there any? Well, there's the union. I've never been there but then nothing's ever been this clear-cut.

"Rachel, what do you think I should do?" Joe explained the issue to his former supervisor.

"You should go to the union. That woman – she loves to tangle with supervisors. This isn't right but I think you already know that."

The walk to the union rep's office seemed long. *Am I doing the right thing? Maybe I should just accept this and move on.* His feet felt like lead. The office was in the basement, down a dark hallway that resembled a dungeon. Her office door was secured so Joe had to buzz her. The door creaked from lack of oil, emphasizing the dungeon image.

"Salli, I need some help. At least, I hope you can help."

"What is it? You've never been here before. Are you even a member? Not that it matters. In the government, we have to help all as long as you're not management. You're not are you?"

"Well, no. At least, during the period for the issue I want to talk about, I was a non-supervisory worker."

"Then I can help. What's the issue?"

"My supervisor denied me a top score on my evaluation. I met the criteria. He never denied that." Joe showed her the documents.

"Did he give you a reason?"

"He said he didn't feel comfortable giving me a top score. He said that he's concerned about giving me a top score and then the other workers finding out and wanting it too."

She laughed. "Just a moment." Tap, tap, tap, and just like that she sent Lee an email. "The Union wants to know, what does your comfort level have to do with an honest appraisal?" Sometimes it can be just that simple.

The answer came back in a few hours. "I'll change the rating. Sorry you had to get involved." That Salli was one scary woman.

Rachel laughed too. "Well, it's nice to see that things work out the right way – at least some of the time."

Sometimes the swamp didn't win. Other times, one critter could offset another. Of course, sometimes it seems that you're winning when you're not.

The first day in the new job, Rachel was the second person Joe saw, after Lorna. "If there's anything I can do to help you, let me know. I'm so glad you're here."

"So, you're okay with me as the supervisor? It feels weird to me."

"Oh sure. I know we'll do great. It's only for a few months anyway. Then it's off to retirement land for me." Her advice was invaluable. Many times, she said "you might do this" and other times "I wouldn't do that."

She knew all the players and workers. Some of the workers were swamp critters. But then, so were some of the managers. Joe was now the only male supervisor in the department. The engineers had male supervisors but that was pretty typical for them. It was a good old girls club but Joe was determined to make it work; to show them that a man could do just as good as a woman in this type of work.

Joe had over twenty years of leadership training and experience. Find out what people want and then help them to get it. If you work with them, they'll usually work with you. He decided to use those Army leadership skills, along with the technical management tools that Lorna provided him with. Management without leadership was a cold, unfeeling animal.

Combining them was a great way to create an effective, efficient and friendly workplace. There were times he didn't agree with Lorna, but he also knew it was bad leadership to disagree publicly.

Privately he voiced his concerns but carried out her directions. Of course, he also knew that the workers knew where some of the more questionable directions came from. Officially, he was the bad guy at times, but in reality, all knew swamp gas came from the bloated crocodiles and Swamp Donkeys.

****

"Party time! Everybody gather around. We're doing a video. We want to show our people in their everyday habitat, doing what they do. If it's not interesting then do something wild. Stand on your head, throw a kiss, and roll around on the floor if you want. But make it interesting. This is a competition and Darnell wants us to win. Losing isn't an option."

"Huh?" Joe had missed the meeting and didn't know this was coming. The videographer came along and asked him if he wanted to participate. "No. I don't think so. I look bad in person and worse on film. You're going to have to do it without me."

"This also looks pretty iffy," he thought.

"Okay. But Rabbi is on your team and wants to help. Is that alright? Come on Joe, don't be such a stick in the mud."

"I guess so, since this comes from Darnell."

It wasn't long before the video was available on the internal website. Within a few days it was on national news.

...And this tonight. The nation's cost savings agency, GSA has been creating humorous videos on the taxpayer's dime. Coming on the heels of the Las Vegas scandal that cost taxpayers nearly a million dollars to host, and included a mind-reader and a clown, Congress is now asking if this is how GSA is spending the billions appropriated to it. GSA is supposed to save us money – not spend it on clowns and videos. Some are even calling for the dismantling of GSA.

Joe held his tongue – the words I told you so would not help anyone. The old soldier also knew when silence was called for. He always tried to save money – in the Army and in the Civil Service. Was this what he was saving it for, so others could make videos and have their minds read?

The Las Vegas reception was almost a hundred dollars a plate; what were they serving, beluga caviar on tartan crackers? It made him sick. Everyone wants to be proud of their work and organization. How was that possible here? Even without being attacked by swamp critters, just the smell was enough to make one sick. The smell got worse.

"Joe, I want you to move Verny and Eloiise. Some of the younger workers are complaining about Birna. She has some, well let's just say, unsavory habits. Anyway, please move Verny and Eloiise to where Tricia and Zoe are."

"Umm, why move Verny and Eloiise? They've been here for years and always done great work. They have a lot of the institutional knowledge that we still need to tap before they retire in a few years. It just seems to me that they have earned a few benefits from their loyal service including not having to deal with the Birna issue."

"Tricia and Zoe are the future. We need to keep them happy. The other ladies are on the way out so they're not what I'm concerned about. Do you see it differently?"

"Well, I just thought the workplace was kind of like the interstate highway. When you're new, you need to wait for an opening in traffic, merge, and when you're in a good position, then you can influence the traffic speed. Showing preferential treatment to the young workers who haven't earned special consideration yet seems very unfair to those who came before."

"I see." For a half-minute she just stared. Then, biting her lip, she said, "Well, thanks for sharing that with me. But I still want the move to happen. Will you see to it please?"

"Yes. Of course, if you want it, then I will do it." Some things seemed wrong but if they were at least legal, Joe would carry out the instructions. Just like in the Army – if it isn't illegal then do it. *I hope they get mad and complain to the union.*

Verny was a very faithful worker. She had been at GSA for almost thirty years. Eloiise had almost as much time and was the most pleasant person Joe had ever worked with. This was not going to be easy for him. It downright stunk – literally.

"Joe, why do we have to move? Why do we have to trade places with Tricia and Zoe?"

"I'm very sorry but Lorna wants it that way. She's afraid of losing Tricia and Zoe if they have to remain near Birna." For once, he was telling them where this was coming from. There was no way he was going to take the heat for it.

"I guess she's not afraid of losing us, huh?" Eldana asked.

"I don't want to lose you. I mean that. You're the best people we have and I want you to stay. I know you could retire any time but I hope you won't."

"We won't but we're not doing it for Lorna."

"I understand. Thank you."

The following week it was "Team Building Day," and the office met as a whole group. Many were out of the office on various days of the week to "telework." A computer, internet, and phone were all that workers needed. They could work from home or from the bar for that matter. As long as their work got done, nobody cared where it was done.

But on Team Building Day, everybody had to be in the office for training, getting reacquainted with their fellow workers, and doing something as a team.

It was almost Christmas so each group of workers had to compete on building a "Gingerbread House." GSA provided the materials and the winning team even got a cash award.

Of course, this was all on duty time since it was about building the team and working together. It never made any profit, the goal of GSA, and never provided any supplies to the rest of the government, its other goal, but it was fun.

I wonder what the taxpayers would say if they caught this and posted it to the internet. Joe wasn't disloyal so he wouldn't actually do that. But he also hated waste and this sure looked like it.

In the Army, they said, "If it walks like a duck, quacks like a duck, then it's probably a duck." Well, this sure looked like a boondoggle to Joe, but what did he know? What he should have known was more to the point. He never even saw the quicksand.

Chapter Nine

The air in the swamp was still and putrid as the saber-toothed swamp donkey made her way to the water. Believed to be mythical, and nothing more than the creation of fertile imaginations, she depended on this agnosticism to escape notice. A body like a donkey, tangled hair hanging straight down to her knees, long, razor sharp teeth protruding from mismatched jaws and feet like a duck, enabling her to swim, she couldn't possibly exist in nature and yet, here she was. No other swamp critter could stand up to her. Fortunately, her smell preceded her and warned most of the other critters off. Only those in the water missed that warning and were captured and eaten alive. She actually preferred the continuing struggle and the look of fear in their eyes as she ingested the small, still-squirming critters. It made her feel more powerful and alive.

This is illegal! How can they do this? When Joe found the contract that Saldana had created worth millions of dollars, he asked for an explanation. Saldana was smooth talking and usually very convincing. Few would challenge him since he seemed to know everything.

"Well, I just wanted to save some money for GSA so I put this contract together."

There was more to the story and Joe had heard it all. GSA

had been caught in an improper practice and was ordered to take a lot of tools off existing contracts by the Inspector General.

Joe knew Saldana's personal stock had gone down through his own misdeeds, and he was anxious to rebuild it, but this? Saldana had messed up time and time again. He was determined to buy back the boss' favor no matter what it cost taxpayers.

Saldana had been pre-selected for several promotions until he was now a GS-15 – the highest grade possible. He also flaunted his close relationship with the boss.

"I don't think there's anything wrong with a supervisor helping an employee. Selecting someone and helping them to move up by being a favorite is okay," Saldana had told him.

No, nothing wrong, except that it's illegal. Joe held his tongue.

"Saldana, this is illegal. We can't hide it very long."

"So, what can I do now?"

A GS-15 was asking him? "If you like, I can help you to resolicit this and then we can cancel the current contract. I'm busy but I would like to help you to make this right."

"Hey, that's great! Sure. Let's do it."

A few weeks later Saldana had changed his mind. "I don't think we need to do anything about this."

"Are you kidding me? What do you think will happen when the Inspector General gets through with it? They always find out, sooner or later. You may even be looking at prison time."

"I don't think so. Look, Joe, you need to drop this. I mean it. You're the only one who cares about it. If you know what's good for you, you'll forget you ever heard about this."

Joe just looked at him. Joe's name wasn't on it so he wasn't responsible. That satisfied his conscience a little, but rationalizing it that way was getting old. He had signed a document when he was hired that said he had to report it if he found anything that wasn't right.

Trying to keep this low key, he asked Lorna. "I've been talking with Saldana. He awarded a contract illegally. We both have an obligation to say something. I'm letting you know so you can pass this up to the right people."

"Thanks, Joe. But what's wrong with it?"

"No competition. He just awarded it. He didn't even run it by the attorney for review – probably because he knew what she'd say. Most of the documents were not reviewed by anybody. Now, he's adding more items to it after the award. That's what caught my attention. He directed one of my workers to add items to it without telling them why."

"I'll look into it."

The following week, Joe asked her what had happened with the illegal contract. "Nothing. I'm still looking into it. I'm not sure there's anything wrong."

Is she really that stupid or does she think I am? Well, this isn't going anywhere.

"Joe, this can be a great place. You can make it to the top. You just have to work with us."

"How's that?"

"I don't think I need to spell it out for you. Loyalty. You're a former soldier. You know all about loyalty."

"Yes, but to whom? You're right that I know about loyalty. I took an oath to support and defend the Constitution. But I owe my loyalty to those who pay my salary. That's the taxpayer.

Like an old cowboy, I ride for the brand. I don't know any other way. Look, if you won't report this, then I will. Please, don't make me do this."

She stared and just shook her head. *Dumb. So stupid. What am I going to do with him?*

Joe had the soul of an old cowboy. It had served him well in the Army – not so much now. Since Dave was responsible for managing the contract, he told Dave. Dave knew this was illegal.

"Well, I'm done. Thanks for telling me."

They went to the attorney and to the Inspector General and reported it. The investigation was a long one.

"Joe, we should talk – about that illegal thing." Dave was talking very low, unusual for him.

"What's up?"

"Saldana was whitewashed."

"What!

"Yep, he got away with it. He should be doing time for it. Rumor has it that he got a choice. Resign or be prosecuted."

A few months later, Saldana resigned his position. GS-15's don't give up a six-figure salary short of retirement unless they have an even better salary to go to. Allowed to resign, he was guilty but received no jail time. Even future jobs would not be affected by his actions. The swamp takes care of its own.

"Well, at least it's over." Joe and Dave were getting lunch together at the catfish restaurant across the street. The special included catfish, cornbread, and black beans. It was comfort food and both wanted to be comforted. They didn't need to, they just wanted to.

Dave wasn't so sure. "I don't know. I saw how Lorna looked

when you had your back to her. If looks could kill. You just watch yourself. You want to believe the best of people. But remember, I used to be a cop. I saw the other side of humanity and I developed a sixth sense. I can read people and what I'm reading in her is no good."

The next week, another supervisor position was filled. It was Eldana. The cookie lady had moved up and was now in charge of her own branch.

The swamp had clearly made a mistake and mistook her for one of their own. Joe wanted to tell her it was about time she was promoted. He also knew there might be some bad feelings. Maybe she was holding it in and bringing it up would only make things worse. Discretion again – it was best to let it lie.

She and Joe talked about almost everything. Both were Christian so they had that in common. She was so easy to talk to and she came to Joe to learn the supervisor ropes that Joe had already sampled. In return, she shared diet tips.

"My counselor told me to not eat anything white."

"So...do you know that when you bite into that apple, it will be white?

"That's true," she admitted, enjoying every bite. She could also ignore his harassment and that often helped, especially now.

Leadership training was part of the job but consisted of rules, limitations, and processes. What they called leadership was no more than management. Do this, don't do that. Proactive leadership was ignored. GSA was also a free-spending organization. Joe went to a special 'leadership' course in Virginia. Eldana also went since she was a new supervisor.

What a wild first day. And that homework assignment – got

to get it done so I can get some sleep. After the homework, Eldana read her Bible and spent some time in prayer. She always seemed to sleep better after this ritual. She didn't have to share a room so her schedule was her own – nobody to bother her.

She would probably get more sleep here than she did at home. The kids always seemed to need something. "Mom, can you fix this for me please?" Then came the dream. *So disturbing. What did it all mean?*

The next morning, the dream was still there. This was no ordinary dream. Those always passed by the time she got up. Of course, she knew where the dream came from. But why him? Why Joe? They liked each other but weren't that close. Having dreams like that were more like work than rest.

At lunch, the instructor asked all of the students to try to sit with someone new whom they did not know. Joe was waiting for his new 'friend' to get some food and join him. Eldana sat down next to him. She seemed to have something on her mind. "Joe, can I talk with you?"

"Sure."

"Last night I had a dream and you were in it."

Uh oh. "Huh? I mean, wow, was it scary?"

"I'm not sure. Can I tell you about it?"

"Uh...sure." No way to get out of this.

"In my dream, you were outside beating a dog with a stick. You did this several times and then you gave up. You then told everyone that the dog was vicious and to stay away from it. Does that mean anything to you?"

"No," Joe laughed. "I haven't been beating any dogs. Come to think of it, I don't think I ever have. I love dogs."

"Well, okay then. There's something I should tell you. I have a spiritual gift."

"You mean like from God? Like one of the Old Testament things?"

This was getting deep. Joe had never met anybody with supernatural gifts. Oh sure, he had heard about them. But face to face – this was different. It was almost like he could see God looking at him and wagging a finger at him. It was almost enough to make him hide under a table. Of course, there's no table big enough to hide from Him.

"Yes. Do you know what my name, what Eldana means?"

"No, I never even thought about it."

"It means knowledge of God."

Joe said nothing. All he could do was stare at her – and hope God hadn't told her about all the bad things he had done – or thought – or thought of doing.

"Anyway, I dream dreams and my twin sister interprets them for me."

"Wow! You mean there are two of you?"

"Yes," she laughed. "Anyway, if you want me to, I'll call her and get an interpretation. Do you want that?"

"Sure." *Can someone refuse a message from the Almighty?*

That day passed slowly as Joe considered the exchange. This was bigger than big. Why should the Almighty take notice of him? Oh sure, he went to Church, donated to charity and sometimes, even did something good. But, so did millions of others.

Hitting a dog? What could that mean? Lots of questions and no answers. Patience came as easily as the night before

Christmas does to an eight-year old. The next morning, he greeted Eldana.

"Any news? Did you get to talk with your sister?" If it was his Christmas gift, he wanted to open it. On the other hand, if it was bad, maybe it should be left wrapped.

"Yes. It was kind of long so I'll let you know at lunch."

Yes, just like being an eight-year old. Dad always made them wait until he had coffee before the presents were opened. The morning dragged. Joe was anxious for lunch, but not for food. It was also hard to focus on the training going on around him. There were several high-level speakers with a lot to share. They all paled in comparison to what was coming at lunchtime.

Sitting down beside Joe, Eldana started in. "My sister said that something will happen and it will be bad. You will respond several times and think you are doing the right thing but each time you will not be in accordance with the Holy Spirit. We don't know what it will be but that's what will happen. Finally, you will give up and tell everyone that something is a vicious dog and to stay away from it."

"Wow!" Joe knew he had a limited vocabulary but that was all he could think of. Then, "is there anything else?"

"Yes, she also said she sees something like Joseph and Potiphar's wife surrounding you. Does that mean anything to you?"

"No, I'm not planning to have an affair," he laughed. Joe misunderstood the message, but maybe that was by design. If he had understood, maybe he would have tried to avoid the situation.

"Well, I'm not sure that's what the passage meant. Anyway, it's just a message and I'm just the messenger."

"Well, thanks. This is so awesome! I never got a message from the Almighty before. Does this happen often? To you I mean?"

"I can't say...from time to time...I don't remember." Maybe she really was just the messenger. That was odd. Getting a message from the creator and not remembering.

Joe thought long and hard on the message. What could it mean? When would it happen? What would happen? Still focused on the 'affair' angle, he was determined to not do the wrong thing. Thirty-three years of marriage and counting.

God was watching too. Better not mess this one up. That must be it! He was warning Joe not to cheat on Diona. Well, that seemed easy enough.

Joe put the message behind him when he returned to the office. Lots of leadership training and he wanted to try to put some of it to work.

For once, GSA had provided something proactive instead of just rules. He was determined to be the best supervisor and leader in the organization. He insisted on the best from his people but also wanted to give them his best.

Several special projects were assigned to the workers to test the marketplace and find new and better ways to do things. If he could save money for the taxpayers, he would do it. Birthdays were celebrated with designer cupcakes.

As the new intern rotation came around, Joe asked who he would be getting and who he would be losing. It was a mixed bag. One name stood out.

Scooter was a very flamboyant and very gay employee. Sometimes he wore a neon green dress shirt, sometimes a pink shirt. His behavior and unusual walk advertised who and what he was.

GSA's policy embraced all groups – race, religion, sex and now sexual preference. Well, Joe knew he could do that too. Even as a soldier, he was professional and not judgmental. Of course, this one was a bit unique for his outspokenness.

Finding out about the rotation, Scooter checked in with Joe. "I have this special project I'm working on. It takes a lot of my time so I'm just concerned about my workload in your branch."

"I don't think that will be an issue. I'll talk with your current supervisor and reduce your workload. You don't need to worry. I won't give you more than you can handle."

"Thanks! That eases my mind."

Dave and Scooter had worked on the same team. It was just after that when Dave talked to Joe about Scooter while they were out for a walk around the building.

"He's sneaky and will bite you in the back. He's also dishonest. He plans to run this organization some day and couldn't care less how he gets there. You'll have to watch that one."

Joe valued Dave's opinion but this time he was obviously overreacting. Scooter was just a kid. Sure, their worldview was far apart. But everybody just had to do their work and things worked out. He just smiled and said "Thanks for that Dave. I'm sure it'll work out. *I should talk to Josephine and work out some dates for the change.*

She was hard to catch in the office so when he did find her, he seized the opportunity. "Josephine, got a minute?"

"For you, sure!"

"Since Scooter is going to come to my branch, do we have

any dates for the change? Oh, and I understand he has a special project he's working on. How much of his time does that take? He seems pretty concerned about it."

"We should make that change in about two weeks. The project itself doesn't take a lot of time. No more than ten percent of his time. It shouldn't affect his work in your branch too much."

"Great! I'll reduce his workload to compensate for that. By the way, I was also told that there are some issues with him. Dishonesty, someone to watch out for. Have you had any issues?"

"I bet I know where you heard that," she laughed. Dave had already been to Josephine and had that conversation. "But yes, he's not ethical so watch out for him. If you can, just mentor him about these issues and maybe you can turn him around. I haven't had a lot of luck there. Then, of course, you know about his lifestyle."

"Yeah, it's kind of hard to miss that. He's pretty much in your face with it. But it shouldn't be a problem. As long as he doesn't bring it up, I won't either. Of course, if he does, then I will just let him know that I'm a Christian and I believe it to be wrong. But I'll be fair with him on that and on the project time issue."

Joe and Josephine had worked well together. They could have candid conversations like this. It was a lot harder with Lorna. Joe had hoped for the best since they had worked together well several years earlier. Now he saw that she was so politically correct. There were some things best left unsaid.

I don't know. I just don't know. Joe's a fair person but he appears to also have an issue with gay people. Is it fair for Scooter to have to work under him? Will Joe be fair with him? Maybe it would be better if Scooter went to another branch. But that conversation was in confidence. And when has that ever stopped me? I better talk with Lorna. She can just move Scooter to another branch. That would be best for all. Josephine had held back from Joe. She was concerned.

"Lorna, did you know Joe is a Christian?"

"Well, I guess I never gave it any thought. Why do you ask?"

"You've scheduled Scooter to work under Joe starting a few weeks from now. I just talked with Joe and he told me that he believes being gay is wrong. I just thought you should know. Maybe you could just have Scooter go to another branch. That might be best for all."

****

It was a Monday and the day had started out so well, so full of promise. The birds were singing, the temperature was an ideal 75 degrees with low humidity. No delayed projects. With all that, Joe should have known an ambush was coming.

"Joe, please come to the conference room. I need to meet with you about something."

"Sure. Be right there."

This was so unusual. Meetings were always announced and planned in advance. What was going on? *She probably has another task for me, like that one with Birna. Well, she is in charge so...*

Lorna was sitting down in the huge conference room. But there were many others including the Human Resources representative. *Hmm, this is unusual. Wonder what it's all about?*

"Joe, have a seat." She pointed to a chair on the opposite side of the huge table from her.

There were no smiles, no announcements of the subject of

the meeting, just the "sit down" thing. Everybody except for him was seated on the other side next to Lorna.

"I have to tell you that this meeting is to discuss your performance. You are not to talk or to ask questions until I say it's okay. Do you understand?"

This was so unusual, so uni-directional. Sit down? Keep your mouth shut? What was going on?

"Ah, yes, I guess I do."

"On the thirteenth of May, you made a statement about a gay employee. This leaves me believing that I cannot depend on you to treat that employee fairly. For this reason, I have decided to terminate your probationary period as a new supervisor."

"I am reassigning you to a nonsupervisory position, where you will be located in a cubicle and perform duties as a Lead Contract Specialist. You are being removed from the supervisory position and the probation period is considered to be unsuccessful. Do you understand what I've just explained to you?"

Was this even happening? Joe knew what failure looked like, what it felt like. He had failed at some tasks in the Army. Nobody could be good at everything. But he also knew that he had expected the failures before they happened.

This – it came from nowhere and knocked him on his backside. The thoughts were whizzing by at light speed. He had done his best work. His branch had the best stock coverage rates. He had new projects in the works that would make a lot of money for GSA. The team was motivated, due in no small part to Joe's creative leadership and the feeling that he would take care of the people.

Why would they even want to remove him? Do you send your best racehorse back to the stables in the middle of the race?

Oh yeah, there was also that thing. What did she say, gay employee? Can't trust? Him? She must have him confused with somebody else. He was the best she had. As honest as was possible to be in this world.

"Joe, I asked if you understand!"

"Yes, I guess I do. But, don't I even get to defend myself?"

"No."

Huh? Did she really say that? Since when? The accused always have an opportunity to present their side. This wasn't happening. A dream. He would wake up and be in bed. He would say, wow, what a dream. That's it. It had to be.

"This is a one-way conversation. The decision has been made. If you have something to say, put it in writing. For now, you will sign the document we are providing to you which outlines the action being taken, the reason, and your rights. The action will be effective one week from now to give you time to close out any actions you are involved in."

"You also have the right to request reassignment in order to avoid having this appear on your record. The staff attorney has been advised to not talk to you about this so she is off limits."

"One more thing. You are not to discuss this with anyone. Do you have any questions about this action or what action you need to take?"

Just like that? Fired but still employed. Career advancement ended with almost no explanation, no chance to explain his actions, no rights whatsoever.

"Yes, why are you doing this? My work has been outstanding. You said so on my evaluation. I just don't..."

"As I said, Joe, we aren't here to take comments but to advise you on our action. You can go now. I'm sure you have a lot to do ... and to think about." In other words, "get out of here. Suck it up. Deal with it. I make the decisions and you have no rights." It was like that.

"But can't I just ..."

"No. This meeting is over. If you have anything to say, put it in writing and send to me by email. Don't come to my office. You are also authorized to take the rest of the day off. I'm sure you will have some thinking to do." She was afraid of Joe. He had a mild temperament but he was still a man. After what she had just done ...

To say Joe didn't see that coming would be a huge understatement. Blindsided. Unfair. Biased. Prejudice. Discrimination. Thought police. Hypocritical. Violation of civil rights. Indecent. Even unconstitutional since it violated the First Amendment. All true.

Yet, when the swamp comes after you, it wins. Even running fast or climbing a tree won't save the victim. Snakes climb trees and panthers run faster.

His stomach churning, the room seemed to be spinning too. Joe was always hungry. Snacks were his friend. Now, he couldn't even think about food. In shock, Joe found the only one he could trust. "Dave, I was just fired."

"No! What is it? What really happened?"

"Like I said, I was called into a meeting and told I have one week to complete all actions. They got a complaint against me for being unfair to a gay employee. No, scratch that. She said I might be unfair in the future. I can only think of one employee that fits that bill. I never discussed anything with him except to say I would accommodate his special project. Who else could it be?"

"Wow! Well, you know it wasn't me. Who else have you talked with?'

"Well, I discussed Scooter with Josephine. But I didn't say anything bad about him. Could it be her? I thought she could be trusted."

"So did I. Let's go ask her."

"Josephine, I was just told I'm being removed as supervisor for being biased against gay employees. I just remembered a brief conversation we had. Did you tell Lorna about that?"

Silence. Panic was in full control. What could she say? She was caught revealing a confidence. A lie would just add to it. Joe and Dave were waiting. She had to say something. But what?

"Well, yes I did. I'm sorry. I just wanted her to put Scooter in another branch. I didn't want her to remove you."

"Why couldn't you talk with me if you had any concerns? I told you I would be fair with him. That conversation was confidential. I thought you could be trusted. But I guess you can't, can you? You're a piece of work!"

****

What am I supposed to say when others ask? Do I say I wanted a cubicle? Yeah, right. Who trades an office with a door for a cubicle? Maybe I didn't like supervising them? But I did. Most were great people and I got along fine with them. I even loved them and I prayed for them when they called in sick. Why is this happening Lord?

Then, the message occurred to him. It wasn't about an affair at all but, just like Joseph, about being falsely accused. He was warned but missed the point. Maybe that was the point. A warning only becomes clear after the event comes about. It's not about avoidance but about what to do next.

One week later, Joe was working in a cubicle. The workers were not told why, only that Joe had moved to a non-supervisory position. One-by-one, they stopped by and asked what happened.

"I'm not at liberty to discuss it. That's straight from our division chief."

Held up for display in a short-walled cubicle which all the workers passed throughout the day, the humiliation was extreme. With all eyes on him, Joe couldn't talk about it, explain his side, he just had to bear it.

He felt as if he was in an occupied country. The NAZI swamp critters had their eyes on him but he couldn't even tell his side of things. The goal of draining the swamp – that dream was probably ended for good.

Rachel's daughter Zoe also worked there. GSA had become the family business. Where Rachel was tactful, Zoe was abrasive. "What are you doing out here?"

"Taking up space I suppose."

"Ha! Well, I heard it was sexual harassment and that your days here are numbered."

"Is that what they're saying?"

"Yes. Serves you right too. Did you know that I never cared much for you? This couldn't have happened to a more deserving man."

"Did they also tell you that I found a way to embezzle from GSA?"

"No!" The look was of pure shock.

"Well, I hope you'll make sure everybody else knows before

the end of the day. I wouldn't want that one to fall through the cracks."

"You're playing me, aren't you?"

"If I'm not, it wouldn't be for lack of trying." The deadpan look and the unsmiling face told her more than the words.

"Well, of all the..." She stomped off.

At least the workload was light – too light. Eldana was Joe's boss now. She was trying to make the transition easier for him. The first month had been filled with soul-searching and humiliation.

"Joe, I'm so sorry this happened to you. I guess I better watch my step around Lorna if this is how she does things. Joe, I just want you to mentor the younger people and review their work. Eventually, you'll get some complicated stuff to work on but I don't think you're up to it now. I know I wouldn't be." She was right about that.

Dave regularly stopped by the cubicle to talk. Still walking around the old building for exercise, Dave asked him how he was doing. "I wish...I wish..." but the words wouldn't come.

"Joe, you need a break. You know we get a fifteen-minute break. I know you usually don't take your break but let's go down to the cafeteria. We can get some coffee or something."

"Well, okay. It's been a while since I was down there." As they walked in, Joe was thinking about a piece of hot apple pie – ala mode of course. There wasn't any out yet. Maybe there would be at lunch but not now. Then...that voice. It sounded so familiar.

"Anyway, that's my story and that's why I don't say I served. I did time. This Army guy cured me of that."

Joe knew that voice. Where was it? *I've got to find out.*

Around the corner and there he was – Felix from the cafeteria at the fort. He was working here now. How many years had it been?

"Well, I'll be a pig's foot. There he is now. Hey, Joe! You remember me, don't you?"

"I sure do." Joe smiled for the first time in weeks. "What are you doing here?"

"I work here now. I moved up. I'm a pastry chef and the assistant supervisor. How about that? I was just telling Amber – you know Amber, don't you? She's the supervisor. Anyway, I was telling her about you and just then you showed up. So how are you doing? Are you working here now? Is there anything I can get for you?"

"Yeah." The response was weak and Felix noticed. "I was hoping for apple pie with some ice cream but I guess I'm too early."

"But it's not too early for me. I just finished several pies for lunch. You get the first piece. Sometimes it's who you know."

"Say, Joe, you seem kind of down. Do you need to talk? I have a break right about now." The three of them sat down in a corner of the cafeteria. Joe poured it all out to him. Felix felt like he owed something to Joe and now he could return a favor.

"I'm still new at this church thing but thanks to you I'm doing better. I even go to a study class once a week. I'm sorry for your troubles but I just wonder if this could be one of those spiritual things. Any chance of that?"

Joe thought for a moment. Then he remembered the warning from Eldana. Briefly, he told Felix and Dave the story. "Wow!" That was all either of them could say.

Felix the ex-con was the first to see it. "Don't you see it Joe?"

"Huh?"

"I know I'm new at this stuff but I can see it. Joseph was not about being tempted or doing wrong. His story was about a false accusation. When Eldana – was that her name?" Joe nodded. "When Eldana told you about Joseph, she was warning you that you were going to be falsely accused."

"I never saw it before. Why didn't I see it before?"

"Maybe if you did you would have taken steps to avoid the trouble. Maybe this is something you have to go through. Joseph was in prison for years before he was released. Maybe you will have something like that too."

"I know it doesn't sound encouraging, but check this out. I got this from my pastor at the Bible study last night. 'If you are found worthy of persecution then God must have plans for you.' Joseph eventually was released and placed in authority over those who had done him wrong. He may have other plans for you, but it may not be for a while."

"Maybe that's why he brought you and me into contact – so you could open my eyes and I could help you?"

Suddenly the pie, the ice cream and even the hot tea tasted a lot better.

In spite of the cheering up, each day seemed worse than the one before. Formerly talkative and cheerful Joe was now silent Joe. Eldana noticed that he seemed moody and depressed, and asked the big question. Since they were friends and Christians too, Joe told her the complete sordid story – including her role in it.

"Joe, did you ever read C.S. Lewis?"

"Who?"

"He wrote The Lion, the Witch, and the Wardrobe."

"Oh, him."

"Well, anyway, he said that 'we're living in enemy-occupied territory.' You are a casualty but all wars do end and the good guys win."

The dog. GSA was the dog. So that's it. But can I give up without doing what I think is right? What is right anyway? What was it that Edmund Burke had said? 'All that is necessary for evil to triumph is for good people to do nothing.' Yes, that was it. But the dog. She had said he would be doing something out of the will of the Holy Spirit. But what was his will? Maybe nothing was the wrong thing.

Joe decided right then to do what he thought was right. He complained to the Equal Employment Opportunity Office and even the Office of Special Counsel. He couldn't complain through the attorney. They had fixed that. Human resources? No, the swamp had her on its team.

Loyalty is just a word in the swamp. Friends? Only when they need you more than you need them. Joe's attitude was changing from the positive one that he had developed over two decades as a soldier. The swamp had its grip on him and was changing him. Better get out while he could. Eldana, Dave and Felix were the only friends Joe had here.

Two weeks later, Lorna saw Joe in the hallway and greeted him. Silence. He just stared at her. She was shocked. Hurrying off, she looked scared.

It was like Joe was threatening her with a look. Maybe she was right. Maybe he was a threat. He had never committed an actual act of violence – except in self-defense. But everybody has a limit. Push them too far and they can respond with violence. He had never found his limit. Was it just around the corner? Through the rest of the day, the thought continued to haunt him.

He saw her – heading alone to her car. He kept a gun in his car. Maybe she kept one in her purse? No time now to go get it. He followed her. As she reached her car, he reached her. A long two-by-four inch piece of wood was in his hand. She saw him and then the dirt-encrusted piece of wood.

She laughed. "You don't have the guts."

He said nothing, just stared and slowly raised the piece of wood. All the shame, the anger – came boiling up. Loss of career, the daily humiliation – they just added to the fire. He was no longer in control and he didn't care.

As he walked away, he suddenly realized what he had done. He could have walked away – before. It was too late for that now. Diona would be ashamed, would ignore and reject him for all time. The children. The grandchildren. To all of them, he was now dead. Worse, he had never existed.

How did that happen? If he could just take it back. Run. That was it. Run. But where? There were video cameras everywhere. They would look for him and they would find him.

Walking down the street, he passed a neighborhood bar. Glancing in the window, he saw the TV with the news. He saw himself on the news. There would be no hiding now.

Suddenly, there they were. "Get him!" they yelled. "It's him. Get him!" Guns drawn, the lieutenant laughed and said "fire!"

Drenched with sweat, he was holding his chest, the pillow and the sheets were wet. "What did you say?" Diona asked.

"Huh?"

"You said 'No'. Did you have a bad dream?"

"Yeah, it was a bad one." Now he knew, he had to get away. He was no killer – or was he? It would be better to not find out.

Help. That's what he needed – maybe for the first time in his life. Jeannie was still available. Unlike the others, the critters, she hadn't changed. She was still the same old Jeannie, so Joe talked with her.

"I wish I had known. I could have told you to not trust Josephine."

At home, it was no better and was getting worse. "Joe, you just need to get past this." Diona was trying to help as best as she could.

The soft brown eyes now seemed so hard. She didn't smile, she didn't talk to him, she just ignored him. Joe had seen her back him through his Army career, numerous college problems, two children, in-laws and outlaws, she was always the same. Strong, courageous, willing to face down a hoard of violent people to protect those she loved. But now …

"I'm trying. I was treated unfairly but if I can get a new job somewhere else, then things should get better."

"Joe, I've been thinking about this a long time. I know you think you did the right thing but did you? I think you were wrong to say anything."

"But…I didn't say anything." Joe had never stammered in his life. He was always self-confident. Having Diona beside him only reinforced his confidence.

He never thought he had a chance with her when they first met. They came from different backgrounds. She was upper middle class and he was far from that. So, when she returned his smile, he couldn't believe how God had smiled on him.

Her statement was so unexpected, and so abandoning. "I

thought you of all people would understand. I thought you were a Christian. I said nothing wrong. I hardly said anything at all."

She said nothing. She just stared down at the floor, unspeaking, hardly breathing.

Then it came out. "After all these years ... I thought I knew you! I thought I could count on you. I guess I was wrong."

"But Joe ..."

"But nothing! If you want us to continue, you'd better think about that. Now, leave me alone!"

Catching heat at work. Catching heat at home too. Humiliation on all fronts. What was it his Navy friend Bob had said years ago?

"You can handle it if things are bad at home but good at work or if they are bad at work but good at home. But it's almost impossible to handle if things are bad in both places." He sure knew what he was talking about.

A few days later, she brought it up again. "Maybe you're right. Maybe we should separate. At least, for a while, so you can sort out things."

Things are never so bad they can't get worse. Lorna had not only taken his career, she had done this to his marriage too. Joe was now lonely and becoming despondent as he traveled life's road alone.

Diona had to get away – for her own sake. She and Joe weren't talking and she was beginning to sink in her own pool of misery. She went to stay with her father who had been sick and welcomed her help. That small ranch in the Colorado mountains gave her peace.

For Joe, peace was elusive. Each day he went to work. Each

day he kept a low profile. When training was held, he contributed almost nothing. "Any questions or comments?" they asked. Joe had always had something to say. He knew his job and tried to share that knowledge. Other times, he tried to keep it light with a joke. But he always had said something. Now, he was home alone and at work alone.

The depression was getting worse. Not exactly suicidal, he just didn't care anymore about anything. He thought about alcohol but the bars had one big problem. There were people there and he didn't want to be around anybody. That would only drive home his current misery.

Finally, about six months later, Diona called. The small talk was very small as they searched for something to say, something to open the huge Grand Canyon between them. Then, it came out. "Joe, I had a checkup and they found a big spot. It's cancer. I'm scared."

Connection at last. Joe was scared too. Diona's mother had died all too young from the same thing. Until the recent trouble, he had always planned to grow old with her.

His own problems forgotten, he dropped everything and went to see her. Brought together by a crisis, the other problem seemed small. Time off was easy to get. Joe had too small a workload to be missed. Lorna was happy to see him leave for an extended period.

As Joe and Diona met in the hospital room, they embraced. A hug that neither wanted to end displaced loss of trust and tears took the place of frowns.

"I've missed you," they both blurted out at the same time. A spontaneous laugh replaced the tension. No words of forgiveness – none were needed.

The treatments were coming along fine. Lorna had almost ended a long marriage by her accusations and persecution. She failed and Joe was exhilarated in that knowledge. Strangely, Diona's condition revitalized him. Or was it their reconnection? It mattered little.

I wish I could get out of here. I'd resign if I had another job to go to. But I've got to support my family. I can't quit and let the critters win.

The justifications were many as Joe tried to get a new direction. The swamp at the fort was now unimportant. He hadn't been unemployed since 1980 – over thirty years ago. He didn't want to start now. Work was life, and life was work. It was his identity.

The Army had converted him from an undisciplined college graduate into a man that his family was proud of. He couldn't be a soldier anymore, but at heart, he always would be. A man works, doesn't he? Yet, a man also has pride.

Continuing to work under the swamp critter who persecuted him for his values; who put him in this humiliating situation; seeing the wagging tongues at work and the unanswered questions; less than gainful employment; it all weighed on him and left him ready for ... what?

Chapter Ten

The Toxorhynchites rutilus – also known as the elephant mosquito – is big. One and a half inches long, it looks scary. The truth is very different. It does not need human or animal blood, unlike its much smaller cousins. In fact, it even feeds on the larvae of smaller mosquitoes that do need blood. It also feeds on nectar from flowers, cross-pollinating plants – at least those close to the swamp.

The occupation of GSA by the swamp critters continued, so it was time for Joe to move on. He was an old soldier. The Corps of Engineers had a good reputation. Maybe it was earned? Maybe it would even be the right place to retreat to.

Two openings meant two chances. Both meant a reduction in grade, a demotion. It would be worth it to get out of occupied territory. Money wasn't everything and his career goals were pretty much shot now anyway. Quality of life – that was important.

"Joe, you have a lot of great qualifications. We're very impressed. So, our final question, if you are offered the position, will you accept it?" The interview had gone well. The job was for a Procurement Analyst. Joe didn't know what that was, but he knew where it was and it sure wasn't at GSA. With all the interviews he had been through, nobody ever asked this question before.

"Yes, absolutely." *Procurement Analyst. What do they do anyway? Analyze procurements?* He knew how to write a contract. Now, he would not be writing contracts but would be reviewing the work of others. That's a little like being the boss but not getting paid for it.

The work was located in a thirteen-floor federal building with numerous other government agencies. Modern to the extreme: security, great lighting, electronic access, on-site cafeteria and childcare for those who needed it – a lot of money went into the building's construction.

There was even a coffee bar to get him started in the morning – Colombian coffee and Danish pastries, the American way. The Corps of Engineers had computers that were almost as good as GSA.

He groaned when he saw that he would be sitting in a cubicle again, with almost no privacy. If one person sneezed, all of the others caught a cold.

"Welcome to the Corps!" Mark was the first person Joe met. Tall, slender, and almost totally lacking in hair, he was full of energy and enthusiastic about almost everything – he could even get excited about ice. He was also very meticulous. Mark loved computers and expected them to do almost everything, even to the point of overtaxing them.

"Now, Joe I want to introduce our other partner. Bart has been here a long time and can probably tell you things that I can't. If there's anything you need, just say the word. Between Bart and I, we should be able to help with most things. Those we can't, well, that's why you're here. We need a miracle worker."

A retired Army Reserve Officer, Mark was not a swamp critter but would probably have had many of them in military formation, dress-right-dress and demanding the gators to close their mouths and act as a bridge across the swamp and the pythons to tie themselves together to act as

rope to benefit others. Seventeen-foot pythons looked elsewhere for a place to stay.

Bart was blind and had been so from birth. Tall, strongly built and still a lot of hair for his age, he was the least blind, blind man Joe had ever met. Reaching out with his right hand, he greeted Joe. "Welcome to the Corps. Glad to be working with you. Let me know if you need anything."

Bart was staring straight into Joe's eyes, so Joe was unsure for a moment if Bart could see him or not. Joe briefly considered winking one eye at Bart to find out, but Bart was a big man and just might smack Joe hard. The risk wasn't worth it and the moment passed.

Bart seemed to see more without eyes, than most people did with them. Once accused of being 'a bad representative for the blind community,' he behaved as if he could see as well as anybody and lived his life (with the aid of a dog) the same as anyone else.

His work as a Procurement Analyst was made possible by technology that put the text of emails and other documents into sound, very rapidly spoken. Occasionally, the technology or some new program would not work right and he would have to get technical help.

On one occasion, he was on a phone call getting that help. The person on the other end asked him what he saw.

He said, "Nothing, I'm blind."

The other person made an adjustment and again said, "What do you see now?"

"Nothing," he said. "I'm still blind."

"Do you mean you can't see anything?"

"No."

"Are you totally blind?"

"Yes, that's what blind means."

Bart just didn't fit the mold. He was hard-working and ready to volunteer for new tasks as they came along. Always ready with dry humor, he said, "You know Joe, things don't look the same to me as they do to you." There it was – the vision-influenced vernacular that he always used.

The stories he told of his life's experiences were those of a sighted person – not those of a blind man. Bart was more like somebody who wandered into the swamp and kept shooing the mosquitoes away, as well as the more vicious swamp critters.

He could also be a bit cantankerous. He once belittled a female supervisor for drinking tea instead of coffee. Witnessing that, Joe never told him that he drank hot tea every morning, referring to it instead as a 'hot caffeinated beverage'.

Bart also would not participate in potluck lunches. He had experienced a bad food poisoning incident on a business trip years earlier where everyone on the bus was violently sick – except him. Everyone but Bart had the egg salad sandwiches available at the restaurant the bus stopped at. He alone was not sick. After that experience, he always said, "I won't eat anywhere that I cannot sue."

Terri McMason was Joe's supervisor. Average height for a woman, she was full of energy, demanded that all workers do their best, but also that they treat each other well. A retired Marine Corps lieutenant colonel, she knew management and administration.

More importantly, she knew leadership. She had everyone's back. That was never clearer than when her boss, Ms. Finley called. The door to Terri's office was open. "T.M., I need for you to have all of your workers increase their work output. We're getting demands for more production. You know the heat we're under here."

"But they're already doing more than they should be doing. We should be getting some more people with all the work we have. We need some relief."

"Not going to happen." Now the volume was increasing.

"What you're asking isn't right. You need to think about what is right here."

"I have. I need for you to make this happen."

"It'll be a cold day in Hell!" The New England accent was very pronounced. She was immediately sorry for her outburst but it was already done. Several people heard it. Amazed. Laughing. But she wasn't laughing. She stepped out of her office and apologized.

"No need for an apology," said Mark.

Bart agreed. "Not at all."

Joe nodded in agreement. Coming from GSA where he had experienced just the opposite, he had almost forgotten that there were still people like this.

As a Christian, Joe didn't curse. But as an old soldier, he was not offended and respected the boss who would stand for the right thing. People with a backbone and values to match were in such short supply.

Almost from the start, Joe experienced the Corps' version of the swamp. As a government agency, it followed the orders of Congress and the president. When the economy declined, the keepers of the swamp provided money for almost anything that could provide jobs.

Shovel-ready was what they called the projects. They were anything but. However, money was available and the Corps was expected to spend it.

Although these projects helped to double the national debt, they also provided jobs for some people. Nobody seemed to care how it was done.

Many of the projects went to foreign companies and to large businesses. The effect on small companies was often negative since they were too small to take on the large jobs and the emphasis was on large projects. Smaller businesses had to wait for the crisis to be over.

With the workplace stress mounting, every day Joe went for walks outside the building. At lunch he was gone for a half-hour. On the morning and afternoon breaks, he walked around the building. It was all for exercise and to clear the mental cobwebs.

It was on one of these occasions that he saw the transient. A young man, clothes not dirty, with a backpack. He was living on the street but hadn't been that way very long.

"Do you see them?"

"Huh?" Joe came back to reality as he approached the young man.

"Sugar Plum Fairies. They're all over the place. I've never felt so much love in all my life."

"Ah. Okay. Have a nice day." Joe usually went around the building twice. Today, on the second round, he saw the young man, asleep on a bench. *Good place for you.* He hadn't been threatening but, wow! He sure hadn't seen things like that in Lamar.

In the Army ... well, there was the soldier who used LSD which the usual tests didn't identify. He had said "God sent me to tell everyone that it's better if they don't wear clothes." Maybe they both used the same thing?

On another occasion, Joe met Paul. Taking advantage of his lunch break, he walked around the streets of the big city. The architecture was old and there was a lot to see. Going down a side street he hadn't been down before, he noticed several men standing around. "What's going on?" he asked.

"Nothing, man. They just kick us out every morning unless we're going through their program."

"Whose program?"

"This is the Rescue Mission. They have classes and Bible studies to reform us."

"Oh, wow. I didn't know." *I should go in and check it out.* Walking into the office, Joe introduced himself.

Paul did the same. "So, would you like a tour?"

"Sure. Why not. I've got time." Twenty minutes later, Paul had him signed up. Joe agreed to help promote the mission at his church. True to his word, every year he conducted a drive to provide clothes and other items to the mission. Money contributions also came in from the church.

The Corps also spent a lot of money for training, though

not just as an excuse to take a vacation, as GSA had done. After a year in the organization, Joe was approved for training in Alabama. The conference center that the Corps used for the training also had lodging.

Great, I can stay there and not have to drive. There's a restaurant there too. It just doesn't get any better. As he was about to confirm his reservation, he thought maybe he should ask Mark for his perspective.

"Have you heard about *Motel 6*?"

"Yes."

"Well, this is *Motel Five and a Half*." Point taken, Joe reserved another location with great reviews. When he attended the training, he found the training rooms to be substandard. The air conditioning in the building was always going out. Internet for computer use was very iffy. The noise was always loud, especially for those who lodged there.

Mark was nothing if not straight to the point. This time, he may even have been generous in his assessment.

A few months later, Joe asked Mark about one of the processes he wanted to simplify.

"Joe, when I was training to be an engineer officer in the Army, I had this old sergeant. I asked him if I could do something another way. He said, 'Sure, you *could* do it that way. But then you'd be wrong and why in the world would you *want* to be wrong?' You have to love those old sergeants. So, do you want to do this wrong or right?"

To ensure the workers did the job right, Mark conducted weekly training. Only thirty minutes in length, the sessions were online and recorded, providing workers with the right way for just about everything but focused on those wrong things that had become a trend.

It was a few weeks later that Mark reported in on his family's farm operation. He lived on a country parcel and had a milk cow and a calf. He got up early to milk the cow before leaving for work and then milked again when he got home. He raised his own hay too.

Eventually, he tired of the long hours and sold the cow and calf. His chores were much reduced though he continued living on the edge of the grid. No television in his house. However, he shared some television interests with Joe. Often, one would use a line from *Star Trek* and the other understood immediately. It was almost like sharing a second language.

Joe's duties included making sure others did their jobs right and complete. On one occasion he told Mark that one engineer was way behind on required reports.

The engineer had a ready excuse on each occasion. He was also a retired Army lieutenant colonel. Joe knew that officers would find fault with those in their command who didn't do their jobs completely but here this one was doing the same thing.

"I wonder how he would react if I pointed out to him, as a retired Army officer, that the maximum effective range of an excuse is zero?"

"Probably not well. Not well at all." Silence was prudent, and tact and diplomacy had to be Joe's mode of operation. Another day, another critter.

Joe had started on his doctorate in business while he was still at GSA. During his first year at the Corps, he completed it, using the contracting world as the basis of study.

Mark was visibly thrilled at the accomplishment. Bart would now ask every day, "Is the doctor in?"

Terri – she was also excited. "This is so great! I want that on the *Good News Report* to Headquarters."

The doctor was in but the old swamp nemesis was coming back around again. When things look too good to be true, they probably are.

The big change came with a new supervisor. Joe greeted him, "Good morning Major. Welcome to the Corps!" Major Kim was new at the Corps.

The general idea was to give those in uniform some actual contracting work to do while they were waiting for the next emergency. Military units are usually training until they are needed. A unit has an ideal situation when it can train and also produce something of value. But how can a unit produce diamonds out of cockleburs?

Major Kim was a bull in a china shop, immediately demanding many things for himself including the right to sign contracts. Terri would have none of it. "I want him to prove himself first. Don't do anything." A year later, he was approved and signing million-dollar contracts.

Engineers love to tweak things and so it was that a new idea came to the organization. "Kim's an officer, which means leader, so he needs to be put in a leadership position. Assign him as a supervisor over those analysts." The Corps district commander was adamant, even if badly informed. He was probably a bull in the china shop too. Joe had seen both types as a sergeant.

The major was seldom available and did little in the way of leadership. For Joe, that wasn't a problem. *Stay out of the way and you can be in charge all you want.* The old soldier knew the role and place for an officer. Officers were seldom needed as long as sergeants of Joe's caliber were available.

The benign neglect became malevolent when an evaluation was needed. The swamp was tired of being ignored. It demanded something of Major Kim. Feed me, it kept saying.

Only two months after Terri complimented Joe for one of the programs he ran, Major Kim was tasked with a performance evaluation of Joe.

All of Joe's accomplishments were missing from the report. Hadn't Terri, in front of the whole office said, "Mr. Trask said we have the best program in the entire Corps?"

Hadn't she been looking right at Joe when she said that and given him that *you did great* smile?

The best of anything should be reported on an evaluation report. Joe had looked forward to a great report card. But when it came, it was a surprise, and not a good one. For the servant accustomed to only giving the best and overproducing, a less than stellar report was more than a disappointment – it was an insult.

Major Kim ignored Joe's concern. He said "You didn't do that by yourself. At most you were part of a team that did that." Joe was incredulous but this critter was the boss.

"What about the other program that I ran? It was one of the best and I got lots of calls from officials who want to copy our approach. Shouldn't I get credit for that?"

"Same thing. You were part of a team but didn't do it by yourself."

Is he serious? Why would I self-report something that could be easily checked out? The major was not budging.

"Actually, Terri mentioned these in her meeting with the staff and gave me credit for them. Can't you accept her position on that?" Still no budging. The major was not smart and also inflexible. The combination could be a killer.

"Well, let's move on then. How about the new procedure I wrote for the Credit Card program? I wrote that after improving the program. "We didn't have one before."

"You also didn't do that!" He was getting louder now.

"If you don't think I did that, why didn't you say something before? When I claimed these things as my accomplishments, why didn't you call me on it? Honesty is required in this field. If I was lying, you should have brought that up and fired me."

Now, the major was getting mad and was yelling. As an old soldier, Joe knew that losing his bearing was inexcusable for an officer.

"I think we'd better end the meeting, Sir. We're not getting anywhere." The yelling continued. So did Joe's requests for ending the meeting. It had been a long time since Joe had been yelled at. Even Lieutenant Colonel Dick hadn't yelled at him, not like this.

****

"Mark, is this how you see me? Joe pushed the evaluation across the table to Mark.

"No!" His eyes were wide. He was almost in shock. "Not at all! Is this what you got?"

"Yes. So, what should I do?"

"You should talk to Terri about this. She's the only one that can fix it."

"I will. I just need to get prepared for it."

"Good luck. Let me know if you want me to talk to her about it."

****

"Good morning Ma'am. Joe always used the military approach with her. He was an old soldier and she was an old marine. It worked for them.

"I got this evaluation from Major Kim. I don't think it's fair. I got an overall low score and when I mentioned some of my accomplishments, he denied them. He said I hadn't done them. If I didn't, then I should be punished for lying and claiming them. As you know, honesty in this job is absolutely necessary. But if I did do them, I should get credit."

"So, what are you claiming but not getting credit for?"

"Remember when you said I was responsible for that program that was the best one in the Corps?"

"Yes."

"Also, do you remember the other one that was one of the best?"

"Yes."

"I also wrote the procedure for the Credit Card Program after doing it on an emergency basis for six months including during a government shutdown. He said that I didn't do any of those things."

Her mouth started to open, just kind of hung there, and then closed. Finally, "This doesn't seem right at all."

"One more thing. He spent a lot of our meeting yelling at me. I never yelled back but repeatedly had to ask for the meeting to end. When I was in the Army, we called getting mad and yelling, losing one's bearing. He's wearing a uniform and that's not the standard expected."

"I need some time to think about this and look into it. You are right. You should get credit for those things you did. Also, the yelling, that should never happen. Give me a few days."

Joe didn't expect her to change the rating. She had a subordinate supervisor to support. That's how it usually went. A few days later, she called Joe in. "I'm changing your evaluation. You're getting the top rating. I'm so sorry this happened. I'm also counseling him about the yelling."

"Thank you." Joe was in shock. He had prevailed. This never happened in the swamp. The Corps was truly a different place. More like a meadow, surrounded by the swamp. Occasionally, the critters entered the meadow but found it not to their liking. Joe hoped this swamp critter would leave too.

****

"Look, I did what you told me to do. No, I really did. I wrote it just that way. Can I help it if my boss changed it? No, I understand what you said. Look, I would never go against you. Yes, I know what you've got. Yes, I know you'll use it too. Of course, I value my career. No, I want to live here – not in that gated community in Leavenworth. I understand. Yes, I said I understand. I'm still on the hook."

What am I going to do? What can I do? I wish I'd never heard of Vegas. It really doesn't stay there. She must have an awesome network. She can't be everywhere can she?

The conversation had been tense. As he came out of his office, he glanced around to see if anybody was watching. *I hope I wasn't so loud that they heard me.* His forehead felt hot. He touched it and found he was sweating. Pulling the Army handkerchief out of his pocket, he wiped it away. It was very wet. *I'm probably red-faced too.*

Guilt wasn't one of his companions. That was for others. It was all about him and he lived life to the fullest. Of course, sometimes the fullest didn't mean the wisest.

As he walked down the hall, he saw Joe. Joe didn't say anything. He just nodded. *Well, I guess I know what he's thinking. So what?* As they passed each other, the atmosphere wasn't just mental. It also felt physical.

Probably hates me. Like that could matter. I'm a major. He was just a master sergeant. Now, he doesn't even wear a uniform. If Terri hadn't interfered, I'd be off the hook now and Joe would be history.

"Sir? Your orders are in. It's that trip they were talking about. Just going to be you and Staff Sergeant Henry. Hurricanes will do that. Contingency contracting can be a bugger."

Another weather disaster had hit, and the soldiers were being deployed to write contracts to fix the mess. FEMA had its job. So did the Corps of Engineers.

"Thanks." He said the words but didn't really mean anything. Pleasantries like this were expected. Just like the staff sergeant. He didn't really care for the officer. Staff Sergeant O'Mallion knew that Major Kim didn't have his back. Some officers believed in leadership and taking care of those under their charge. This one only took care of himself.

This too shall pass. That's what Mom always said and O'Mallion knew sooner or later he and Kim would part company. It was something to look forward to.

Major Kim saw the silver lining in the deployment. *Well, at least I will be out of here for six months. She can't blame me for not doing anything about her nemesis for a while. I wonder what she's got against him.* It must be huge.

"Hey, Sergeant Henry. We need to talk. We have that deployment coming up in two days. I want you to get with reservations and get us a flight and some lodging. Probably not much down there left so get the best you can. Don't mess this up like you did last time."

"Last time, sir?"

"Yes. You and I shared a room. I don't like to share rooms with enlisted people. I'm an officer and expect to be treated like one."

"But sir. That was the only available lodging. We were lucky to get it. What was I supposed to do?"

"I don't care what *you* do or *where* you sleep. Bring a tent if you want. I want my own room."

****

"Tami. I want you to know that I value you so much. But we have a few issues we need to work out. I want to see what you and I can come up with."

Tami hadn't been doing her job very well and Terri was determined to make a final effort to save Tami's career – if she could.

"That's what you want? Well, let me tell you what *I* want. I want to get through the day so I can go home and drink beer and watch *Awesome Man* get whomped. In fact, I even keep a cooler in the car so I can get started early. That's what I want. That's what this job means to me. It keeps me in beer money."

"One more thing. You haven't been here nearly as long as me. I've kept this office afloat by my knowledge. You can't do anything to me because you need me. You can't fire me because I have rights. I also belong to the union. You just need to get off my back!"

Terri just smiled that hard smile. It wasn't humor-driven – more like grim acceptance.

"Did you hear about Tami?" Bart caught Joe just coming in. A twenty-car pileup on the freeway had kept Joe from being on time. Joe had been feeling pretty good lately. Five months without Major Kim was like a vacation.

"No, I just got here. Boy, you should have seen that pileup. I bet there were fifty cars sitting around every which way. On second thought, it's probably good you didn't. I hope nobody died. I did see a few ambulances though. Some nut cut off a tandem truck with two trailers hauling spools of heavy cable. It looked like a war zone."

"Well, you had an interesting morning. Glad you made it. But back to the latest. Tami got fired."

"No! Nobody ever gets fired in the Civil Service."

"This one did. Terri had counseled her repeatedly. Terri even tried to help her get out on disability. But she refused. She came from an autoworkers union family. I guess she thought our union would protect her. It's not that kind of union."

"Terri sent an email to all of us. It doesn't say much except to not help her get in the building and to report any attempts."

"I didn't know there was a problem. I got along with her fine. What was she doing or not doing?"

"She alienated a lot of people. She didn't know her job…behind on her work … rude on the telephone. Tami had talked to me and I tried to get her to just take the retirement but she was hardnosed about it."

"I didn't know all that. She was nice to me. Still, to get fired. That's a big thing. I think this may be the first firing I've ever known about."

"Terri is very supportive, but she's also the boss. She takes the job seriously."

"Hey, Mark, I guess you heard about Tami?"

"Yes, really a shame. You got a minute, Joe? Something I need to talk to you about." He had that 'really bad news look.' The office door shut, he started out very candidly.

"Major Kim is coming back from his deployment. Terri just told me that he will be in charge of this branch again. I told her that you would be unhappy. She already knew but said there was nothing she could do about it. The orders come from above her. I even told her I would be willing to take the supervisory job. That's not going to work either."

"Mark, I had a terrible time when I worked under him. I won't do it again. I'd be willing to retire early if necessary to avoid that."

"You should talk to Terri. However, I don't think it will do any good. Her hands are tied."

Here it was again, another hostile work situation developing. Joe had left the GSA for similar reasons.

There he was falsely accused. The major was similar. He refused to give Joe credit for accomplishments. He was a lousy officer but knowing that was of no help to Joe. Stay or go. Fight or flight. It was all the same. Joe wanted to retire but he was not sure he would make it to a typical retirement.

These critters just keep coming around. I thought the Corps was free of them.

Joe had that talk with Terri. Mark was right – there was no change. It was then that he started the old escape approach. He had been here over three years anyway. Maybe it was time to go.

As an old soldier, he believed in keeping his backup fighting position in case a retreat was needed. Now, it was.

Was Joe ready to leave the swamp? On the other hand, maybe the swamp was coming to the Corps. We make the best decisions we can with the information we have at the time. So it was, this time too. Only later did Joe find that the Swamp Critter he was trying to avoid would retire instead of coming back. *C'est la vie.*

Chapter Eleven

The heron was fishing. It would eat almost anything but it liked fish. Sitting motionless, it often waited for fish to come close. If that didn't work, it would then stir up the water and catch whatever moved. It would work if it had to, but always preferred to let the prey do the work.

The pain was coming back and was worse than before. An old, broke down soldier, Joe got some of his medical care from the Veterans Administration Hospital. It was time to get in and get the medication increased. While he was there, he decided to drop in on Sherry. He hadn't seen her since they had worked together in the Army. She also worked in the Contracting Office.

While they were talking about people they had known then, her boss passed by. "Hey, Jaeck," she said. This is Joe O'Flaherty. We worked together for the Army at the fort. Joe's working for the Corps of Engineers in contracting now. Didn't you also work for GSA?"

"Yes. I had that too." He wasn't going to volunteer any more than that. The pain was still too fresh. Even with the passage of three years he still loathed the place and even the name.

About middle-age, not very tall, a full head of styled hair and manicured nails, Jaeck offered his hand. Joe was accustomed to a strong grip from men and this was soft. He was the image of the office worker. The pot belly said him and the gym were not on a first-name basis. The smile was big as he held onto Joe's hand and looked up at him; he wanted something from Joe.

"Hey, we've got some positions to fill and someone you may have worked with applied for one of them. Do you remember Artie?"

"Sure. We worked together at Fort Prairie for about three years."

"Could you recommend him? What can you tell me about him?"

"Well, he trained me on my first purchase. He completed the intern program at the fort. He worked in Army supply before that. He's great. Most of this you already know."

"Yes, I was just looking for a second opinion. If you've got a minute, could you come back and talk?"

Oh great. Now he's going to ask me something about Artie that he doesn't want any witnesses to. He's on a fishing expedition.

After they were sitting down, he said, "So, tell me what you've been working on."

Well, that was unexpected.

Joe went over the laundry list of projects, types, what he was doing, what he had done at GSA, and far too much more. Jaeck acted interested so Joe kept going. Joe wondered where this was going but Jaeck was very pleasant. *He probably just wonders how the other half lives... maybe even looking for alternatives to what he's doing now.* Finally, both realized they needed to be doing other things.

"By the way Joe, we have openings every once in a while.

You should think about coming to work with us." Jaeck had been fishing – for new talent.

Coming out of Jaeck's office, Joe suddenly realized he had just been interviewed, and he was wearing old jeans and a t-shirt. Jaeck was very different from any other boss Joe had known.

Jaeck was pleasant but worked under his own rules – he could have sold used cars. Then there was Sherry. Joe considered her an old friend – it would be nice to work with her and also not commute two hours every day. The Contracting Office had quadrupled in size to accommodate the spending demands put on the VA when a lot of veterans were dying from insufficient medical care capacity.

So, they had job openings? Might have to apply for one, just to see what would happen. This might be the escape he had been looking for. About three weeks after the job announcement closed, Joe called to see if he was going to get an interview. Sherry passed him off to Jaeck.

"No, I don't think I'm going to interview you."

Joe's heart sank. "Why not?" he wondered.

"We already met and I think I already know what you're about. I'm just going to select you without an interview."

Can they do that? "Wow, that's great! I'm really looking forward to working for you. So, when do you think I can start there?" *Hope I said all the right things and not too forward.*

"Be patient," Jaeck laughed. "This is still the government."

The time passed quickly. Joe told Mark about the new job as soon as he found out. He was almost as excited as Joe. "Joe, I'm really going to miss you. Your work was always great. You were like my right arm. Well, maybe more like my left. Yeah, that's it. You were like my left...thumb. We're all going to miss you."

Failure. Quitter. Those old inadequacies were making themselves known. Am I? It did feel like he was a failure. Joe told himself it was a good move. But here he was, taking the fifth job in ten years. *What's wrong with me? Why do things keep going south?*

As Joe walked into the old building at the VA for the first time as an employee, he noted it was a lot like the fort had been. Same old interior. The lighting here was worse. Overall, it looked like something out of the 1950s. It was. This was one time where the government's actions made financial sense. The VA was cash strapped, with money going for actual medical care and clinics. Administrative offices got the leftovers.

The buildings were brick, made of clay dug on-site. The hole that was left behind was filled in with water, christened a lake, and became a recreational spot for people ... and for thousands of geese. Originally an old soldier's home, it had since become a Veterans Administration Hospital.

Reporting to the supervisor's office, he was offered a seat and told to wait. It felt like being in the Army. Others were talking about the poor computer support. One of the repair people was Danny and reputed to be worse than no help at all. "If he touches your computer, it will really be broken." Since it was time to break the ice, he offered to help Rebecca.

"Hey, I know Danny and I can get him to work on your computer."

She laughed. "I don't care what Jaeck says, you're alright." She had been around old soldiers and knew how to take abuse as well as give it.

An office with a door – wow! The equipment was somewhat less. The government bought from the low bidder so the computers were slow and weak. The VA had a very limited budget so the computers were always behind the times.

Peeling paint on the walls, old floor tile that had been popular about fifty years before – the building was not much to look at or even to work in. From his third-floor window, Joe could even see the building he had worked in at Fort Prairie. The sight of it reminded him of his failure and he had to look away.

The mission was better than what Joe had at GSA. There it had been all about saving money and making profit. Here it was all about serving veterans. Millions of veterans had served in America's wars. Here he could serve them back.

As a service-disabled veteran, Joe had received some medical care from the VA. He knew that the equipment, facilities, and even some of the doctors were not top notch. He hoped to remedy that as much as he could from inside the organization.

As always, his need to make a difference was his driving force. Lower cost equipment without lowering the quality would leave more money for more medical care. Joe hoped he would be needed. He was not disappointed.

"Joe, we heard you're a miracle worker and we need one now. We have this issue in Omaha that we need you to take care of. There's a national mandate for improved security and communications at the hospital. Your predecessor in this office, Peggy Sue, was supposed to take care of it but didn't get anywhere on it. I'm not sure why she couldn't handle it but we need to get it done. Sorry to drop this on you at the outset. Could you do something with it?"

"Sure, I'll get it taken care of." This was a challenge and a chance to make a difference. This was a chance to get off on the right foot and show his ability. Security at a VA hospital was very important. Joe knew some veterans are not stable and some go off, losing control of their actions and even threatening or harming those nurses who are there for them.

After talking with the security chief in Omaha, he knew he would have to go to Omaha, see the situation and the hospital, talk to the people with the knowledge, and get this moving before the deadline came. *Stat, that's what they call it in hospitals. Well, I'm going to have to get on this, stat.*

Creativity was called for and Joe was good at thinking outside the box. Only one supplier could provide the equipment and install it. Unfortunately, they also had bad past performance and Joe knew he wasn't supposed to award to a company like that. After investigating, he found that the bad history was a fluke. He made the award and the job was done in near record time.

The engineer in Omaha was full of praises. "Joe, I can't thank you enough! I was beginning to think we'd miss the deadline. Hey, if you ever need anything, let me know. You're my hero!"

I bet he'd even let me marry his daughter ... if he had one ... if she was older ... if I wasn't already married.

Now, there was time to look around the office. He found another mess to clean up as he looked into the files. Hmm. Five drawers of files covering five years. No wonder Peggy Sue left. She ran out of space to file. Joe started getting the files closed out and boxed up.

When Joe first met Abby, he was sure he wouldn't like her. Full of energy, she was just the opposite of Joe. Where Joe was calm, Abby seemed ready to go skydiving. She also reminded Joe of a favorite country singer, Reba, with her country twang. *I wonder if she can sing too?* When Joe needed help, she was there and ready.

One day, Joe found more contracts that Peggy Sue had messed up. A contract with almost no clauses – another with confusing renewal terms, a third with an informal contract issued against another. It reminded him of the movie line, "you can't do that! What you're doing is illegal!" What did she care? She was gone and nobody had caught her doing these things.

Abby was as surprised as Joe had been. "Well, you know we were friends when she worked here but…dang! I'm sure glad you're here. I'm especially glad it's not me that has to fix that."

"If I knew what was going on, I would have been down there to straighten it out." Jaeck was apologetic but wasn't he supposed to know what was going on? Isn't that what supervisors do? Jaeck was more like a politician than a government official.

Joe maintained friendships with those he had worked with before. Roberta was no exception. He visited or called her every few months. They called it networking but allowed them to get ideas from each other.

One day, Jaeck came to him and asked him if he knew any of the people on the hiring list he had. Jaeck danced to his own tune and Joe knew this question was improper. However, like Jaeck, he was more focused on accomplishment than worrying about rules. Jaeck had a position to fill and the finalists had worked for the Army, some at Fort Prairie.

"Well, no, but I know someone who might. I'd be happy to ask her about them."

"Great! Here's the list in priority. Just let me know how they are and if I should hire one of them."

"Will do." It was always in Army talk.

When he met with Roberta that weekend, she was right to the point. Taking the list, she drew a line through the first name, laughed and drew a line through the second name. She circled the last name on the list. The lowest ranking applicant – she said that Carrie was the one to select. Carrie was also not a veteran. "What's wrong with the others?" Joe asked.

"The first one did terrible work. The second one was bipolar and we were never sure if she was going to hurt someone. The last one I worked with for a few years. She sucks up a lot but also does good work."

Joe thanked her and, after some small talk, he left. At work, he provided the list to Jaeck. "Are you sure? I mean, these others did better on the interview. Aren't they any good?"

"Not according to my contact." Jaeck was surprised but followed the advice. Joe wasn't sure he was doing the right thing, the smart thing.

The following week, Joe got what he really wanted – what he needed – the opportunity to make a difference.

The VA had a lot of contracts for medical laboratory equipment. They were all due at the same time. Joe worked through each one of them but then spaced their expirations over the next several years so they wouldn't be such a load in the future when they had to be renewed.

Jaeck looked at him like he was crazy. Maybe he was. But then, in the Army, they called it prior planning. Army people often expanded it into an even more colorful metaphor.

"If we plan then we can avoid crisis management." Jaeck just nodded, surprised but not unhappy. Joe might leave one day, but he wouldn't leave a mess for someone else. No respectable janitor did.

****

"Joe, I'm sorry to keep doing this to you."

"I'm sorry too. What is it this time?" He was grinning but had to give Rebecca a hard time anyway. Joe wasn't the first old soldier she had worked with. It was a good thing she had gotten used to the warped Army personality.

"This could score some points or have you on a time out. It depends on what you do with it."

"You have my undivided attention. What's the make-or-break problem?"

"We have a huge contract that has expired. Baoth was working on it – until she admitted she didn't know what she was doing. That took a whole year. Now, Jaeck wants someone competent to handle it."

"Is that what he said?"

"Well, not exactly. That's what I'm saying. Jaeck said that he wants to free Baoth up for other things. He refuses to admit she's worthless. Anyway, you drew the low card so you get this."

"Great, just let me get on my coveralls."

"What? Coveralls?"

"Yes. If I'm going to be the janitor and clean up another mess, I better dress for it." Rebecca just shook her head as she left. Sometimes those old soldiers were hard to understand.

Baoth was the senior contract writer but she had dropped the ball. She did that a lot but this time the impact was huge. She had an essential contract for medical supplies that was expiring. Renewal should start a year out at the latest. She waited till it was about to expire before she did anything, ignoring the fact that the supplies were needed for ailing veterans.

Trying to make up some of the lost time, Joe worked nights and weekends to get the job done. All of this overtime took its toll. Loss of sleep, crankiness, increased health issues. As a government employee, Joe didn't even get extra pay beyond the regular hourly pay. No time and a half for him.

The preliminary work that Baoth did was worse than worthless. It almost cost Joe the whole project when only one contractor could meet the requirement. Then, Baoth had the audacity to ask Joe to reduce the time for responses.

"Joe, we need that new contract – now."

"It's a long way from being available. Be patient. It takes time."

"Denver Bob told me that you only need to give companies two weeks to respond."

Well I guess it's true what they say. She doesn't know the job.

"You do know that this is complex and worth over thirty million dollars, right?"

"What's that got to do with it?"

"Everything. But the bottom line is that we need at least a month."

"But it's an emergency!"

"Well, I guess you would know since you created the emergency. But lack of prior planning on your part doesn't create an emergency on my part. If I try to cut corners now, this will get bungled and we will lose the whole thing. Is that what you want?"

"You're being unfair. It's not my fault!"

"It's all your fault. Until you handed this hot potato to me, you had a year to work on it. You did nothing. You get paid a lot more than me, and you did nothing."

I did some research on it so …"

"You bungled that as well. In fact, you almost totaled the project. If I did something that lousy, it would only have taken a week or so to complete the bungling – but not a whole year. Also, I would be fired. I'm not sure why you're still here. Maybe if I had the same relationship with Jaeck, I could do whatever I wanted too."

She stormed out.

Well, I didn't handle that very well.

Then Rebecca came in. Her office was next to Joe's and she heard everything. She and Baoth detested each other. "Joe, I just overheard that thing with Baoth. As your supervisor, I have to say, don't get into a shouting match with her. You know her and Jaeck are tight."

Then leaning forward, she said in a hushed tone, "I loved it. I've been wanting to put her in her place ever since she came to work here. You're my hero. I think I saw the old sergeant coming out!" As he saw the twinkle in her eyes, he knew – just like his good supervisors at GSA and the Corps, Rebecca also had his back.

After a few weeks, Joe had to negotiate with his only offer. They wanted all they could get out of the government. "This is crazy. No way I'm going to sign off on this."

"But Joe, we need it. Maybe we just need to bite the bullet." Jaeck was getting nervous. Baoth could be contagious, even if she didn't really know what she was doing.

"It's not just us doing the biting. It's the veterans and Joe Taxpayer."

Joe contacted other companies and asked them how much they would want if this was opened to them. "Just a ballpark figure in millions please." The price was about what Joe expected so he let the current supplier know that they would not be getting the contract.

Joe also knew that they were a one-contract company. They were getting fat on the VA and losing the contract meant going broke. Joe also knew that the best way to negotiate was when he was willing to walk away. He was willing.

In desperation, the company rep called Joe. "I need this. What do I have to do to keep the contract?"

"Well, like I said before, the cost is too high. Get it down to thirty million and you can keep the contract." What Joe didn't tell him was that it would be painful if he had to start all over.

The pain would be worth it. Veterans were being taken care of because Baoth had gotten a temporary supplier. It was painful for her, painless for Joe, and a hoot for Rebecca.

The contractor was desperate. He got paid very well by the company owner for this contract and any others he could get. Lose the contract, and the gravy train ends.

"Okay. I'll have it for you by the end of the day. Thanks." He didn't sound very enthusiastic. He had just lost seven million dollars and had to explain it to his boss. The veterans had kept the same amount for other things.

Jaeck had told him the previous contract amount was too high but he allowed the contract to go forward anyway. Joe wasn't Jaeck – he worked for the veterans and the taxpayer.

Joe was in a different part of the swamp from where he had

been before. However, it was still full of critters. The varieties were different, but still just as vicious and just as deadly.

From the boss on down, there were many crocodiles and few flamingos. Birds with redeeming values just couldn't thrive in a swamp where crocodiles could, and would, eat them.

Jaeck was an unusual critter. He had unique ways to deal with problems. Marcus was not so unique – he had come to work for the government, expecting to do little work and be a manager. He found he was one of the workers – not a manager. He resisted learning anything about the job. His greatest talent was in managing the office coffee fund. So, when he had an interview for a promotion in Washington DC, Jaeck helped him as much as possible.

"His work? Yes, he's awesome. I don't have any other employees like him. I hate to lose him but my loss is your gain. How soon would he have to leave? Well, for the greater good, I'll let him go. It wouldn't be right to hold him up just for my needs here. Hey, no problem. Let me know if there's anything else I can do for you." "Or to you," he thought.

Finishing the call, he brushed his hands together, washing his hands of the situation, and displayed a huge grin. The office was already getting better. Jaeck's problem was about to belong to someone else. The problem was not getting fixed – the critter was just relocating to a different corner of the swamp. Jaeck was getting rid of one of the critters. Of course, he had also hired him.

Jaeck had his flaws but taking care of his subordinates was not one of them – he backed up his workers when needed. When one of the supported medical centers called near the end of the fiscal year to complain about Joe and a contract Joe had not completed, Jaeck asked Joe for his side of the situation.

"I tried several times to get the information I needed. They just ignored me. I have the emails, but you know as well as I do that I can't help them if they won't help me with the information. This stuff doesn't happen in a vacuum."

"Forward the emails to me. I'll take care of this." After Jaeck got the emails, he said, "Thanks. That shut them up real fast. It was all on their end that the project fell apart." It was great having a boss that had your back. Not like some of the other corners of the swamp at all.

Jaeck was also good at finding shortcuts and ways around the system. On one occasion, a million-dollar contract needed a modification that would cost the VA a thousand dollars. Joe had never handled a situation like this one. He asked Jaeck for advice.

"Let me take care of this real fast. 'Hey Bob. Yeah, this is Jaeck. Great to hear from you too. Hey, Joe is one of my people and he got a letter from you guys for a change to our contract. It's only for a thousand dollars but that's a lot of paperwork and time. Since we're paying you a million for the X-ray machine, how about you just give us the upgrade for free and skip the modification? Great. I knew we could work this out. Hey, next time you're out here, let's get some lunch. Thanks! See you.'"

This was not the right way but it was the easy and cheap way to get it done. That made it the right way in Jaeck's – and Joe's eyes. Save the government time and money and avoid the paperwork when possible. Joe remembered this trick and sought Jaeck out in the future for other shortcuts.

One day, Jaeck came to see Joe again. "Joe, I had this guy named Menti from Fort Prairie in an interview today. Did you work with him? What can you tell me about him?"

"Did you ever hear the saying big hat, no cattle? That's him."

"But he gave such a good interview."

"Like I said, he talks a good game but doesn't follow through. I had to fix several of his contracts. He violated the Anti-deficiency Act. He tried to get me to violate the Competition in Contract Act. He's very incompetent. Is that the kind of worker you want?"

"Well, when you put it like that ..."

Joe had not forgotten the fort – or his mission. Menti wanted to move up. So did Joe, but for different reasons. When an opening with a promotion came up at the same place where Peggy Sue had gone, Joe applied. It was a chance to move up and get closer to his real goal. It should be a breeze.

If she can make it there, someone who knows what he's doing should do well.

Sometimes, Joe was totally clueless about how the swamp thinks. Joe applied only to find out that the opening had been canceled. A few months later, the opening was again available. Joe again applied. Again, it was canceled.

What's going on? Joe got a copy of the referral list and saw several, blacked-out names on it just below his. Again, the opening came up. This time, the VA followed through with interviews. The interview was easy.

Joe knew his job and had all the answers. He should have gotten the job. He didn't. Joe found that his nemesis, who left him so many problems, had been selected. The VA kept re-announcing the job until Peggy Sue completed her four-year college degree. They had wanted her all along and refused several service-disabled veterans in favor of an incompetent, non-veteran.

Selecting her before interviewing applicants was illegal. The government called this pre-selection. Joe complained to the personnel office. They ignored his complaint. The swamp had struck again. Law, ethics, morality – all were antiquated concepts in the swamp where it was critter-eat-critter.

I thought the law was supposed to protect me from stuff like this.

His attitude was beginning to morph into a more mercenary viewpoint. The old sergeant had been more right than he knew. There really was nobody directing traffic.

****

Two months later, Jaeck was selected for promotion. He knew contracting. That much was certain. He knew how to massage people to get them to do what he wanted. A visionary, he also knew how to grow an organization. That talent was essential to the bureaucratic mindset. An organization that was not growing was suffocating or dying. A bureaucracy is like any other thing that is alive – it is either growing or dying. Jaeck wanted the organization to grow and take him along with it.

One day, his boss who was having some illness issues called. "Hey, Jaeck. I want you to come up to headquarters and be my deputy." The arm twisting needed to get Jaeck to leave was minimal. The pied piper was playing his tune and Jaeck danced his way to a Senior Executive Service position. Most civil servants don't dream of being an SES. Jaeck not only dreamed of it, but made it happen.

A vacancy was created by his departure, so Jaeck had to put someone in charge. He nominated Baoth. She still didn't know the job, but while Jaeck had been massaging his boss, Baoth was massaging him. Birds of a feather, they had similar goals in mind.

The primary difference was that Jaeck had political talent and Baoth preferred to hide out. She was best qualified to be a hall monitor and, when she was busy, she often sent a proxy to check on workers and supervisors. She didn't trust anybody so they didn't trust her. It was becoming a hostile work environment.

Baoth had also not forgotten how Joe insisted on doing that contract right and wouldn't play her game. She didn't say anything about it. She didn't say anything at all. When he passed her in the hall and greeted her, her eyes had said all that was needed. Joe had been through one hostile work environment already and knew the signs. He was determined to avoid a repeat experience. He had no desire to work under another saber-toothed swamp donkey.

Rebecca helped him with his decision. "Joe, you need to get out of here."

"Sorry! I'll leave your office right now. You don't need to tell me twice."

"No, not that. Look, you've done great work. But Baoth is a vicious critter. You know she doesn't like you, don't you?"

"Yeah. I guess I figured that much out."

"So, get out of here. Find another job. Go get a promotion. You should have already been promoted. I'm leaving or retiring. I can't work under that woman!"

"But I like it here. I like the mission. Also, I hate a long drive to work. The last time almost killed me."

"There's something that you don't know."

"Oh?"

"Baoth and I were on a call one day. A woman – I really can't call her a lady – called and identified herself just as 'me'. It's *me* she said. Baoth knew immediately who it was. She told this woman that I was there. *All the better*, she said. *I want you to find a reason and fire Joe.* What for, Baoth asked. *Never mind that just do it. You know what I've got and you know I'll use it.*"

"I didn't know what was going on but I didn't want to play. I said so. She said, *Do you remember that Trade Fair you attended in Vegas about five years ago?* Vaguely. It's been so long. *Well I remember and I also remember what happened.* What did happen? *All those men, chasing you around, showering you with attention. Work with me or I'll tell your husband.* Go ahead. Maybe he'll appreciate me more. *Well, of all the... You don't think I'm serious, do you?*"

"I really don't care if you are or not. If that's all you have on me, I'm pretty safe. Tell my husband. He'll probably laugh about it even more than I am. I'll tell you this though. *Yes?* I don't know you and I don't want to know you. You may have something on Baoth here but I'm not going to play."

"Joe, that's where it ended. You have an enemy out there. You made someone hate you beyond most typical bounds. I'm leaving here so I can't protect you. You should get out while you can. I'm sorry but that's how it is."

Joe frowned. "Well, I don't know who it is but I do appreciate the warning. Thanks for sharing, especially that part about making your husband appreciate you more. We must be related."

Joe really did like the mission, taking care of old soldiers through the hospitals provided for them. It was almost like he was still on active duty. Army formation with physical training had always been a team building thing. *Esprit de corps* they called it. Shared hardships, challenges, laughs, and sweat just made everybody bond together. They were like a family is supposed to be.

Joe wasn't ready to go – not just yet. He was approaching retirement and only had a few years left. Also, the situation with Diona was ongoing. For a while she had beaten the cancer. Then it came back. Then more treatments and things would be good for awhile. It was just sort of a back and forth thing and he was afraid to take on a commute that would leave him an hour's drive from home, from Diona, and from his ability to go to medical appointments with her.

Chapter Twelve

The weasel slowly crossed the open marsh. Watching him, the nutria decided he was no threat and ignored him. They each had their place in the ecosystem. The weasel's job was to be, well, weasel-like. He took over the homes of other critters after eating them. The nutria, a large rodent, kept an eye on all but was a vegetarian. He had teeth for show but not for fighting. Considered invasive because of his destructive feeding and burrowing, once he became established in the swamp, eradicating him was nearly impossible. Both were present in the VA swamp. One was harmful by what he did. The other was harmful by what he didn't do, just by being there.

Jaeck had made a difference at the higher headquarters. He was building an empire and needed a trustworthy local governor. Baoth fit the bill. As the organization grew, it needed new space. They found an old *Walmart* building that was just about right. It was converted into office space and the department moved in. Now about five times its original size, almost everyone was promoted – everyone except Joe. Baoth still had someone looking over her shoulder and she despised Joe in her own right.

The converted building was nice – too nice. Somehow, the local media caught wind of it. Don't they always? There was an exposé and it even made the national news. Wasted money by the agency that needed money the most – that was the way the television news opened the story.

Joe had been out of town when the move occurred so he was as surprised as anyone with the quality of the new offices. Diona had to travel to Minnesota for treatments by the Mayo Clinic. That used up a month of leave for Joe and left Diona's once silky hair just a memory. She had to wear that wig, that awful wig that just never seemed to match her face.

Returning to work, he walked into the new building. *Is this a luxury hotel or a business office?* Joe was surprised by the splendor of the facility. Fireplace, lounge chairs, sculptures, fountain: the lobby looked so grand. Joe was immediately confused. He didn't know what he expected but this wasn't it.

It used to be a retail store so it should bear some resemblance to that. A remodel had been needed to convert it to professional office space. But the more the remodeling changed the appearance, the more it cost. "Who paid for the remodel of the building?" he asked.

"The VA did," Julie advised. "How do you like it?"

"Well, it's nice but I thought the VA was cash-strapped."

"Probably is, but I think we deserve a nice place to work, don't you?"

Looking around at the artwork, the statues, the sofa and other chairs, Joe wasn't so sure. "Yeah, I guess so. This is just so much more than I expected."

"I'm glad you like it." Julie clearly misunderstood what Joe was thinking.

During Joe's one-month absence a lot had changed. Baoth had been *volun-told*. That's what happens when a boss is told to retire – or else. All the workers had complained about her and management hates complaints. It's often easier to just make the source of the complaints go away. Sandy was the new boss now.

"We've got a vacancy coming up in construction. I was just telling Chuck that you've done that kind of work. We really need you and your experience on this team. How about it? Interested?" Artie was asking but not pushing.

Artie was in charge of the Construction team and he knew Joe would be a good fit. He just had to get him moved from the team he was on. Chuck could make that happen.

"Sure! I started in construction. It would be great to get back to it." *And do it till I can retire in a few years too.* Joe's retirement plans were still his own secret.

"We may also have a supervisor job coming up, if you're interested in moving up," Chuck offered.

"I think I should just focus on learning the ropes here for now." *After what GSA did to me no way I'm going there!* Joe had already been burned and was not going near the fire if he could help it.

Joe didn't know that the "vacancy" was currently filled by a worker who was being removed for poor work. Her delays were hurting a big medical center. She would be reassigned to another team and given a fresh start.

Joe had heard about Tawnya. She had left the Corps a few years ago, just before Joe started there. If a leopard doesn't change its spots, neither do some workers.

"We're going to let you support the medical center in Denver. You have to go there every other week to meet with them."

Dang. I thought I was done with having to drive in the big city and deal with that traffic. Should I just say no? The word *no* just wouldn't come out. "Ah, okay. I guess I can handle that."

"Be advised. You're getting the worst station we have. Those guys are well known for all kinds of issues."

"Like what?"

"You'll have to find out for yourself. I don't want to poison the water. Just be prepared – and watch your back."

This doesn't sound good. What have I walked into? Is it too late to say no?

"Mick will be working with you. I think you'll get along great."

At least Artie gave him that. Mick *was* easy to work with. Like Joe, he seemed to be more of a lost soul, wandering in the swamp, than a resident. A former Marine, the two of them had lots of stories to share and a common work philosophy.

Mick was medium height, medium weight, average looks, and like Joe, of Irish descent. In fact, everything about him seemed average. He was so nondescript as to be nearly invisible. Though he was a former Marine, he was incredibly pleasant and very smart. Buck at the Corps had been a Marine too but he was as abrasive as Mick was pleasant.

Mick rapidly became the go-to guy for any questions. He was a great listener and usually had the right solution for any problem. He was so pleasant that one might think that he was carefree and had no problems of his own.

Ah, if only! On one occasion, he was working with a former military officer located in another city. That man may not have been entirely stable – one day he was irritated by the processes the VA used and challenged Mick to fight.

"When are you coming out to Salt Lake City? I want to go a few rounds with you."

"Are you challenging me to fight?"

"Whatever you like, boxing, wrestling, karate, you name it." This was so beyond the pale that it was hard to believe. Professionals work together to get the job done. They don't challenge the other person to fight. Fighting man only wanted to quarrel.

****

Artie was also right about the hospital. The engineers were responsible for maintaining the buildings and putting up new ones. They were also swamp critters. They did have at least one skill – deflection. Whenever something went wrong as it always seemed to, they were ready to throw Joe under the bus.

One of the more interesting critters was Mike. He was a politically focused supervisor who was often more of a hindrance than a help. Like the nightingale, he loved the sound of his voice. Unlike the nightingale which eats insects, he contributed little.

On one occasion, Joe was preparing a small team for negotiating with a contractor to settle a problem that had been festering for over a year. Mike came in and started giving the group a long-winded pep talk. Finally, after about twenty minutes, Joe pointed out that he had limited time to prepare. Mike seemed hurt.

"So, you want me to leave?"

"Well, yes," Joe agreed. Mike laughed but also left the room. Joe's candor left him with little to say. Joe knew that if someone could just get him to stay in his office, surfing the net, and drinking coffee all day, things would go much better.

Mike appeared to be rather fit and, aside from the usual

middle age health issues, would be a thorn in everyone's side for a long time. How surprised Joe was, when word came of a sudden heart attack and passing soon after.

After Mike's passing, his subordinate was moved up which left a new position to be filled. All eligible employees were rotated through the position to give each some experience and exposure. That also included Reggie. He was every bit the quality of the swamp critter. He hated paperwork which was what his office did. He was really good at one thing. He was pleasant and could socialize with the best of them. His ideal position was probably to be the Walmart greeter.

After numerous issues with the vipers in Denver, Artie asked Sandy for a meeting. Appointed to be in charge of an organization which had so many military veterans, Sandy seemed so out of place. He appeared physically fit. When he spoke, his voice was quiet and seemed tinged with fear. He shouldn't have been afraid of anyone. At six feet, five inches, and with obviously a lot of time spent in the gym, he had a build that said don't mess with me. The eyes were a different story. Looking this way and that, it was clear he lacked confidence in himself.

A lot of military veterans worked there and were used to a straight ahead look in the eyes. Sandy was the boss but seldom looked workers in the eyes and hid out as much as he could.

His deputy had no problems with direct talk and often had to pick up the slack. Although he could easily have intimidated anyone, he became the welcome mat, someone to wipe shoes on. He had no problem with enforcing his will on subordinates as long as he could do it by distance, but those who the department served were another story.

Workers needed some support against unreasonable demands. Terri had proven that at the Corps. Here, the workers received none. Some subordinates – those who were really trying to do a good job – wound up in a hostile work environment because of the lack of support.

Aggressive subordinates also violated his orders with no adverse effects. His support of the workforce in the face of outside opposition seemed equally timid. "I've talked with their director. She assures me that she's aware of the situation and doing what she can. What else can I do?"

"Have you told her directly the things that are happening and not happening? Does she know about how these guys change the truth to fit the need of the moment? All projects are late and they are taking on even more, even though contractors are tripping over each other. Does she know all of that?"

"I told her what I could. We can't beat her over the head with this. What else do you want me to do?" Joe kept quiet for once. The way this conversation was going proved nothing good would come of it.

"Nothing, I guess." The sarcasm was barely disguised. Sandy was a definite politician and wanted everyone to get along. Was he afraid of being fired if others complained?

Since his predecessor had been removed, the fear was not entirely unreasonable. However, she had been removed for being overbearing to the workers and because of complaints from outsiders. Sandy was pleasant but not strong. In a swamp with many wanting to eat you for breakfast, everyone liked Sandy – few respected him.

****

Why can't these engineers do what they said they would do? For Joe, it was inconceivable that a man could say he would do something and then not do it. Reggie was also an Army veteran so he should understand what responsibility is. Knowing that only irritated Joe more.

"Reggie, I need that work from you now or we're going to pay a lot of extra money to the contractor for delaying him. You've been promising it for weeks now. We're at the point where we have to get this done." Reggie's supervisor just remained silent, staring at the conference table. He was about as helpful as ice in a blizzard. A kumbaya kind of guy, he hated conflict.

"I'm sure trying. I've just got so much to do. But I'll get to it. You have my word. I just need some more time." Joe knew when he was being put off. With Reggie, it happened whenever his lips moved. A new tactic was needed. This had become an emergency.

"So, Reggie, are you saying that you've been very busy but will get that work done as soon as you get around to it?"

"Yes, very busy but I'll sure get it done. Just as soon as I can. As soon as I get around to it."

"Okay. Here you go. Here's your very own round tuit." Joe handed him a round piece of wood with the word *Tuit* emblazoned on it.

"Now then, I expect you will be working hard on that work and getting it done today." *Can I negotiate or what?* Reggie and everyone else broke out laughing.

The problems with Reggie didn't end there. He regularly made deals that he didn't tell Joe about. He behaved like a used car salesman – the kind that gives the other kind a bad name. *Why don't the managers just fire him? He makes things worse than if his position went unfilled.*

Since Reggie's boss was a kumbaya sort of man, Joe had to go back and try to determine what really happened every time Reggie fed him a bull story. *Is he receiving money under the table?*

One day, Reggie drove up in a shiny red corvette. The new tags were still on it. A lot of mouths opened; Joe wasn't one to let it go. "Hey Reggie, tell me your secret. How does a GS-12 afford that and a house and a family?"

"What's it to you?"

"I want a new red convertible too. Share your secret. How about it? Huh?"

"I just manage my money well, invest well, and do a little baseball umpire work on the side."

Hmm.

Then came the diversion. "Joe, come over here, I need to show you this." It was a hole in the ground. A very big hole. Men are still boys at heart and they like nothing better than a hole in the ground.

Joe had dug holes in the yard in Lamar – until Dad stepped in one at night. He dug holes in the Army (they said it was to put foxes in). But this one was way bigger. The best part was that Joe didn't have to dig it. Impressive. The diversion worked and Joe ignored the new car. This was an awesome hole!

Chapter Thirteen

The oil was leaving its tell-tale sheen on the water of the swamp. Neither motor vehicles nor oil spill had caused it. The swamp's microbes and plants had produced it. In small quantities it causes little harm. However, this is no ordinary swamp.

"Joe! This is an emergency! The power is out in the hospital building. We've restored most of it but we can't take X-rays or MRIs. Those things take too much power for our backup generator."

"How did it happen? What do you want me to do?"

"We need a backup generator rental."

"Okay. We can do that. Now, how did it happen? Was it the rain we've been having? Was there a lightning strike?"

"Actually, we saw a video of that contractor who's been doing some trenching work. Remember that big hole? He dug that one too. The same time the power came down, the video shows sparks coming from the backhoe. Then the driver took off with the backhoe as fast as he could. Like something on television. He must've hit a main power cable. We told them it was down there. They weren't careful and hit it. We want our power back, we want this fixed, and we want the contractor to pay for it. That's what we want."

"Okay. We'll get on it. I need some evidence from you."

"You've got it."

As they all trooped into the room, the look was serious. This would cost a lot. But the contractor was supposed to have insurance to cover stuff like this.

"Well, Bob, you know why we're here. The power outage was very costly." Joe was hoping for cooperation from the contractor.

"We don't think our work caused it. Can you prove it?"

"Yes, I believe we can," Joe said. There's a power cable running just under where you were digging. We told you about it before you got the contract. We inspected and saw where it was cut. Our video shows the backhoe going down at the same time the power went out. Sparks are seen coming from the trench. Then, our video shows your subcontractor taking off like he was on fire. First this way and that way. He almost ran over an elderly veteran, hobbling along on crutches."

"Oh, check out this part. It's my favorite. Do you see him dodging a police cruiser? Now he's driving over a speed bump, the backhoe leaping into the air and then bouncing down hard. Finally, he makes it to the gate to leave the facility and continues down the side road at a high rate of speed."

"It would be funny if this wasn't so serious. The incident could have cost lives. The people getting care at the hospital depend on the power remaining on."

"Then there's the backhoe operator who could have been electrocuted. We're all very lucky nobody died. This was careless on your part and your subcontractor's. At this point, we want to be paid for the damage. You need to fix the cable, pay for the temporary generator, and establish new safety protocols to keep this from happening again."

Bob was more than slippery – he was oily – as he tried to weasel out of responsibility. "That doesn't mean anything. Pure coincidence. Look, we're very responsible and the fault isn't ours. It's yours. You never told us about the cable or where it was. You've got a thousand cables and pipes under this old facility. You don't even know where they are. How should I know?"

"You should know because we gave you a map that showed the cable."

"But a main cable repair could cost us a half million dollars. Then there's the generator rental. I'm not sure our insurance will cover it."

"It had better. That's why we require it from you. Regardless, we'll provide you with a modification to cover the additional work at no cost to us. There will be a bill coming to you for the emergency generator rental that we had to pay for, and that will be for about one hundred thousand dollars."

"But we're a small business. Can't you give us a break?"

"No. The responsibility is yours. That's what we're paying you for."

After the repairs were made, Bob submitted a bill to Joe. Joe laughed and handed it back. "Nice try funny man. But seriously, you should be getting the bill of collection from us on the generator. You need to pay it right away so we don't have to withhold funds on the contract."

"If I don't? What can you do?"

"I can withhold payment on this contract and do the same on all your other contracts. We call that 'set-off.' Also, I can give you a bad rating. That might keep you from getting any more government contracts. Do you want to go through all that?"

Bob saw the futility and paid the bill. He was mad, but he understood Joe a lot better. Joe had a backbone. Bob wasn't used to that.

However, Bob also had a few tricks up his sleeve. Numerous changes had to be made to the construction contract. All the things that changed or were unknown at the start led to contract changes. Each time, Bob inflated his charges for the change. He also found accounting tricks to use. He overcharged for almost everything. He had moved beyond oily – he was now greasy like Greasy Thumb Guzik, Al Capone's right-hand man.

Joe referred the situation to the lawyer. "Let him finish and then we'll pursue a fraud case against him. We're asking for trouble if he doesn't finish the work. Imagine trying to get another company to come in behind him and take on the liability for the work that's already done. Nobody would do it. No, let's wait and build a case, doing our due diligence to minimize the costs."

A year later, all the contracts were done. Bob received the summons as he was celebrating a great financial year for the company. "What the ... what is this?"

"Looks like a summons," said the police officer delivering it. "You might want to read it, but my job is done."

All through the trial, as the attorney for the government presented its case, Bob just stared. First at the floor, then at Joe, then at the floor again. When it was his turn, his attorney looked at Bob. Then he rose slowly, "Your honor, in all my years of practicing law, I've never seen a case develop like this one. Why didn't the government pursue these charges earlier? It's clear that they waited till they had what they needed from my client and then brought the charges. This is unconscionable!"

"Maybe so," the judge said, "but I don't see anything illegal here. Are you ready to pursue the defense?"

Momentarily staring at the floor, the attorney continued. "No. After consulting with my client, we have decided to forego the defense and change the plea. However, we also ask that Your Honor consider this progression of events and mitigate the punishment that my client receives. He has a family. He has been an outstanding member of the community for all of his life. Surely, this counts in your decision."

"And for many of those years he has been cheating our disabled military veterans," the prosecutor pointed out as the judge paused in thought.

Raising his eyebrows, the judge finally responded, "I see both points and will let you know my decision one week from today."

The decision was fair, prompt, and met the demands of blind or nearly so, justice. "I understand the points raised by both attorneys. However, one thing could not be ignored. Bob willingly and knowingly defrauded the veterans who served our country at very low rates of pay and loss of limbs, literally. His apparent lack of conscience in depriving an already stressed medical organization that cannot care for those who need it goes beyond almost anything that has come before me in twenty years on the bench."

"Bob, I sentence you to twenty years in confinement, fifteen of which are to be without possibility of parole."

The gasps filled the room. Even Joe was surprised. He was the agent for the people and for the veterans. He wanted to make sure others didn't cheat the veterans, but this? It was totally unexpected.

As he stood up, Joe couldn't meet Bob's glare. He should feel good about the victory but that feeling was elusive. One more year. That's all he had before retirement. This job was increasingly one he was uncomfortable with.

Reggie was also present during the trial. Since he had approved many of the changes and recommended them to Joe, he was more than concerned. That new car, his bank account – it could all go up in smoke. "Joe, can we talk?"

"Sure, what about?"

"Just thinking about Bob."

"Yeah, that's really something, huh? I sure didn't expect the sentence though. Still, it might help us to get what we need without being cheated."

"Just, wondering, are you looking at anybody else. I mean, are they still investigating anything, anyone?"

"I'm not sure. Is there anybody we should be looking at?"

"Oh, no, not that I know. Just wondering is all. Thanks! See you around."

Hmm. That was odd. I wonder.

Chapter Fourteen

The brown recluse spider is dangerous and resilient. Without food, it can live for several years. It comes in a variety of shades and hides very well. Get rid of the hiding places and you may be able to get rid of the spider too – or at least limit its numbers.

It's been said that old soldiers never die, they just fade away. Joe had no intention of fading away – not as long as the swamp remained. He was still the old soldier and candor was the only way he knew how to behave. Sometimes that upset people.

When Joe had a meeting with an architecture company, he told them how he would evaluate the performance of the company.

"I don't intend to sound mean but I would want to know this up front so I have to believe you do also. Surprises are seldom good – unless it involves ice cream. I will evaluate candidly and fairly. If you are substantially late, I will say so on that written performance evaluation."

"A few days isn't a big issue but it's all relative. You have to give us a design that's within the limit. When we tell you that we only have so much money to spend, then that's your limit. Although there can be some variance, if it's a lot more than the limit, I'll say that in the evaluation, accompanied by a less than successful rating."

"Since this affects your ability to get future government contracts, you need a good rating – and I want to give you one. Help me to do that."

Joe never forgot who he worked for. As a former soldier, he often thought about the people who paid his salary; they had his first loyalty. This was not his supervisor, not the Congressmen who appropriated funds, nor the president who headed up the Executive Branch.

It was those who paid taxes and deserved the best value for their money. It was people like Dad who still detested government largesse. This sometimes made enemies for him.

Joe felt bad when he prepared a negative report on a contractor who had previously earned high remarks – but not bad enough to not do it. If they were no longer doing a great job, that had to be reported. Each time he wrote an evaluation of a contractor that was less than glowing, someone was going to be irritated. Sometimes they would be outright mad and call Joe or someone in his chain to complain.

He recalled the first sergeant's words, "I'm not doing my job until I start seeing my name on the bathroom walls." Some say that "doing the right thing is its own reward." Joe's intransigence would not allow him to do anything that did not set right with his conscience.

The only ones who should be upset with his candor were those who had not provided the best product or service. They were also irrelevant. The old soldier in Joe had come out. Approaching retirement also made it easy to ignore the consequences of unpopularity.

The evaluation system of contractors was there for a reason. That reason was to provide a good picture of past performance.

If used honestly, candidly, and accurately, it was a great tool. However, too many swamp critters just wanted to get along with the contractors and were willing to whitewash poor performance.

Joe was having none of that. He told them upfront what he would do and then he did it. Some didn't believe him when he warned them that he was going to be honest and accurate.

"What's with this rating you gave me on my contract?" Bob Mankin asked.

"I didn't give it to you. You earned it."

"But it says marginal in several areas. This is going to keep me from getting future business from the government."

"And?"

"I need a better rating. Change it."

"No. You earned that and I even warned you at the start I was honest and would be reporting what happens on a contract. I work for the people and the veterans. I'm an old soldier myself and there's no way I'll betray my fellow soldiers and veterans. We want the best and that requires honesty and candor."

"You ... you're just a golem."

"A golem?"

"Yeah, that's what I said. You probably don't even know what that is."

"Actually, I do. According to Webster's, it's a Yiddish word meaning an artificially created human being, supernaturally brought to life. That's kind of like saying that I was sent by God. I think I like that – sent by God."

"That's not what I meant!"

"But that's what you said. Maybe you should learn the meaning of a word before you use it. Hmm?" *I wonder if I can get that put on my business cards?* Joe knew he was taking liberties with Webster but, why not?

A few weeks later, a contractor failed to provide what the government had paid a great deal of money for – a corrected design for a construction project. Joe discussed it with them and thought he had reached an agreement. He was wrong. Finally, he sent them a warning letter. Feigning surprise, the owner called him to discuss it.

Joe said "I don't know why you're surprised. I've been patient and asked for these corrections several times. I shouldn't have had to ask for them in the first place. But when I pointed out all the problems, you should have fixed it. You only fixed a little each time. Did you expect me to accept that?"

"So, what are you going to do? You need us so you can't fire us."

"That's true," Joe said. It would be foolish of me to do that. But what I can do is withhold payment. I can also discuss this with the government engineer and order specific changes to fix the problems. Then, when I do your past performance evaluation, I'll rate your company as less than successful. That means that you're unlikely to get any more government contracts. Do you really want to go there?"

"So, what do I have to do to get past this?" the critter asked.

"Fix everything by Friday and have it in my hands, fully corrected by Friday. That would resolve it."

"Okay, I will do that. Sorry for the issues." He had seen the light.

Joe's peers began to see the light too. After too many problems, Big John cornered Joe. "Hey, Joe! Got an issue I need to talk about. A contractor installed equipment, damaged the walls, and won't pay for the damage. We've already paid them. What can we do?"

"Well, I'd call them, tell them to either pay for it or we do a negative performance evaluation that will probably keep them from any more government contracts. We can also have the finance folks send them a government collection letter."

"Hmm, that just might work!" Sometimes we need a rabble rouser to be unpleasant so we can get what's fair and right. The old sergeant could definitely rouse the rabble.

****

He was an older fellow, but no older than many others. He only stood out when he took a break. All workers were entitled to a fifteen-minute break for every four consecutive hours that they worked. He was no exception and took his break religiously. However, he also napped during that break.

Most people can't fall asleep that quickly and particularly, in a public place. He went to the common area in the fancy lobby with overstuffed armchairs and slept right there, watching the false fireplace. At some point in the past, he had aroused concern. His age, coupled with apparent lack of consciousness, caused some co-workers to nudge him and ask if he was okay.

Now, he always took a cardboard sign that read, 'I am napping. I'm not dead. Leave me alone.' He wasn't so much a swamp critter as one of the unusual sights of the swamp. He was like the mangrove tree that drops its branches which then take root – totally unexpected.

It was a few days later, birds were singing, fresh grass cut with the smell filling the air, the temperature was a perfect seventy degrees. Everything was so perfect; something was bound to go wrong. It did.

Joe went into work and found... almost nothing. The processes which everyone used were paperless. There were no paper documents. Everything was electronic in a computer system, accessible by all workers. The files that Joe looked for were just not there. For months he had been diligently working to update all of the records. These were important. If a court case came up for who knows what reason, this was the evidence. Half of Joe's files were gone. What could have happened?

Traci, the miracle computer worker couldn't figure it out. Fortunately, she had a lot of friends. They looked into it and found the files had been removed. Deleted. Recoverable due to backups, but that would take weeks to resolve. The deletion also left a computer trace.

Nothing happens in the cyber world without leaving a trace. It was tracked back to Jody. He never let bygones be just that. He had deleted Joe's files. He had finally gotten even with Joe over the trouble he got in. Joe had reported him for sleeping in his office when he was supposed to be working, and Jody had waited for a good time to strike back.

Well, at least he had timed it well. This couldn't have come at a worse time with that court case coming up. Sandy called Joe in along with Joe's other supervisors and let him know what had happened.

"So, what are you going to do?" It was more of a demand than a question.

"Well, we have asked to have the files restored. That should fix everything. Sorry for the delays and inconvenience."

"No, I mean what are *you* going to do?"

"Huh? I'm not sure I understand."

"You have a worker - no, scratch that. You have a weasel who has just cost the VA lost productivity, thousands of dollars to restore the files, violated every norm of the VA, not to mention decency. This is not his first action that has imperiled this agency. So, what are you going to do about him?"

"Well, that's a personnel issue that I'm not at liberty to discuss. You can be sure though that it will be taken care of and he will be counseled. This will not work out well for him"

"That's what I thought. More of nothing. I think I have bought into the right to know, with what he did to me and my projects." Joe wanted to call him a nutria but decided he'd already said enough.

Sandy just stared. The other supervisors said nothing but their faces said it all. They agreed with Joe.

"Boss, you need to fire that sorry waste of skin. He did this intentionally. You know this. If you don't remove him, your inaction will lead others to ignore your directions. This is called vandalism and provides you with grounds for termination as well as criminal prosecution." Joe was letting it all out and leading the boss to a right decision, something he shouldn't have had to do.

For a moment, Sandy just stared. "You're right of course. I have no choice." He was thinking out loud now.

"Okay, Moe, Artie, put him on leave and start the immediate termination process today. We need to get him off our computers and out of our building right away. Get with our attorney and find out what is done in cases like this. I don't want to do anything trendsetting. We just need to resolve this as quickly and as quietly as possible. Don't announce anything. Let his empty desk tell it all. Does anybody disagree with this action?" Of course, nobody did.

Walking back to his office, Artie said, "Joe, I've never seen you like this. I thought you would bite his head off. And they thought I was bad." Both were laughing hard now. The stress gone, Joe had to start putting the puzzle of files and documents back together. Even with the recovery help from the computer guys, it would take months, if ever.

Chapter Fifteen

The beaver was active. One of the most industrious creatures in nature, it was building to meet its needs. Other creatures were taking advantage of the beaver's labor. Fish liked the deeper water and sanctuary that the dam provided. Crocodiles ate the fish that took shelter there. Other species ate what is left over when the crocodile was done. Nature is like that. So are other swamps.

"We lost $150,000 when we cancelled that contract. Now I have to explain that to the Medical Center Director. What should I tell her? Why did you cancel it when there was still work to be done?"

Joe had been listening to Jesse, the Chief, Engineer drone on. Now, he was yelling at Joe. Easily over sixty years old, he had a stocky figure, receded hairline, punctuated with white hair, and wrinkles on top of wrinkles. His best days were behind him.

Jesse was excited but Joe remained calm, infuriating him all the more. "Why don't you tell her it was canceled because you asked me to cancel it? While you're at it, tell her also that we were unable to get it complete because you refused to give me the one word answer I needed to an easy question. A simple yes would have saved the project. Tell her that she lost all that money because you didn't do your job. Tell her that."

The engineer was red in the face. "I can't tell her that. You canceled it. You work for us."

"No," Joe said. "I work for our veterans. I work for the taxpayer. I even work for my boss. But I only support you within the limits of the law."

"Also, while we're on the subject, I don't respond well to yelling. You're supposed to be a professional. You're a retired, full Army Colonel. You lost your bearing yet again today. You know better. So, I won't even be supporting you until I get a full, heart-felt, and public apology."

"Have a nice day gentlemen." He picked up his note pad, donned his "made-in-Ireland" Donegal Tweed hat, and left the room.

Two weeks later, Joe was again visiting the engineers in Denver. He hadn't received the apology but Sandy insisted he go back anyway. As usual, the engineers had bungled the process and now wanted Joe to do something – it smelled illegal.

As he explained, the old man decided to weigh in. He usually got what he wanted by being a bully. The lecture started and twenty minutes later was still going on. He might be old but he still had wind. "... You're just not taking care of our veterans. Now you better get this done and get it right. Forget a legal review of the issue. Just do it!" Jesse wasn't taking no for an answer.

As the old man finally wound down, Joe said, "It sounds as if you're directing me to do something illegal. Is that what you're saying?"

"Of course not. Just get it done. That's what you're there for."

"Yes, but I'd like to do it without getting a prison sentence in the process."

Another twenty minutes of lecturing followed. Joe needed to leave but wanted to work with these guys too. Jesse had repeatedly denied that some of his own engineers had failed to get their jobs done, expecting other departments to pick up the slack and to do pretty much anything. He demanded that a dozen projects get completed when he had the resources for less than half that number. He was still droning on.

"... and about that parking garage. I want it awarded now. It's part of my performance goals and affects my evaluation. Get it done!"

"We can't," Joe said. You asked for a Cadillac design for a Ford requirement. Now the bids are for more money than it's worth and more than we have. Awarding it would be illegal and a major waste of money. We've already wasted a million dollars on the design. I'm not going to throw away another nine million."

That was the final straw for Jesse. His face turning red, veins bulging, eyes bugging out, he started yelling at Joe. Cursing, banging his hand down on the conference table he suddenly jumped up – and collapsed forward on the conference table. A few hours later Joe got the word on Jesse. It was a stroke. After Jesse got out of the hospital, he retired.

When Joe heard about the retirement, he asked Bob in Jesse's office if it was true. "Yep, sure is. I saw him in the hospital and he said he couldn't take any more. Said he was done. You know, I saw the strangest thing when I was there. There was this one woman who came in and Jesse turned even paler than he had been."

"Oh?" Joe was interested now. What could scare old Jesse? He was mean but also tough. Joe still remembered what Rebecca had told him. Bad things kept happening. Could they be related? He realized that was just being paranoid. Still, it's not paranoia if they really are out to get you.

"Yeah, he called her ... oh, what was it anyway. Laura ... Macie. Sorry. Any of those sound familiar?"

"No, not that I recall anyway."

"Well, probably not important. Still, I just wonder." Joe wondered too – all of thirty seconds.

****

Some days everything seems to go right, while others are just the opposite. It was one of the latter. Joe came to work and saw the news media all over the place. I hope nobody died. His phone was already ringing.

"It's the water tower."

"What water tower?"

"Your predecessor Tawnya awarded a contract to mothball the old water tower on the VA campus. It was, oh, about three years ago. Apparently, the contractor used the wrong paint, didn't remove rust, and in general did a really bad job. Anyway, it collapsed overnight."

"The tower crushed ten cars and the hospital director's antique Harley-Davidson. Good thing nobody was around when it happened. The only casualties were the cars – and the motorcycle. Really sorry about that. It was a classic. Fully restored too.

Anyway, the press wants to talk to everybody. Since you're responsible for the contract, even though it happened before your time, they want your blood too. Better not answer the phone and just let the Public Affairs guy handle it."

"Wow!" It took a moment to take it all in. Again, "Wow! So, who was the engineer watching the contractors? Why didn't he catch the sloppy work?"

"That was Ann. She no longer works for the VA. The TV reporters don't care. They just want blood and an award-winning story."

"Okay. I'll keep my head down and let the director know. Do we have a plan for what to do with what's left of the tower?"

Salvage. That was what was left. Scrap iron and a lot of it. The tower hadn't held water in decades. It also couldn't be torn down since it was historic. Well, it was down now. The director wasn't answering the phone either. He avoided stressful things like this. Not that this happened with frequency.

Joe thought about the critters he was coming into contact with here at the VA. He remembered the beaver. It is unwittingly a participant in the swamp, driven by nature to build dams which block streams to provide a home for itself (and fish). However, that water also backs up, providing a habitat for other, less desirable forms of life. Was he becoming the beaver and making the rest of the swamp possible?

****

Joe provided contracts to several VA Medical Centers. He had been trying to make the people in Teardrop Park happy. Their VA Medical Center needed a new MRI Suite. However, the hospital director had reduced the staff in the engineering department to below half of the authorized strength in order to hire more nurses. No veteran would conclude this is a bad thing.

However, the nurses and doctors need a place to work such as a hospital or clinic. The engineers' job is to provide for that including new or remodeled facilities that keep up with current technology. At the reduced level, they were unable to get their work done. Yet, the Medical Center Director continued to expect the remodeling and new construction to take place.

This was the gift that keeps on giving. The Contracting Office lost time following up with the engineers on work or documentation that should have already been done. It wasn't their fault – they were doing the work of several people.

The director little understood that her actions were delaying the facilities she wanted and needed. It also reduced the effectiveness of the Contracting Office which had to keep calling about actions her reduced engineering staff hadn't been able to do yet.

Finally, the Director summoned Joe to her office to attend a meeting with the Engineers. She came right to the point, impressing Joe with her willingness to dispense with the usual pleasantries. "Why isn't my new MRI Suite available yet?"

The engineers locked eyes with her and then glanced at each other, and finally, at the floor, totally unsure how to proceed. Joe wasn't as shy – she wasn't writing *his* evaluation. The old sergeant was always candid.

"Well, actually we haven't awarded the contract yet, Ma'am."

"Why not?" she again demanded.

"There have been a lot of delays in the process."

"Such as?" She was unwilling to let things drift along this way.

"I haven't gotten the responses and information I need from the engineers. Often, weeks go by without a response to key questions."

"Well?"

Dale was the head engineer for the hospital. "We're doing the best we can. There's only the two of us now to do the work."

"That is unsatisfactory!" she exploded.

Joe interjected, "Ma'am, if I may ..."

"Doctor!" she demanded. "I'm a Doctor!"

"Fine," Joe said. "I will if you will. I'm also a doctor."

She looked at him, then at the head engineer. Dale nodded, "That's right. He is."

"Well, okay then *Doctor* O'Flaherty," she emphasized the Doctor part, "you were saying?"

"*Doctor* Shelby," Joe returned the favor, emphasizing the title, "my work has been delayed because of slow responses from the engineers. The engineers have been delayed by numerous tasks involved in these contracts but also in their other routine work such as inspections. Their department has been reduced to less than half their authorization."

"According to the grapevine, that's so that you can provide more nurses and other medical specialties. I have no problem with that – I'm a veteran also and I receive care from the VA.

However, I believe it's worth mentioning that the Doctors, nurses, and others work in buildings that the engineers provide. They provide them through contracts that my office awards.

We can't award them without all legal requirements being met including the answers to our questions."

"If they are doing the work of two people, they will only get half of it done, delaying the projects to twice the typical amount of time which

easily adds months."

Joe noted that she seemed unimpressed so he took off the gloves. "You asked why the delays are happening. It's starting right here – in your office."

The Director was absolutely fuming but Joe didn't pause to give her an opening. "If you want projects to move along more rapidly, may I suggest you restore the full staffing in the Engineering Department? That is unless you want to practice medicine out in the parking lot. But oh, my bad. The parking lots are also the result of their work. Hmm. Where does *that* leave us?"

He paused now, waiting for the explosion and the order to get out of her office. To his surprise, she just stared at him. Then she too stared at the floor. It was sure getting a lot of attention today – the housekeeping staff better be on their toes.

Then she looked at Joe. She smiled and then laughed. "I guess this is what I really needed to hear. Is there anything else you want to add?" she said to the Head Engineer.

"No, I think that about covers it all. It's sure more than I would have offered."

"Okay then. We'll look into restoring your staffing. Get with my secretary and schedule a meeting for us – without Dr. O'Flaherty – for next week." This hadn't gone exactly according to anyone's plan. It did seem to offer promise for a better tomorrow though.

As they left the office together, all were silent until they were out of the building. The Engineer laughed. "Geez, I'm not sure what to say. I'm not even sure what just happened. I thought you were going to throw us under the bus for a moment back there." They all laughed – all the way back to the Engineer's office.

****

Trina was Joe's work buddy. She hadn't been around as long as Joe but she had been on the team for five years so she was an excellent go-to person. "Good morning, Trina!" Joe had seen her in the breakroom. *Guess she didn't see me.* "Hey, you alright?"

"Yes, just tired I guess." She still had her hat on, pushing the bangs of hair down over her eyes. "Rough night."

"I have those too. It's worse when I have caffeine late in the day or I'm worrying about things … or excited about things…or just thinking about things. So, what's your excuse?"

"Nothing. I guess I had better get to work."

"Hey, hold on. What's up? This doesn't sound like you. You never even called me *old* today. That's not like you."

She turned around and looked at him. Shrugging her shoulders, she started away again.

"Trina, talk to me. What's with the sunglasses in the building? It's not that bright in here … except maybe when you look at me."

"Maybe in private."

She was having marital issues. The sunglasses were just camouflage until she could get to the privacy of her small office. "Look, you can't go on this way. You need to get help and get this reported."

"You just don't know. He – well he wouldn't let that set. He would do something. I'm afraid to do something and I'm afraid to do nothing."

"Do you want *me* to do something? Maybe I can talk to somebody? I have a friend on the police force. I have other friends who can get you a safe place. What about reporting this to management for some help?"

"Management? You've got to be kidding. Look at what we've got for leadership. I'm also not ready for police or to leave yet. But I'll think about it. Please keep this between us." Joe couldn't help thinking about her the rest of the day and the next. He wanted to help but how?

Chapter Sixteen

The mangrove jellyfish was floating, waiting, hoping for a lunch. Plankton is a favorite dish, sucked into the jellyfish's many mouths. The jellyfish doesn't exert a lot of effort but just floats on the water, waiting for lunch to come to it. Some of the swamp's critters can easily be compared with it.

Hey, they missed me! Joe heard the awards being announced. Some were for years of service. Joe had thirty-five years including his Army years and he knew they counted. "Artie, when am I getting my thirty-five-year pin?"

"I guess we missed it. Sorry. I'll let the boss know."

A few weeks later, Sandy had the award. "So, Joe, we'll be presenting this tomorrow at the group meeting. Just want to make sure you'll be there."

"Umm, something is wrong here."

"Oh, what?"

"This plaque says fifteen years of service."

"And?"

"I have thirty-five years."

"Well, this is what they sent."

"Okay, but I think it should be changed, corrected."

"I'm not sure I can do anything about that."

"But it's wrong and more than that, it's an insult to someone with my years of service."

"There's no insult intended here."

"Well, can't you ask them to fix it?"

"No. They know what they're doing." *I sure don't want to stir things up.*

"Apparently not."

"So, are you saying that you would rather have nothing than this?"

"Well, since I already have a thirty-year award on the wall, I guess if those are my only choices, I *would* rather have nothing than this."

"Okay. Works for me." Here it was again – the backbone of a jellyfish. It was easier to do nothing than to do the right thing.

Why did stuff like this keep happening? It was almost as if a dark cloud hung overhead. Maybe he was born under an unlucky star. It was as if someone was always out to make his life difficult.

Some people would just quit under these conditions. Joe thought about it and got mad. *No way! I'm too close to a retirement. Diona and I will need the income from a retirement. I'm not going to just walk away.*

The next day, the awards were given out. Joe's name was not mentioned. He had made his choice. Then Sandy made his week. "We've hired a new supervisor. Douglas MacArthur Kim will be joining us from the Corps of Engineers."

Joe heard nothing else at the meeting. The same thought kept running through his mind. "What? I left to get away from him." Things were never so bad that they couldn't get worse.

Even that name. It was so pretentious, but he had even insisted on the full name when he was in uniform.

Joe thought about both developments for a few weeks. He couldn't do anything about Kim. The award was probably the same. The resentment welled up inside him: the frustration, then the anger, then the determination to embrace the anger. It was then that he called the Human Resources office.

"So, what's the issue? What can we not do for you today?" There it was again. The HR guy was very down to earth and flippant too. Joe had to laugh in spite of the problem.

"Look, you guys recently sent down an award for me for fifteen years of service."

"What's wrong with that? Wrong color? Did you want a box of donuts with it?"

"Ha! Well, I have twenty-one years in the Army and I believe those years count."

"Let me look into it." A few hours later, "Yeah, you're right. We dropped that ball."

"Well, here's the rest of it. My boss refused to do anything about it. If you send it down through him, he'll know I went over his head. Not cool for old soldiers like you and me to be doing – and I don't want to leave here until I can retire."

"Hmm. There's no way we can get the certificate past him since he has to sign it. I can get you the pin though."

"Okay, let's do that." Not a complete fix but it was something and validated Joe once again against the swamp.

Chapter Seventeen

He looked out of place in this corner of the swamp. The deer had a backbone while the frogs, fish, leeches, and slugs had none. Surely, he couldn't last long?

I like this guy. He's got a backbone. When was the last time I saw that? When a new president came into office, he was challenged on every side. He seemed to have few allies – Joe and Mick were among those who were happy with the change. *I should send him a letter. Let him know what I know about this swamp he wants to drain.*

Dear Mr. President,
I would like to take this opportunity to congratulate you on your election and on the actions you have taken so far. While you are catching a lot of heat for them, your actions are necessary and definitely in the public interest. I would like to also provide a few thoughts from one of your supporters and one of your employees. I did vote for you and I currently work for the Veterans Administration as a contracting officer where I support two Veterans Administration Medical Centers with construction-related maintenance contracts. (I

am also a retired U.S. Army master sergeant.) I hope you can take the following words as just "a view from the trenches." As you are aware, the overwhelming majority of the Civil Service is neo-liberal in its political views. However, there are also a sizable number of us who support you and are pleased with the opportunity to work under a president who cares about our country. One point that I would like to make concerns the General Services Administration where I previously worked. Beneficial in concept, the GSA has been corrupted. We've all heard the stories and seen the videos they made in-house on government time as well as spending government funds on magic shows. In addition to that, it is liberal to the extreme. GSA belongs to the people of our country and the workers need to be reminded of this. I worked there and I was required to attend a one-week orientation in Washington DC. We had private rooms at the Madison in downtown Washington DC. The purpose for attendance was "to imbibe the corporate culture." If the training is necessary, why not conduct it onsite at each regional headquarters annually. This one change would save millions of dollars each year. However, I saw little benefit for too much cost.

The budget of GSA is mostly self-generated by volume buying and reselling within the government. However, the workforce has come to believe that because they generate profits, the money is theirs. Too many times I saw where individual workers repeated that statement "it's our money because we earned it as profit so we should be able to spend it as we see fit." If profits allow, prices for goods resold to other government agencies could be reduced. This is the original reason for the GSA. The bonuses that the workforce has come to expect are very substantial. One of the services – Public Buildings Administration – receives an inordinate amount since they receive awards within the organization as well as cash awards from other agencies when they do something well for that separate agency. Incentives, for excelling workers, need to continue for motivational purposes but too much is not a good thing. I would recommend an executive order limiting total cash awards in any given year be limited to a percentage of the employee's salary. Two percent might be appropriate.

An additional point I would like to provide concerning the GSA is about the organizational mentality. I was removed from a supervisor position because I made a private confession of faith to a fellow supervisor who immediately took it to our supervisor since as a Christian; I might have an issue with a gay employee. I clearly stated that I would treat him fairly and not discuss his orientation unless he brought it up.

The entire supervisory chain supported removing me from the supervisor position, alleging that I could not be counted on to be impartial. I would submit, it was they who were not impartial since, at no time did they give me an opportunity to defend myself or ask for my side of the conversation.

A final point concerns an issue you are already pursuing. Overregulation has caused a great increase in costs. Similarly, laws that require goals and actual set-asides for various socioeconomic categories add billions of dollars to our costs. Although I am a service-disabled veteran and readily support this particular set-aside, I also know that it adds 10 – 20 percent to each acquisition. Getting rid of these preferences will generate huge opposition and great savings. We are often asked how we can cut costs but when we mention the above, we receive a polite smile and the question, "are there any other ways?"

Again, please accept my sincere goodwill concerning your actions taken in our behalf. If there is anything I can ever do for you or any way I can facilitate your goals as our president, I hope one of your staffers will let me know.

Thanks for all you are doing!

There! I wonder if he'll read it. Might even go into the trash on delivery. Well, nothing ventured, nothing gained. It didn't go into the trash. That would have been better.

Chapter Eighteen

The possum was hiding. He was not typically violent and preferred to play dead. However, he has large teeth and knows how to use them, if a predator gets too close to them. Snakes in the swamp are one of its favorite meals, making the possum a beneficial critter.

The day started like any other. Come in, get a cup of coffee. Realize it's not very good, shake his head, and proceed to his office. At least he could get a cup of tea. Joe could control the quality of that.

There was even a piece of good news. Kim had completed his one year as a supervisor and was now qualified for a promotion. Even better, GSA had offered him that promotion. He would be leaving in a month. It was an undeserved promotion but Joe cared little any more. The swamp could keep its critters and muck for all Joe cared.

About ten o'clock, Joe was focusing on yet another problem. This looked like a case of fraud. Retirement was looking better all the time. Walks with a dog and lots of time for reading the classics. It was going to be all he had hoped for.

I wonder if I could even write something that ... Suddenly, he awakened from his daydreaming to the sound of angry shouts.

Then he heard it, the infamous "Allahu Akbar" followed by what sounded like gunshots.

"Is there no consideration? Who's watching a video on the internet with the volume up?" he asked out loud. He was getting irritated until he realized – it was not a video. This was the real thing! Here in the heartland of all places!

Joe had served in the Army and saw firsthand what weapons can do. He had no weapon – they were prohibited on government property. Down the hall, he heard Kim.

"Please! Oh, no, please!" He was even praying out loud. They had found him. He was curled up under his desk as small as his six-foot frame would allow. Then came the laughter as the gunmen just passed him by.

The training had said to try to hide and only resist when hiding is not an option. Hiding in his office did Joe no good. A few rounds eliminated the lock on the door. Joe was hiding out of sight, just to the side of the door, but they would be coming in.

"Okay! Okay! I'm coming out! Look, we don't have to do this. Can't we talk it out first?" The look on their faces told it all. Conversation was useless.

Joe was still holding a copy of Webster's dictionary to his chest – he had just been trying to decide on the spelling of a word he hadn't used in years and was unsure the spellcheck on his computer had it right. It didn't.

Almost forgetting he still had the book, he moved faster than he had in years. The adrenaline was in overdrive as Joe jumped toward the first one. He took a round in the book-covered chest before knocking down one of the attackers. The second one was twenty feet behind and moved to join the struggle.

Suddenly with the shooters' attention on Joe, other workers emerged from their offices and tackled the second attacker. Kim still huddled in his office but all the others were joining in the fight. The office was staffed by a lot of military veterans. They hadn't had to fight in a long time, but they also hadn't forgotten how.

As they took the second one down, he fired, grazing Joe in the leg with a stray shot. Focused on the struggle, Joe didn't even notice it. The adrenaline was just like the scud incident. Only after the attackers had been subdued did he notice it. A co-worker said, "Hey Joe, are you alright? You're bleeding!"

Joe looked where he was pointing and there it was. "Wow!" That was all he could think to say.

Kim finally emerged from his office, ready to take charge. "Yes, yes. That's right. I'm in charge. You, take off your belt and use it to tie his hands."

"No, you just get out of the way!" Mick was irritated by the interference.

The ambulance was there almost immediately, or so it seemed. They were very easy on Joe and gingerly lifted him to the gurney, all the while applying pressure to the wound.

The nearest hospital was very close, only a two-minute drive. After getting the wound cleaned and stitched, it was bandaged. As things began to calm down, he began to ask "Why?"

This was a question nobody could answer and, in spite of the shock and suddenness of it all, Joe probably could make as good a guess about the attackers' motives as anyone else could – and he was dumbfounded.

That afternoon, Sandy showed up and thanked Joe for what he had done. It looked a lot like groveling. "You might be interested in the investigation. The detectives found that those attackers were actually not Muslims. They were just using terrorism as their cover."

"Actually, they were hired by a disgruntled husband of one of our employees. The yelling was apparently just cover for them. You undoubtedly saved lives by your action. If there is anything you want, just say the word."

"Who was the employee that was hooked up with those nuts?

"Well, I probably shouldn't say but I guess you earned that much. It was Trina – actually it was her husband. Do you know her?"

"Yes. I was afraid it might be her. Well, at least now she'll be safe. Oh, and I am kind of hungry. Could you tell those nurses to give me some ice cream?"

Sandy turned to the nurses and said in a mild tone, "Can Joe have some ice cream?" Without doctor's instructions, they just glanced at each other.

Joe said to Sandy, "You're doing it all wrong. You're a GS-15. You need to walk with a big swagger and cut a wide swath. Don't ask them, tell them! Now, put your hands on your hips, turn around and say, 'I said to get Joe some ice cream and get it now!' Say it loudly!"

Sandy turned around and for what may have been the first time in his life, showed a backbone, not to mention a lot of decibels. Within three minutes the nurses were back with a tray holding a dozen different flavors of ice cream. They were scared. Joe asked Sandy, "Didn't that feel good?!" Sandy just grinned.

****

"Mr. President, the news reports say there has been a workplace shooting in a federal facility."

"Where? Who was it? Who did it? Spit it out!"

"It was a VA facility in Colorado. They're reporting that the shooters came in and yelled Allahu Akbar and started shooting. No deaths. One wounded but expected to recover. They're calling the victim a hero. The news media is calling it a terrorist attack."

"Turn the plane around. Let's go see this victim for ourselves."

"But Mr. President, we're already over Utah."

"I don't care. Do it."

Two hours later, they were landing in Denver. Two hours is a lot of time to make things happen when you're the president. Air Force One carried drinks, snacks with the White House logo on them, lots of fast food for this president, and medals. Anything the president could award without Congressional approval was in the safe.

"I want to give him something. What medals do we have on board?"

"Well, there's several. The Presidential Medal of Freedom, the Presidential Citizens Medal, President's Award for Distinguished Federal Civilian Service the..."

"That's enough. Get the second one you mentioned, the..."

"The Presidential Citizens Medal, Mr. President?"

"Yes. That's what I want. Get it and have the paperwork done when we land."

"That's usually reserved for a long-term accomplishment. Are you sure ..."

"Yes. Do it. I want to send a message. Terrorism has no

place, no opportunity in our country, and we will recognize our heroes."

The trip from the airfield was short. When you have emergency flashers and an army of police to clear the way, traffic is no problem. As they started to announce his unexpected arrival, Sandy regained his typical composure. The detectives had arrived and briefed Joe on what had happened. They stepped aside fast enough when the president was announced.

"So, this is the hero! I love you. You stopped terrorists and saved hundreds of public servants."

"Ah, actually, they weren't terrorists and there were only a hundred workers in the building."

What, you're correcting me? The president icily stared at the detective. Lieutenant Murphy stepped forward.

"Yes, Mr. President, that's correct. It was a workplace violence incident that resulted from a domestic dispute. But Dr. O'Flaherty did save the day and stopped all the violence. He even saved the Muslim community from a false accusation."

"Well, that's fine, fine. Thanks for correcting the matter for me." He glanced at his aide with a look that told him to tweak his resume. "Anyway, you are a hero. A real hero. I have something for you. No, don't get up; just lay there...stay where you are."

The aide opened the envelope and handed the medal to the president. Clearing his throat, the aide began, "Award of the Presidential Citizens Medal is made..."

Joe had heard these readings of medal citations hundreds of times in his Army career. This was little different and time to zone out. Usually, they started with something like *Attention to orders...* Well, Joe certainly wasn't going to come to attention.

The enormity of what was happening hit him. He felt woozy and slumped back down on the bed. Sandy retreated even further into the shadows.

The president's aide then stepped forward and whispered something in the presidential ear. "Really?"

"Yes, sir, that's him. The same one we were talking about." The aide's job was safe again.

The president turned to Joe again and said, "I got your letter. We've been wanting to talk with you."

Oh, crud. Just what I need now – to be in trouble with the Secret Service. "I can explain," Joe started.

"Why would you want to? I enjoyed the letter. It was great. Great! Read it to the staff. Even shared with our new administrator – what's that place called? Oh yeah, GSA. We need to change that name. Your letter was eye-opening and confirmed some of my own thoughts. What are your career plans now?"

"I'm due to retire in two months."

"Great. Just great! Take your wife on a retirement trip. Come to see me in the White House. Would you like a tour?"

"I'd love that. I've been to D.C. several times and never got a tour, though I did get to see the Capitol Building. I'd be happy to settle for the F tour of the White House."

"So, you heard about my letter rating of the tours."

"Yes, I watch TV too."

"I can't give you an F tour. But I can give you an A plus tour. It's that or nothing. Then, we can eat in the White House Dining Room."

"Can we have meat loaf? That would be great! I love meat loaf but it's better with tomato sauce, just like Mom used to make. I heard the White House has the best meat loaf." Joe could negotiate almost as well as the president and he was going for all he could get.

"Ha! I like you more and more." He gripped Joe's hand, avoiding the IV needle.

After the president left, it took Sandy several minutes to come back out of the shadows. He looked pale. "I've got to get back. Get well, Joe. Everybody wants to see you back in the office." He couldn't leave fast enough.

The hospital kept Joe for a few days for observation, just to make sure there would be no infection. The stream of visitors was never-ending and left Joe wanting privacy and sleep.

The local Congressman showed up. Joe didn't care for the Congressman but was polite and even offered him some of the ice cream that was still flowing to his room. He also remembered to ask the Congressman to give the president his warm regards and a bear hug. That would be good enough payback to the Congressman for taking the strawberry cheesecake ice cream.

When he returned to the office, Joe was a week closer to retirement. Douglas MacArthur Kim hadn't been in lately. Word was that he was on extended leave. That made it even better.

All he had to do now was to wrap up outstanding business or pass it off to someone else. No more frauds to investigate and no other critters to hold accountable for bad work. It felt like the day after a final exam in college when he had been freed from the stress, but also left with an empty feeling, wondering if he had done his best.

Retirement was one of those bittersweet moments. It was Joe's day. It was also the realization that his dreams and goals would never be fulfilled. The swamp remained, and he had done little to affect that. He considered himself lucky to make it through the swamp without being eaten alive.

He remembered the pledge that he and Artie and Jock had made. They were going to bring in leadership. They were going to remake the swamp into something approaching paradise. Good management, leadership, caring for each other and for the taxpayer. The soldiers they had served with also deserved better.

He felt like he was slinking off with his tail between his legs. He had failed.

Artie could almost seem to read his thoughts as he changed the mood. He had been there at the start and now, he was also there at the end. "How do you want to celebrate your last day?"

"Potluck." That said it all. Potlucks with the variety of great foods – Joe always ate too much, but wasn't that the point?

Looking forward to some ease, not having to get up at a particular time in the morning, though knowing he still needed to get up if only to walk the dog. The dog. At least *that* dream was still there. However, it was also a major change in life and the routine of the past. How many years was it anyway?

There was a ceremony with speeches, recognizing over seventeen years of civil service and another twenty-one years of military service – they gave credit for all 38 years of federal service, even if Sandy wasn't willing to do the right thing. It no longer mattered. He could keep his plaque. If only he didn't feel so empty, so … what was it? Was it like what the Vietnam War veterans felt when they came home? Reviled or, even worse, just ignored. Had it all mattered?

That last day came up fast. Joe emptied his office with a lot of mixed emotions. Of course, government property stayed where it was. But the other stuff. The accumulation of seventeen years would not go home with him.

He had so many certificates already as a soldier, what could he do with these but box them up and put them in the back of the closet.

Other things were in demand. Copies of regulations and other stuff he gave to his favorite coworkers. The microwave went to Mick. A personal clock, typing stand, Christmas decorations, and a lot of other small stuff – all bought with his own money so he gave them away.

At the bottom of his drawer he found the back brace. The doc had given it to him to help with the back pain. Who could use that? Sandy. He gave it to the boss. "You might be able to use this," he said.

"Why me? I go to the gym every day. I feel great. My back is in great shape."

"If you say so." Joe just smiled. There was no way he could have gotten away with this a year ago. Now, he was leaving and nobody gets fired on his last day. It's so hard to fire a federal employee anyway; it's just not worth the effort that last day. Sandy might be irritated, even mad. Burning bridges can be a bad habit but in this case, it was worth it.

The speech by the supervisor was lengthy and felt like more than was deserved. One member of the audience would miss Joe – of that he was sure. Joe had worked with her when he was a soldier and she cried then as he left for another military assignment. Joe hated the down mood. *I better do something to lighten the mood.*

"Thanks!" he said to the supervisor, "for those kind and undeserved comments. However, I also acquired some gray hair in performing my service and I'm not sure I deserve that either!" The mood had changed and a general, if muted chuckle was obvious.

He added, "However, I think you forgot one thing."

"What's that," Artie asked?

"You forgot to mention that I was the best looking one in the department for many a year."

"Actually, I wasn't going to say that," he said.

"You weren't? So ... what are you trying to say, anyway? Man, you are so ugly, the general appearance of the department is about to go up by ten percent. Hmm, is that it? That's okay, I've been abused before."

"Kick me to the curb. Had that too. I think I'll just go off and cry by myself." The mood had definitely changed so Joe felt able to move on to more sober things.

"I was told I'm supposed to say something helpful and inspirational. I don't know if what I'm about to say will do either, but here goes. Seventeen years ago, I started as a contract specialist. That followed twenty-one years as a soldier. I had no idea what was coming or even what my job title really meant. Boy did I learn!" The group laughed with that.

"As a soldier, I had seen things that made me wonder what you all were thinking! It never made any sense to me. Why not just take a credit card to the local store and get what you need? If the roof springs a leak, use the card and get it fixed."

"After seventeen years, I now know that I was a really smart soldier! But I also know that there are reasons why we do what we do. Congress forces a lot of that on us to get themselves elected to another term."

"What escapes me sometimes is when we don't do all we can

do. Yeah, this is where it gets serious. Some of us know we work for the Veterans, for the taxpayers, and for our country. We have college degrees. Many of us served in uniform. But when we came here and started spending the taxpayers' money, we acted like we were at a buffet and money was no object. If a contractor wanted to rip us off, as long as it saved us some conflict, we ignored the problem."

"At other times, we forgot that the contractor who is trying to do the right thing is our partner, not our enemy. See what I mean? It works both ways. We have to be honest and do the right thing."

"At the same time, we have to hold our contractors responsible for giving us what they said they would. Sometimes that's a hard thing. But that's why we're here. To get the most bang for the buck and meet the government's needs."

"Here at the VA, we are all about the veterans who served in uniform. If we don't do our job and insist that contractors do their job, then veterans suffer and the taxpayers' sacrifices were wasted. Please. Please, please, please! Don't forget who you work for."

"Now, let's advance to another point. Who's got your six! Yes, that's a soldier's phrase but it applies here too. If we're doing the right thing, we're going to ruffle feathers. Someone will be unhappy. If people aren't saying anything bad about you on occasion, then maybe you're not doing anything good either. Doing the right thing might even mean that a contractor gets found out and goes to prison. If we're doing our job, we'll take heat. Conflict is inevitable –

but not always."

"To survive the heat rounds, the individual needs to know

he has management backup. He also needs to know that his fellow worker will support him and share their knowledge. If you don't have those things, you're already beaten. With them, and the right ethics, you can each make a difference. Why not try? If you haven't done what is right, why not change now? It's never too late."

"Well, that's my two cents and probably worth a lot less." The laughter was more nervous this time as if offered grudgingly. Nobody likes to be preached at. Joe knew that but still he had to say something and this would be his last chance. God willing, he would never be back in this building or any other as an employee. Free at last!

He should have felt good. No, he should have felt great. Now, he could finally relax and spend his days walking a dog. At long last, he could get a dog. Maybe it would be a golden retriever? The smile on his face said he felt great. The pain inside told another story.

I should be happy. Why aren't I? Here I am retiring and I no longer have to work for a living. The mission, the goal – I failed. These people see me as a success. Why can't I? I should've retired a GS-15 and transformed at least one office into something Dad would respect. Instead, I'm just sneaking out of here with my tail tucked between my legs. Shoulda, woulda, coulda – those three thieves took my destiny. I never would've done this as a soldier.

Chapter Nineteen

The walking catfish, more formally known as the clarias batrachus, is a freshwater, air-breathing swamp critter. When the pond dries up, it simply gets up on its pectoral fins and goes in search of another pond. Swamp critters are like that. They don't really leave the swamp but just relocate – unless the swamp itself is totally drained.

Joe knew he would follow through on his White House invitation. Who wouldn't? First though, he owed Diona a cruise. They went to Alaska. Summertime was a great time to see the forty-ninth state – the wildlife, some snow-capped mountains, and a lot of water. Then there were the glaciers and the day trip to fly-fish for salmon. They fit a lot into one week. The cruise ship had a lot of food and Joe was going to get his share.

Not everyone on the cruise was pleasant. One of the younger passengers was surly and kept using that "O" word on Joe. Only he knew why he needed to mess with Joe.

"Hey Old Man, what you up to today? Napping again?" When he wound up on the same salmon fishing trip, and seated at the same table in the restaurant, Joe decided it was time for some payback.

Leaning forward, he said very quietly, "Buck, do you see those seven Marines sitting over there?"

"Yeah, so what?"

"I'm going to go tell them that you've never been in the military and hate Marines and said you could take them all." Then Joe got up and started for the Marine table, glancing at Buck long enough to see the fear in his eyes.

He stopped at the Marine table. "Hey guys, how's it going? I'm here with a cruise ship group. We're sitting over there." He pointed at the table. Again, "Over there at that table," emphasizing it with his finger.

They all turned and looked at the table. "I served twenty-one years in the Army and retired from it." Joe's look was serious as he nodded his head vigorously.

Buck turned around when he saw that and held his head in his hands. He could already feel the beating coming on.

"Well, enjoy your highly deserved time off. Hoorah!" Joe just continued on to the restroom, enjoying the moment.

After the cruise, Joe and Diona flew to Washington DC and stayed at the Madison. Years before, he had been here, with GSA footing the bill. Now he was paying the full cost himself, a once in a lifetime trip for the couple. It was nice, but not cheap.

As he walked through the lobby, Joe again thought about the massive waste of money his earlier stay had cost the government. The concierge helped Joe find a great restaurant. He was a constant source of information during their stay.

"Joe, you shouldn't bother him so much. He must have a lot of other things to do, other people to help." Diona was embarrassed at the level of attention they were getting from this one man.

"Why not? I'm paying for it. Do you know how much we're paying for our room?"

"How much?"

He whispered it in her ear. Her eyes widened. She looked pale. "Joe! We can't afford that!"

"It's a once in a lifetime trip."

"I thought the cruise was supposed to be our once in a lifetime trip?"

"This is the other once in a lifetime trip. We have an invitation from the president. Who do you know who got that?"

"Well then, let's get our money's worth." Her attitude had shifted.

Joe had already contacted the president's aide about the tour and was expected. The guard at the White House looked at his identification, "Ah, so you're Dr. Joseph O'Flaherty. We've been expecting you."

In two minutes, a cheerful young blond woman with a huge smile arrived at the checkpoint and greeted Joe and Diona.

"Please come with me. You're expected." Tall, shapely, and a lot of leg, the president had standards and they weren't all about academic credentials. He knew the camera was always watching.

Joe expected to go to a foyer or conference room to join other tourists. "This is the Oval Office. Please go in. He's waiting."

"What? I'm just here for a tour. You may have me mixed up with someone else."

"I don't think so. We have your complete dossier including your picture. Not too many look like you." *Was that a compliment or...?*

Joe started to knock but the aide smiled and opened the door. "Follow me please."

Confused, Joe entered the room and was in awe, unable to speak. "Mr. President, Dr. O'Flaherty is here on your invitation."

"Would you like a great cup of coffee Mrs. O'Flaherty?" The aide was pleasant but clearly, it was more than a polite offer. Did she know how much Diona loved her coffee? This morning Joe and Diona had been running late so the stop at the coffee shop didn't happen. "The president wants to talk to your husband and I would like to show you around."

The president noticed Joe's overwhelmed look. "Yeah, it did the same thing to me the first time. It's yuge, yuge. All the things that have happened here. The people who have been here. I think you're also a history buff. This must be even more impressive to you than it was to me. Have a seat." He motioned to a chair across the room from the Resolute Desk that was so famous to television land. The president stood and came over to join him in a similar chair.

The president eyed the aide as she left. Beyond attractive, she had a unique walk. Sort of like the Pink Panther without the tail, she was undoubtedly gifted in many ways. Joe hoped this president was able to keep his hands out of the cookie jar. The cookie jar mystique had nearly ended previous administrations.

When the Chief of Staff came in, the president said, "I'd like for us all to get acquainted." The old general nodded in agreement and took a seat on the sofa. Never smiling, he just sat there, taking mental notes.

"It's great seeing you again and I see that you're recovered from that shooting. Just great. So, tell me about your time in the Army. What did you learn? How would others describe you?" The president already knew a lot about Joe and the Chief of Staff was ready to interpret any vernacular that Joe used. Joe knew they had a dossier on him so the question confused him.

"Well, some would call me *Mr. Nice Guy*. Others would call me *Sergeant Meanly*. It depended on the situation. I tried to be effective and a man for all seasons."

"The officers that I worked with typically respected and valued me. One of the best compliments I ever received was "Sergeant O'Flaherty, I hope you never retire. You are an old sergeant and I mean that in the best possible way." The old general just nodded.

"The bottom line is that I was a doer. The officers were more about telling and I was fine with that. Is that what you wanted to know?"

Changing the subject suddenly, he asked "What should I do about Wikileaks? They keep releasing a lot of stuff."

"They helped you get elected by releasing information that the people should have had. A free society depends on the free flow of information, even when it's embarrassing. Compliment them. Encourage them. Put them on the payroll."

"What about the press? Isn't it their job to keep the voters informed?"

"If they were truly a "free press" then yes. However, they're not. They refuse to provide stories that benefit their conservative opponents. They've been bought and paid for."

"Wow, you're a bit of a radical, aren't you!?"

"A bit?" he responded almost hurt.

The president laughed, "I like you." His look was intent as he stared at Joe, kind of hunched and leaning forward like he was ready to jump up.

He grinned at another aide and nodded to the Chief of Staff. "My aide will take you and your wife on a tour now. We'll get lunch in the dining room. I still want to talk some more with you." The New York accent was ever-present.

The president skipped out on lunch but the aide was there. Meatloaf as promised. The chef, a culinary snob, even used the tomato sauce – a big compromise in his estimate.

"I don't usually do it this way but the boss said to do it today, just for you." The chef had stopped by to see Joe and make sure everything was as it should be.

"It's great. Even Mom didn't make it this good – and the rolls are a slice of Heaven. And the banana cream pie – can I get the recipe?"

"No."

After lunch, the aide escorted Joe and Diona to the Oval Office. However, she asked Diona to join her in an adjoining lounge. Plying her with another cup of the best coffee Diona had ever had, they had a long visit.

Diona realized she was being entertained while Joe had the official visit, but for coffee this good, they could do almost anything they wanted. Smooth, with no bite, Diona wondered how much this coffee cost. The aide seemed to read her thoughts and simply said, "You don't want to know."

The president came right to the point. "I want to let you in on my dream. This actually came to me in a dream. I want to remake this country into what it can be and bring back the best of what it used to be. My dream includes ending GSA and returning contracting actions to each agency to do on their own, or we can fix it by remaking it."

"You know about the scandals, the wasted money. The politics. There have been too many scandals, yuge scandals, and it no longer serves its purpose of saving us money. What do you think of my plans?"

"Well, it would be an easier sell to Congress to fix it than to shoot it like a horse with a broken leg. Otherwise, I agree completely. You've read my letter. You know what happened to me. I wanted to make the government better and save tax money. Instead, I was kicked to the curb, my career effectively ended. No hope, no appeal. A deaf ear from everybody there and from other agencies that were *supposed* to hear my appeal and stand up for my rights. I hope you're successful. Something needs to be done."

"You still don't get it. I need you. How about it?"

"Huh?"

"I'm offering you a job in my administration. You'll take over the GSA region you worked at before. I won't let you leave without a yes. Security, lock the doors!"

Joe thought the president must be joking about locking the doors and smiled – until he heard the bolt click. A smile was totally missing from the presidential face.

"Are you serious? Me? I was just a master sergeant. I only went to a GS-13, thanks to the swamp. You need someone with experience. Someone who has done this before, who has cracked the whip and drawn blood."

"You let me worry about what I need. What I *want* is you. Well?"

"Mr. President, with all due respect ..."

"Now just hold it right there. In my experience, when someone says with all due respect, they're about to show the opposite."

"I would never do that – and especially not to you. I just think you should look for somebody else."

"Look, Doc. I understand if you're reluctant but ..."

"I'm tired. I've served for almost forty years. I need a break – probably a long one that will last till I turn ninety. I've been run through the wringer – multiple times – and I even have the scar to prove it." Joe touched the scar on his hand that he had received as a child. No need to tell the president *how* he had gotten that scar.

The memory came flooding back. Mom wouldn't let him push anything through the old-style wringer washing machine so he waited for an opportunity. When he woke up from a nap, and found her gone, he took advantage, putting a washcloth through the wringer. She would never know. However, he was short and couldn't see as the wringer grabbed him and started pulling him through. It almost killed him.

"I see. Well, I just thought you were a patriot and still cared about the soldiers in the Army."

"Meaning what!"

"Don't get upset. It's just that if this agency is overcharging the Army, then that's less money for the things soldiers need. It could mean fewer weapons and less ammunition available to them. Vehicles out of commission due to limited repair funds. Lower pay for soldiers which means lower quality soldiers."

"But I know what you're saying. You're tired and you certainly deserve a break. I just thought you might want to go on one more mission. But if you don't ... if you can't ... I understand. Maybe we can just let things at that agency go as they've been going. I'm sure the Army and the soldiers will continue to get along."

"What! That's just dirty!" *Was that a grin?*

"Well, Doc? What's it going to be?"

"Do I have time to think it over? Like I said, I'm more of a doer than a teller. The officers told and I did. You should find a general somewhere who likes the telling part. Someone who does politics well."

"That's not what I want! Haven't you been paying attention at all? General, I thought you said sergeants listen well."

"Yes sir. They usually do."

"So, when do you need an answer?"

"Take your time. Sixty seconds or one minute should be enough. I want a doer, not a love-himself politico. Well? Well?"

"You don't play fair at all do you?"

"If I did, I wouldn't be a rich man. I'm a deal-maker and right now I want to make a deal. Are you in or are you out? Are you a patriot or another get-what-you-can bureaucrat?"

Joe paused a moment as he considered the president. What was he anyway? It came as an epiphany. He was somewhere between General Patton and the Godfather. An image of Joe being slapped and then at the bottom of the Potomac with his feet encased in cement came to mind, distracting him for a moment. He was also known, and often reviled, as a loose cannon – but he was also an incredible dealmaker.

As an old Army sergeant, Joe tended to ignore the politics and focused on the nuts and bolts of the mission. Unafraid and very forthright, he approached each situation with as much candor as was reasonable and polite.

He considered the president's request – he was what the situation called for. He could never be one of those 'grow the organization' or 'enlarge my kingdom' managers. He would have to go into the job with one focus in mind – to put it on a total economy and efficiency basis while draining the swamp.

To Joe that meant just one thing – those who contributed to the overall savings to the government and worked hard at the tasks they were assigned should be retained. Those who were more political and focused on creating new programs that made them look good, but were not good for the taxpayer, would have to go.

However, Joe also had no illusions. Swamp critters want to stay in the swamp. He would have to find ways to encourage or force them from the swamp. He felt no animosity but only a single-minded determination to succeed at the mission.

But he also wondered if he could negotiate for something extra special. Now was the time to ask. The president was wearing his usual, signature bright red tie. Souvenirs were always good. *I wonder if I could get him to give me that to close the deal?*

"As a sergeant, I never turned down a mission. How can I say no,

especially after that tour, that lunch, and that sales approach? I guess

I'm in."

"Great! That's just great. What's that word you Army guys use?"

"Do you mean hooah?"

"Yeah, that's it. General we've got a hooah here."

"Roger that, sir."

"Then it's done."

"Just a moment. I have a condition."

"For me? I'm the president. I don't take conditions."

"You will if you want me to work for you."

"Wow! You really do have a backbone. Okay, let's have it."

"You can't fire me."

"Did you see that sign on my door? I'm the president. I can fire anybody. I've done it whenever it's necessary."

"I know and that's the point. Your reputation precedes you. I'm not saying you have to keep me. But you can't fire me either. If we reach a point where you no longer want me, then you call me and ask for my resignation. It will always be ready. After that, you can say the usual nice things about me and we go our separate ways."

"Well, okay," he laughed. "I guess I can live with that."

"Unlock the doors," he said to the aide. He shook Joe's hand hard and long.

Ten seconds later, Joe reminded him, "I might need that back – at least if you want me to be successful."

Stepping into the anteroom, the president was gone a few minutes. The old general used the time to distract him with Army talk. Then he added, "It'll be like an Army assignment. Do your best. Just one thing I should warn you about."

"Yes?"

"He expects loyalty. Also, don't ever …"

"Alright. What are you two gossiping about? Anyway, I've already been on the phone with the new GSA director. I told her to give you whatever you want – people, directives, support, regulations. You just name it!"

"You'll be running one of the test cases. I want each region to try a different model. Your model is whatever you come up with to save money and improve efficiency. After one year, you'll compare notes with the other regions and the director to identify what works."

"You have a free hand and my support. I'm counting on you to make a difference! Your country is counting on you! Get out there and drain that swamp!" He had Joe's number. Just wave the flag and Joe would come to attention. If he wasn't the president, he could have been a cheerleader.

After he left, the president asked the chief of staff about what had just happened. "So, what do you think? Can he do it?"

"Maybe. Like he said, he was a sergeant and something like this would typically be more along the lines of a full colonel or even general. Still, some of those sergeants are pretty salty and that might be what we need. He's certainly not very politically-oriented. The best sergeants aren't. That also might be just what we need. Then, there's the expendable factor."

****

"So, what did he say? What did he want? There's no problem is there?" Diona was beyond curious. She was also wired from the second cup of coffee.

"That depends on your perspective. I've been drafted. As Gene Autry said, I'm back in the saddle again."

"Huh?"

"I'm being appointed as regional administrator for GSA in Denver. I'll be over the region I used to work for. He wants me to clean that part of the swamp."

"But ..."

"Hey, I've got a doctorate in business leadership."

"That's the college version of the *been there, done that* t-shirt. You don't know anything about running an organization. How many people are there for you to supervise? Maybe one hundred?"

"Closer to five hundred."

"That's even worse. Joe, you've really stepped in it this time!"

"Yeah, I know. I said the same thing to him. It didn't matter. He demanded I take on the job. He even locked the doors so I couldn't leave until I agreed. I'll need help. Lots of it."

Joe didn't sleep well that night, or the next, so many thoughts, so many emotions. Then, he realized, "Hey, wait a second! This is what I wanted. It's why I felt like a quitter when I retired. Finally! I have a chance to make a difference. I can get rid of those weasels who aren't contributing. Remake one little corner of the swamp into a paradise. But can I do this? What will be the cost?" The laugh was sarcastic – there was always a cost.

Joe also remembered the message, the dream interpretation. *Something like Joseph* she had said. After a time, Joseph was released from prison and elevated over a whole empire. That empire was one of the most powerful of its day. Now, Joe was becoming a regional director of an agency that buys billions of dollars of stuff every year. Was there a difference? This felt more and more just like Joseph.

Two days later, Joe was on the telephone with the president, the chief of staff, and that aide. Joe didn't know everything but he did know that he needed help. Socrates had said "the admission of ignorance is the beginning of wisdom." That was where Joe was. This admission to himself and to the president was the first step to a solution.

"You're the one I want so whatever you need, you can have," the president told him.

"Okay, here's what I need. Two extra lawyers experienced in

labor law and terminations, and four more aides. I also need for you to have my six. Can I have that?"

"Your what?"

"My back. I'm no politician and this is going to get ugly."

"Just a moment." Silence followed by static and then more silence. Ten minutes later, the silence was broken. "You drive a hard bargain. I wonder if we're related. But you've got it. So, what's your overall plan?"

"I believe GSA *can* be useful again, but only if it is returned to its original mission and focus – that of saving money for the taxpayer through volume buying. We should also try to make GSA 100% self-supporting instead of 90%."

"Finally, we need to get rid of those who won't fully support your administration's goals, those who have committed illegal acts, those who are focused on political goals – ignoring the core mission of saving money, and those who are marginal or less performers."

"Alright. Do it." When the president hung up, he told the chief of staff, "I believe we have a winner out there. If he succeeds, I want to recruit more retired sergeants to replace these career do-nothings. We need people with a vision and a backbone."

Joe's first consideration was to get some help in running and navigating the world of large organizations. The snakes were in abundance at GSA. He had first-hand experience of that. He needed help from someone who had been at the top and understood the politics.

It came almost as an epiphany. General Smartwell. He might be available. He had commanded a very large organization for the Army – a whole combat division. They had gone to church together for a time. He knew how powerful people think, act – the games that are played and the knife-in-the-back tendency from many of them. This might be just the person he needed.

After his sudden retirement from the Army, the general was at loose ends. It seemed like they needed each other. Joe definitely needed him.

He had been a great leader in the Army as well as a super manager. He was medium height, medium build, and very good looking. These attributes undoubtedly helped him to great heights, though his decision making and communication abilities were the primary factors. Joe contacted their mutual acquaintance and ran it by him. A meeting was set up.

As Joe walked into the restaurant, the smell of the Thai food welcomed him. Joe liked any food, as long as it was good. The building was on its second life. Previously, it had been a car dealership. *The Really Good Thai* was one of the best restaurants in town and had quiet booths where they could talk.

The restaurant design was incredible with floor level and elevated seating where he could see outside the window and had a clear view of the rest of the restaurant. The high ceiling was a leftover from the car repair shop but all else was new and very Asian in design.

As Joe sat down, he realized this was almost the exact spot where he used to get his car serviced. It seemed like a lifetime ago.

As he explained the mission from the president, the general raised his eyebrows. As Joe talked on, he nodded in understanding. His face was blank, like he was playing poker. He understood all but revealed nothing.

Finally, he said "Joe are you sure you're up for this? What I mean is that you've been asked to serve as a pest eradicator. This won't be like writing contracts nor like what you did as a soldier. You're going into combat without body armor or any Kevlar."

"The swamp doesn't want to be drained – it's resilient. It's happy just the way things are. You're going to have to get really tough, real mean. The swamp will know you're coming and the critters will all be there waiting for you."

"Frankly, I'd rather be back in the sandbox in combat, surrounded by jihadists than what you're going to experience. You're going to have to out-critter the swamp critters. You'll have to be better at their game than they are. In order to succeed, you may even lose yourself in the process."

Joe just nodded. It was probably too late to say no. That should have been done that day when he had been locked in the room with the president. Retirement was now a long way off. Freedom from the swamp was moving into the far rear view mirror. The dog would have to wait while he took on a more vicious one. He needed someone to have his "six" and the general was the best there was.

"Okay, then. I'm in. I'll back you all the way. What's the pay?"

"GS-15. You'll be the assistant administrator."

"Catchy title but can't you just call me the Head Janitor? Maybe swamp cleaner-outer?

Joe laughed, "Let me think on that one."

"We'll need more help."

"I've got a few people in mind. Also, we need to identify a couple of crackerjack labor lawyers. This won't be easy. We need to make sure we dot every "I" and cross every "T". Can you handle that for me? I can get you on the payroll right away so you can prep the objective before I come in."

Previously the worst missions only involved people shooting at the pair. Now, they had entrenched bureaucrats who would be sniping at them every step of the way. There was no doubt in the mind of either that this would be difficult. The fun-meter was not going to be on high.

However, the general pointed out that Howard Schultz, former CEO of Starbucks, had stated "When you're surrounded by people who share a passionate commitment around a common purpose, anything is possible."

The small core was growing and would be entering battle soon, fully prepared. Since battle was soon to be joined, Joe would hate to go into battle without the best soldier he ever knew.

"Hey Top, how's it going?"

"Huh? Who's this?"

"Joe, Joe O'Flaherty – Sergeant O'Flaherty."

"Oh, it's you again. You're not in trouble, are you? Are you still drinking? Do you need someone to bail you out?"

"In a manner of speaking." Joe laid it out for him. "Top" had been Joe's first sergeant. For Joe he had been *the* first sergeant. Tall, the face of a bulldog, flattop haircut, skin like leather, and a backbone of high tensile steel, Top was the very image of a soldier. What Joe felt for Top was beyond respect, it was more like hero worship.

Joe needed people who understood administration, were strong, and could be trusted without question. He needed people of proven abilities who would have his back. He needed his first sergeant.

Top had retired and been working in a paperwork job for the Army – often dull, but at least it paid the rent. The position Joe was offering him would triple his salary. Money was important but the mission was the real attraction.

"Drain the swamp? Good luck with that but sure, sounds good to me. Of course, it won't be pleasant for anybody, but yeah, it needs to be done. Count me in."

Top was also approaching retirement, so a few years in this different type of combat would help his pension substantially.

Next on Joe's list was Sam. He and Joe had served together and had the same political, religious, and moral values. Sam also spoke fluent Spanish and had immigrated from Cuba as a child. He knew first-hand what a bureaucracy run amok can do to a thriving economy. Joe had lost Sam's number and he'd never had an email for him.

A letter is in order. No, scratch that, I'll fly down to Miami and see him. Never been there. Should be getting cooler now that fall is here. Won't he be surprised when I show up at his door!

Surprise didn't cover it. Sam had inherited his parents' home in an upscale neighborhood but hadn't been working. At loose ends since his Army retirement, he spent his days reading the classics and taking history classes.

Sometimes, the local college even let him teach a class. Even there, his Spanish helped. The occasional magazine or newspaper article about everything that was wrong with the country completed his daily regimen.

When Joe knocked at the door, he heard a gruff "Quién es? No quiero. Tengo un perro y tiene hambre de vendedores."

Then he repeated it in English. "Who is it? I don't want any. I have a dog and he's hungry for salesmen."

Joe finally had the chance to say something when Sam paused for a breath. "Sam, it's Joe. You've been recalled. Get your uniform on and get out here. Pronto. Do you need that in Spanish?"

"What the...? Hey, it's you. I never thought I'd see you again." Sam was a hugger. "What's this about a recall? I did my time. Twenty years should be enough for anybody. Look at you – you don't have a uniform on. What's the deal?" *Well, at least he said it in English.*

"I need you. The president needs you. The job pays well, but you'll have to come back to Colorado. Can you leave the sunshine and beaches of Miami for the sunshine and snow of Colorado?"

"Oh, this better be good! I was sleeping."

Joe laid it out for Sam. They had both served in uniform. They loved this country. Even though he was an immigrant, Sam may have loved it even more than Joe. Immigrants like Sam, who had witnessed how bad things can get, tended to be more American than most native-born Americans.

"It'll probably get ugly. But I'll have the lead and you just need to support me and help run the office. You'll get a high GS rating but you can only count on two or three years in that job. Of course, it will give you enough years so that you can get a retirement benefit out of it with what you've already got."

"But it's really not about the money – it's about the job. These guys have been costing us taxpayers a lot of money. They also charge the military more than they have to so they can have parties with clowns and magicians. We're going to stop that, help the military, and clean up the mess. Are you in?"

"Did you really ask that? You already know the answer. If you're in, I'm in. Who else do you have?"

Joe updated him on the duty roster. "I'm also going to try to get Carlos. He speaks Mexican Spanish. Real cool, energized, almost happy-go-lucky. Like you, he retired from the Army as a sergeant in an administrative job. I just need people who have my back and work as a team. There's nothing the Army knows better than teamwork."

"I need a few weeks to get someone to watch my house."

"What about the dog?"

"There's no dog. I hate the shedding hair. I just say that to get rid of the unwanted – which is almost everybody."

"Great! Let's get some Cuban food. I've never had any so it's all up to you. But I don't want spicy. I hate spicy."

****

"Hey, Carlos, this is O'Flaherty – Master Sergeant O'Flaherty."

"Hey, never thought I'd hear from you again. You're not calling about that ten dollars, are you? Who knew he would be elected?"

"No, I already forgot about that. I need your help to drain the swamp. You know, the one the president has been talking about. He's asked me to help and I'm asking you."

"Oh, wow. I wish I could, but my wife likes it here and after twenty years of moving around in the Army, I owe her this."

"Oh. Okay. I understand and you're right. Well, give her my best, will you?"

"You're not disappointed with me, are you?"

"I'm disappointed, but not with you. You have to do what's best for your family."

A few weeks passed as Joe tried to fill that remaining position. There was almost nobody that Joe trusted like he did Sam and Carlos. The hurricane had been massive. Joe knew that Carlos lived in southern Texas but never really considered where.

"Uh, Joe, can we talk?" It was Carlos.

"Sure, what's up?"

"That job, you called me about a few weeks ago. Is it still available?"

"Well, sure – for you. What caused the change of heart?" Carlos told him the whole depressing story. When the hurricane hit Houston, it took out a lot of homes. Carlos had lived in one of them. It would have to be rebuilt from the ground up. There was almost nothing left.

The house, the school, the stores, even the business Carlos had been running – all were gone. Carlos was almost homeless, living with his in-laws in northern Texas. This looked like an act of God's provision to Joe and reluctantly, also to Carlos. Joe glanced up and lipped the word "thanks."

The core team was nearly complete. When the general called with the good news, it just couldn't get any better. "Joe, I found two crackerjack ambulance chasers. They've specialized in labor law and have twenty-three years of experience between them. They hate the swamp and detest government bureaucracy. They served in the Army under me and are as salty as they come. Simply put, they're more than interested. We just have to pay them reasonably and they're yours for the duration."

"Wow, that's great! That's why I need you – well, part of

it anyway. You sure came through. I'll be sending you a list of names. I want them hired – all as GS-14s. The lawyers can get that rating also, if you think it would be right."

"These people on the list – they're all retired soldiers. We need to help them with moving and other relocation issues. I want to pay their costs. Some of them can't afford a move like this and I know the government will do that to get good employees."

"Okay, I'll make it happen. I've been in touch with the office and they know we're coming. Already rolling out the red carpet. We should be able to move in there in two weeks. They're already setting up the offices and computer access."

Later that day, the general had time to review the list. "Joe, are you kidding? These people on the list – they were sergeants and one was a first sergeant."

"And?"

"You may be overpaying them. This pay is equivalent to full Colonels. If the press gets wind of this..."

"We'll deal with that when and if it happens. These are outstanding people in their own fields and I want to make sure they earn their pay. That will be your area. Also, you know I was a sergeant too."

"Look, you recruited me to help you. You need to listen to me now. This looks like a misstep. I can find some real hot retired officers that were as vicious as any of the critters you're going to run across."

"Thanks, and I really appreciate your thoughts and concerns. However, I know these guys and I have ultimate trust in them – just like I do in you. As you said before, this is going to be a firefight we're going into. I don't mind taking point, but I need people who will have my back."

"You're the boss." The tension was thick – the general already had his doubts.

Chapter Twenty

The shrike waited patiently. Appearing to be a charming and gentle bird, she was anything but. As the other animals considered her – and ignored her as no threat, she attacked. Catching the lizard, she impaled it on thorns. She used the thorns to help her rip it apart and then as a place to store the remnants – a convenient snack for later.

The battle was joined the first day in the office. Joe asked the general to schedule a meeting with the work force. After that, the small group would meet with the senior staff.

Top was the first to walk in the room. Wearing his best bulldog *Sergeant Meanly* face, fisherman's waders, holding a shovel and drainage equipment to drive home the message that they were there to drain the swamp, he just glared at the crowd in that special way he had.

The initial laughter died down rapidly as Top continued to stare. The stare that Joe remembered so well as he stood in formation, he saw again. It was all he could do to keep from grinning. Top would remember the laughers and give them his special attention. Along with his business suit, Joe wore a construction helmet that said "Foreman." The general got his wish – his helmet said "Head Janitor."

Government workers were used to the usual speeches. In

the Army, Joe had heard many speeches and saw far too many *dog and pony shows*. This was going to be different and not soon forgotten. Jumping on the stage, he set down the helmet at the front where all could see it.

"This will not be one of those typical kumbaya introductions. Rather, it is about what we will be doing going forward. I was sent here with a mission and I intend to accomplish it. Specifically, I am here to drain the swamp."

"If you are a swamp critter, you should start planning your exit strategy. Great workers with a service focus are needed and we want you to stay. The president sent me here with a specific mission, which means change more than anything else. You should also know that he and I are in agreement. In fact, the only real difference between us is that he has nicer hair." Mild laughter followed.

"The old ways are over. We're here to drain the swamp. If you think I'm joking, you will be the first critters to leave. Our focus will be on service to our country and saving money as our core mission. The focus will not be on the workers and what extra things they want. That's why it's called service." The mood was suddenly somber as eyes bugged out and everyone listened to each word.

"We need to be leaner and meaner. We will go after business, but on a competitive basis. If there are rules and practices that are strangling us, provide that to our point of contact for "leanness and meanness," who will draft it into a coherent strategy. Yes, that is an official title. I just appointed someone to it today."

"Terri is the only one here who I know well enough to believe we have a winner in her." Sitting in the front row, Joe and her exchanged nods. "We've known each other for years and she is the only one I have such a level of confidence in. She is taking this on in addition to her regular duties unless, and until, we prove that she needs to be doing it full time."

"We can avoid regulations if they don't make sense. We just need to get it to the president's desk. He has a pen and knows how to use it. We can get a presidential directive to avoid wasteful practices that do not save the government money. We can get him to put it before Congress if laws need to be changed. We have a pit bull living on Pennsylvania Avenue and we need to use him."

"Don't think this is the same song and dance. We are here to make this organization work for the American taxpayer. If you aren't part of the solution, you will be considered part of the problem. We are here to drain the swamp and make this organization more effective and more efficient. Many jobs will be lost if we're not successful. No longer will we buy the items that do not pay for themselves. If you are buying special order items one at a time, that stops now. Get the word out. We pay our way or we go away."

"We were happy with generating 90 percent of our budget in the past and threw a big party with bonuses all around. We'll now generate one 100 percent of our budget and reduce our prices for our customers. Programs will be analyzed for the profit generated. If you're not generating one hundred percent, jobs and even whole programs will go away. We'll use reverse auctioning and other methods that are proven profit makers. But we will not innovate for the sake of innovation. If it doesn't make money, it ends as of today."

"If you are a union official and spending the majority of

your day on union activities, that also stops – unless you can show me in the union agreement where it's provided for. If I'm found to be wrong in this and you can prove me wrong, know this – when we negotiate the next agreement, that will no longer be the case. Union activities should be done on your own time and your own dime. We won't oppose the union but we will not bankroll it either."

"One more thing. The trips, including the "New Associate Orientation," ends as of now. If anybody is scheduled for it, cancel it. Other trips will be as necessary and I do mean necessary. Run all trip proposals and the justification for them by Top." Joe pointed to Top and the crowd turned to look at Top with his military haircut and bulldog face. Joe knew few trips would be requested.

Joe glanced around the room. It was silence. Everybody present seemed to be in shock. Nobody had ever talked with them this way before. Clearly, they were more accustomed to being served than being the servant. They would need more training on this aspect. They would learn what service meant or they could leave and Joe didn't care which. He was determined to remake the organization into what had been intended at the start. It would serve the taxpayer or would go away. It was up to the workers and Joe made sure they understood.

"Any questions?" Joe didn't wait for a response. He leaped down from the stage and his small group followed him.

When they got back to the office, the general said, "Wow! I never heard such a speech in my life and that includes all those years in the Army. You definitely got their attention. The union officials and those new labor lawyers you brought on will be busy for the next few weeks, no doubt about that!"

Joe could see some doubt in his eyes. But there was something else. What was it? Could it be a newfound respect? He had been the general and Joe had been a sergeant. Now their roles were reversed. But he never expected Joe to hit the ground running *this* hard. Joe saw his step quicken a bit and his back stiffen. It was going to get interesting – and fast.

Joe followed that with a meeting for his small, immediate staff. The rules were the same as those for GSA. "Also, I'm instituting the Billy Graham Rule."

"What's that?" Top asked. The others nodded the same confusion.

"There will be no meetings with a male staffer and a female employee alone in a closed room – unless they are already married. It saved him a lot of grief and should do the same thing for us. I don't need to tell you about the climate in the country nor that we're in occupied territory here."

****

"I have to go see an old friend." The general knew Joe had worked here before and there would still be a few of his old friends there. However, the way Joe said that, just before he left the office – it seemed strange.

"Joe! I heard you were coming back but I thought I was hearing things. Is it true? Are you in charge now?" Joe found Felix was still here and still happy to see Joe.

"Yes. I wanted to see you first, before I see others. How are you doing?"

"Great! Love the work and the people. Well, most of them anyway. Some are kind of creepy. Others seem to look down their long noses at me."

"Well, that's to be expected in a place as big as this. Hey, if you have a few minutes, maybe you could take a break and we can catch up."

"Sure," answered Felix and they retired to the dining room.

When the two entered the dining room, Felix yelled, "Hey, boss, taking my break. This is my old friend Joe." The cafeteria manager just nodded. He worked in the same building but wasn't part of GSA. He couldn't care less about the office politics as long as nobody complained about the food service.

After the meeting with the workers, Joe convened a staff meeting with the department heads. The message was similar to the earlier one but more focused. They were all there and showing their alligator teeth. Joe was ready for a fight but so were the alligators. Terri was there too. Except for the earlier meeting, Joe hadn't seen her since he left the Corps. She looked the same and even smiled at him. Well, at least there's one non-critter here. He already felt safer.

"I am tasking you today with numerous changes and their implementation. You'll also provide me with a list of the employees who have performed substandard and whom you've previously been unable to terminate. I want that by the end of the day and the termination paperwork to Human Resources (HR) by the end of tomorrow. They in turn," he paused and looked at the HR chief, "have two days to process the terminations. I want those identified out of here by the end of the day on Friday. I also want the list of the names and the reasons for their termination. If it's for political correctness-related reasons, I will be looking at the paperwork closely." The gasps were clear and immediate. Their lives had just gotten a lot more complicated.

"Next, I want to set a new hiring policy. In the past, almost everyone in this room has used the so called 'Merit Promotion' method to deprive military veterans of their rights for priority in hiring. Yes, that's right. I mean you. From now on, that method is gone." He slowly looked around the room at the shocked faces.

"The preference law was created to give veterans a level playing field, surely something that they deserve after risking their lives to defend the rest of us. While non-veterans were burrowing in ever deeper in organizations like this and getting the extra resume fillers, veterans were shedding their blood."

"Except for vacancies that have already been offered and accepted, a veteran will get his or her due. All positions will apply the preference required by law. The only time a non-veteran will be hired is when there is not a fully qualified and quality candidate available. Even then, you will process a waiver through me before you proceed."

"Those people in uniform have done what many of you have refused to do. Discriminating against them ends as of now."

Then he added, "Look around this room. Go ahead, look. Before long half of you will be gone."

The response was immediate. One middle-aged woman pointed her finger, "We already heard about you. But you can't fire us! We've done nothing wrong."

"Can't I?" The look was that of a cat, smiling at the cornered mouse.

Darnell Fett was in the back of the room. It was clear that she was trying hard to be invisible – kind of hard to do when she packed such bulk. She was still her same, rotund self. If anything, she had gained weight.

At the end of the meeting, Joe thanked all participants and urged them to go out and "do great things for our country. Don't be the last one without a seat." Standing up to go, just a few feet from the door for dramatic effect, he said, "Oh, Darnell, please come to my office this afternoon ... at One O'clock."

When the time came, Darnell was there. So was Joe, along with General Smartwell. Darnell came in hesitantly and offered her hand. Joe ignored the offer, coming right to the point he had waited so many years to make.

"Please sit down. As you know, several years ago, you participated in the wrongful removal of a supervisor for his religious beliefs and made the mistake of including that language in the paperwork."

"Also, you were advised of a senior manager who had committed serious law violations including violating the Competition in Contracting Act as well as fraud. You also hired and promoted that same manager at least twice with pre-selection which is both provable and a prohibited personnel practice."

"If we take the time, I know we can find more issues. We're not going to. I asked my Special Staff Assistant Attorney to investigate the matter. He assures me that we can and should terminate your employment as well as referring the matter for prosecution. He believes we can get at least a ten-year sentence."

Her mouth hung open but no words came out. She was in shock. Then came the tears, running down, staining the white lace neck scarf she wore. Her breathing came harder too. Although he wondered if she might have a heart attack in his office, Joe said nothing. The general just stared at the floor. He had fired people but they were mature and able to handle the removal with gritted teeth. Finally, the words came. "I can't go to jail, I just can't. I need to talk to an attorney. I have that right."

Joe was getting impatient. "You have three choices. Resign, retire, or be fired. If I have to fire you, I will also refer the matter for prosecution. What's it going to be? You have till you leave this room to make that decision." When she just stared at him, he helped her to decide.

"Okay, I understand you can't make the decision so I will make it for you. General, please bring me that file."

"What's that?" she asked.

"It's a personnel action. I'm signing your termination with a documented file which describes the reasons. The same ones I told you about. There is also a packet in here from the attorney, referring this to the federal prosecutor. The same president who appointed me, appointed him. I'm told he's hungry."

"You can't do that! I've worked for this agency for over thirty years."

"I just did it. Are you having a change of heart? Would you rather be fired and go to prison from the same GSA office where you've worked for over thirty years, or retire from it?" The steady gaze and deadpan eyes told Darnell all she needed to know. This was no joke – it was really happening.

"Fine! I'll do the retirement."

"That would be the other folder." Handing it to her, he said, "Please be out of the building within two hours."

"One more thing. This is a tradeoff for both of us. You will not discuss this with anyone. You will simply be able to say you want to retire and leave it at that. If anyone, the media, your co-workers, anyone at all hears about this, the deal is off. If word gets back after you are retired, we will reactivate your appointment and move to terminate with loss of retirement pension. The prosecution will also go forward. I don't think you'll do well in a gated community. This is similar to the gag order you issued me. Is that clear?" Words were not needed – and there were none.

Her mortification was obvious. She even seemed to be shaking. With her body weight, it reminded Joe of Santa Claus without the joy. Joe wasn't smiling either. He had taken care of it. That was clear. Revenge? No, it was more like what was necessary. After she left, Joe just stared at the desk, waiting for it to tell him that he had done well. This had hurt Darnell but Joe hurt too. Even the old Army sergeant hated the feeling.

"You know, a lot of the others won't be this easy. She was retirement-qualified. Many of the other critters won't be." The general was already raining on Joe's parade.

"I know. I have a game plan and we need to discuss it in detail. We need to get out those new directives too. I promised a new direction and I want to make it happen today, before the ashes of those meetings grow cold and people think I wasn't serious. How are those documents coming?"

"Completed fifteen minutes ago. Here. Take a look." The general slid the folder across the desk to Joe. The changes were sweeping and sure to generate comment from managers and the workers. They were also the result of issues that Joe had noticed."

"When Joe had been a college student, that professor had said, "I have a lot of rules in this class. But at some point, someone has made each one necessary." That's how it was now. Someone made each change necessary.

"Ok, I see that one. Yes, I want all job announcements to give veterans the rights they were supposed to get under law. GSA has been using this merit promotion thing as a way to avoid providing veteran preference to veterans."

"It's a 'good old boys' and 'good old girls' way to help their friends and forget the veterans. All jobs should be giving veteran's preference. If there's no veteran available and qualified then fine, hire the other person. Otherwise, it better be a qualified veteran getting the job."

"Make sure it also includes all of those open announcements that haven't had someone offered the job yet. If anyone complains, introduce them to a military recruiter. Veterans paid for that benefit with their blood. If anyone else has an excess of blood that they want to give, they should be given the chance."

"Okay, what's next?

"The cash awards, the bonuses that workers and managers get. We've been spending a lot of money on that."

"Right. We want to limit the bonuses to two percent of the annual salary – especially for those people in the Public Buildings Service. Those guys have been making out like bandits, getting money from us, and from other agencies, when they worked a project for someone else. Their loyalty is divided so no awards from another agency will be accepted."

"We're going to focus on what's right, not on what generates rewards. We are professionals, not mercenaries. Oh, and make sure the bonuses are earned, not just a 'gimme' for working here. Okay, that's my soapbox."

"You've got it. You can see, that's what this one says."

"Now then, I want managers and supervisors who are leaders. For all job announcements, include leadership training and experience and documentation for supervisory positions. Also, have HR develop weekly training for new supervisors that include what they can do, what they can't do, and what leadership looks like."

"Rules are fine but leadership is about more than rules. It's about what's right, not what's popular, and taking care of people. Get Top to kick that off with them and provide a lot of the training. I never knew a better leader."

"Is there anything else?"

The General had some more thoughts and shared them. "Well, I couldn't help noticing at the meeting that a lot of the people look like something the dog wouldn't drag in. T-shirts, bleached and holey pants, numerous piercings of the nose, ears, face, and so on. Some wear sweats and running shoes. At that meeting this morning, some men appeared in need of a shave, some women had the wildest hair styles, and some outright stunk. I bet those probably don't take a regular shower. Even in the Army, we took a regular shower or at least as regular as we could. I know this isn't the Army but it is a professional place. I think we could do something to make it appear more professional."

"Hooah! Put it together. Prohibit all those things and provide specific guidance on what isn't acceptable and what is acceptable. Include what would be ideal. That could be dark, solid color pants, dress shirt and black shoes for the guys and a dress or pant suit for the ladies. We just need to be clear that the dress is long enough, and doesn't distract others. If we aren't specific enough, people will look for a loophole. I agree that we need some common appearance standards. Include the hygiene thing too."

"You know, I recall one time, I worked in an office in the Army and a wife of a soldier came in for a new ID card. She was unacquainted with soap and deodorant and she stunk to high Heaven. We all laughed and snickered and she never even noticed. Sometimes you just have to be very open with people."

"Oh, and include a requirement for supervisors to be held responsible for the professional appearance of their workers. If a lady needs to do something with her hair or wardrobe, put it on the boss to tell her. If the boss is afraid to say something, we'll get a new boss for that section."

"Maybe even use the words, 'Avoid fads, dress conservatively and professionally.' I want it to be conservative, not flamboyant and at least business casual. No jeans and no short skirts or other revealing attire. Is there anything else?"

"We've already got a vacancy, other than the one you just created," the general said. "The deputy administrator got a job offer and is leaving. Apparently, you're already scaring off some of the critters. Anyway, you will need a new deputy, someone to handle things when you're not here. Do you want us to review the remaining executives and put together an interview list?

"No, not yet," Joe said. "But call Terri and ask her to stop in tomorrow at Ten. I can't think of anybody better but I don't want to assume. One more thing, check out Darnell's division. Find out who her deputy is. Also, get me the files on Eldana Smithers and Willow States. I think they're still there. I'm in a promoting mood!"

When Terri came in the next day, she was all smiles.

"Joe, it's so good to see you. How have you been? I've

thought about you a lot since the last time I saw you. Do you know, you were the only doctor that I ever worked with? That was so good when you got that degree. Now look at you – the regional administrator. I knew you'd go far." She finally took a breath and gave her New England accent a rest.

"Well," Joe said laughing, "I'm okay, I guess. I've got this new gig that was pretty much forced on me."

"No!" The look was one of total surprise.

Joe gave her the abridged version and asked her to sit in the leather chair beside his desk.

"Wow. This is more comfortable than it looks. I wonder if I could get one," she laughed.

"Actually, that's why I asked you here."

"Oh?"

"As you know, Jake Smith left us and he was the deputy. I need a new deputy, but I also need you right where you are. Would you be willing to take on both roles and give up sleeping at night?"

"Why me?"

"I guess you know why I'm here and what I'm supposed to do. But the swamp critters won't behave of their own volition. You are the only manager in the Civil Service I ever knew who was also a leader. Also, you are the only manager I ever saw fire a civil servant.

I need both of those qualities here – a good working environment, coupled with accountability and a service ethic."

"I see. Extra work, no extra pay. Sounds like I'd be back in the Marine Corps. Let me think about this Dr. O'Flaherty."

"Absolutely. Thanks for stopping in. Let me know if you

need anything from me on this or for your department. Maybe we can even get you that new chair."

The timing couldn't have been better as Terri left. The general had those personnel files. "Darnell didn't have a deputy."

"What?"

"Yes, no deputy. After she lost the one who resigned, she never filled the position. Scuttlebutt is that she was saving that to reward somebody down the road. Now, they're unsure who's in charge. Several of them are arguing that they should be in charge."

"Well, that simplifies things then. Do you have those files on Willow and Eldana?"

"Yes, right here. Looks like a couple of star performers who aren't going anywhere. They've been in the same positions for ten years."

"That's even better. They're about to get promoted."

Joe knew leadership. He also knew how to schmooze. A plate of fresh cut fruit and cheese. Coffee for Willow. Tea for Eldana. A chai tea for Joe. The general had his coffee black – he had no flair. "Ladies, come in. Glad to see you again!"

They were less than certain that this visit was a good thing. Word was already getting around about what a visit to Joe's office meant. They came in slowly, quietly and glanced around. Joe invited them to help themselves. Actually, it was almost an order. Seated on the sofa, they continued to quietly watch him. The snacks remained on the plates, uneaten.

Joe took the leather armchair and assumed the most unprofessional pose, one leg crossed over the other and totally relaxed. "Well, I guess you want to know why you're here."

They nodded but said nothing. His earlier speech to the work force had them on edge.

"As you know by now, Darnell has retired, leaving a leadership void. Although, to be candid, the void for leadership existed there for years. She was a manager and a lot of little else, pun intended." The chuckles came more easily now for the ladies.

"There is a director's position and a deputy's position available. I intend to fill these positions with a temporary detail, a more permanent arrangement being my long-term intent. I want the two of you to fill those positions."

To say they were shocked wouldn't come close. The whites of their eyes were very visible as they both seemed to choke on their drinks at the same time.

"I know this comes as a surprise, but I have a reason behind my madness. I remember both of you when I worked with you. This place has all the traits of a swamp and you are among the few who are not swamp critters but honorable and dedicated people."

They seemed more relaxed now. They weren't going to be fired after all. "All I need from you is two things. First thing, are you agreeable? I won't force this on you, but it is a great opportunity."

They were clearly unsure. The shock was still present. "Just say yes," he prodded.

"Ah, okay, if you really want me to."

"Yes, I'm also okay with it."

"Great. Second question, we need to decide who is in charge and who the deputy is. Do you have a preference or do I have to decide? The pay is the same."

Their shrugging shoulders said the shock hadn't fully worn off.

"Okay, then here it is. Eldana, you will be the director and Willow, you will be her deputy. I have to appoint you for a few months and then fill the positions permanently, competitively. If you do as well as I expect you to, the appointments will likely become permanent."

"I also expect your support in the changes that are coming. However, I don't think you will have issues with them. They actually reflect what you are already doing. One more thing. Don't try to change who or what you are. You are what we want and need."

"Well, I think we're done here. I'll have the general send out the notices and other paperwork within the next few hours. When you come in tomorrow morning, I want you to move into the executive offices in your division."

"General, have Top put in a cleaning and fumigation work order to be completed today. I want a fresh start for these ladies." When they left, they were alternating between beaming smiles and shock.

****

The meeting was intense and to the point. "I said it before and I'm saying it again, you were lucky with Darnell. Most won't be that easy. She was guilty, knew it, knew you knew it, knew you had the proof, and what's more important, had an escape through a retirement she would have taken soon anyway. You brought me here to help you with the twisted back room office politics in this place. Let me help you now."

"Okay, what do you have in mind?"

"Find an avatar."

"A what?"

"A stand-in or a spy if you prefer. Someone highly placed but willing to sell their own mother for a dime. You remember that old saying, 'keep your friends close...'"

"But keep your enemies even closer. Yes, I remember."

"Now is the time to take that seriously. This Lorna that you were talking about – she sounds like a good candidate."

"Go on, I'm listening" Joe said.

"Make it look good. Start out with the same approach then give her an out. Don't make it too easy. Then negotiate a deal. She can support you and give you the inside scoop on everyone and everything. She's on the inside. She can be very useful."

Joe had never been very good at chess. He was usually two-dimensional in his thinking. That could be great for a sergeant but not so good for developing strategy. The general was at least three-dimensional.

Lorna Reese had moved up the ladder through hook and crook. She was now a GS-15, which was the highest level, short of the Senior Executive Service. The people she had stepped on over the years to reach that level had either retired or not advanced to be a threat to her.

She was definitely a rising star. She used people as needed and then tossed them under any convenient bus, and this had worked so well, she couldn't imagine she might fail.

Nobody had told her to be nice to the people you meet on the way up because you'll meet them on the way back down. Her rising star was now a falling star.

She didn't know this. Almost nobody did or would have suspected it.

"Oh, Joe, it's so good to see you back here again. Now you're in charge. That's awesome!" Lorna said.

Joe thought, *Does she think I'm stupid? Am I supposed to have forgotten how she hung me out to dry, how she persecuted me for private values that I kept to myself and hurt nobody?*

"Good morning Ms. Reese. Please have a seat. By the way, it's Dr. O'Flaherty." He handed her the file. The charges were clear: Civil rights violations of the First Amendment, gross incompetence, conspiracy to allow violations of the Competition in Contracting Act, violations of her oath of office to report law violations when they were made known to her, pre-selection of employees, and discrimination against male applicants and Christian applicants.

Joe knew some of the charges would be hard to prove. But Joe was also a good negotiator. Start from a high demand point and then give ground till you reach what you really want. There was an implication of prison time, not to mention loss of her career and retirement benefits that she had 'worked' for, for the past fifteen years.

"Are you serious?"

Joe said nothing. Just stared at her with his usual poker face. The Cheyenne was definitely coming out. The old sergeant – he detested people like her. Sympathy was not in attendance in this meeting. Joe knew it wasn't right, but he was enjoying the moment.

"Joe, I have twenty years here. I can't go to prison and I need this job! All I've ever done is try to do the right thing. Let's just drop this and I will owe you. Please, I just want to do the right thing!" Tears were starting to flow.

Waterworks! Well, I guess if one thing doesn't work, then try that.

"The time to do the right thing is before you did the wrong thing." Joe was serious, somber, and immune to her psychological maneuverings.

"Please! Anything. I'll do anything."

"Did you give me a chance? Even a chance to present my side of the story?"

She just stared, remembering all too well what she had done.

"Ah, Joe?" The general decided it was time to make the offer.

"Yes?"

"Maybe there is something."

Lorna looked hopeful, even pleading.

"Oh, for crying out loud general! Well, go on," Joe said.

"She knows the people here. She knows what has been done and what is being said, even now. If Ms. Reese would be willing to work with us, maybe we could just stick this folder in the drawer. Things get lost all the time. I'll try to safeguard the file but, well, things do happen."

For the first time, Lorna looked hopeful, not exactly happy but definitely the tears had stopped. The eyes were wide and the white showing as she confirmed what the general had suggested. "Yes! I want to help. That's what I've been trying to say. Let me help. I've always been your friend. Let me prove it now." The pleading was almost pitiful – almost.

"My friend? No, you were never my friend. You were always only your own friend. I doubt that you know what a friend is. Still... Okay, here's how it will work. You get to keep your job – at least for now. What you will do is act as if nothing has changed. You will not discuss this conversation with anyone except me and the general. I do mean, anyone – not even your best friend, father, or husband."

"You're going to help us with our mission. As you know, the president sent us here to drain the swamp. I want to identify all of the workers who aren't providing the best work, who are below par. I want to identify supervisors who do not fully support the president's goals or who say things suggesting disloyalty or at least encourage limited support for his goals. I want to identify all programs that are not self-supporting or making money."

"You are known as politically correct. Your friends have the same lack of convictions. Listen to them. Record conversations that run that way."

"General."

"Yes Joe?"

"Give her one of those cool spy pens you showed me earlier and show her how to use it."

"Now then, I want you to send a few emails that reflect those conversations and blind carbon copy Top. He'll be collecting those."

"I also want you to go to lunch regularly and have Spanish speaking friends sit in the cafeteria near Sam or Carlos. Encourage them to speak in Spanish among themselves and tell them that nobody else understands."

"When you hear about people going to the union or plotting anything against us, you'll report it. I expect allegations of sexual harassment, setups, and all manner of means to either entrap us or provide outright fabrications. You won't discourage these but just report them to us."

"Sometimes we'll provide specific names to you to get information on – especially Josephine. You know part of what she did. I want you to suggest that she trump up a charge of sexual harassment against me or one of my staff and you can secretly tape record it. That's her usual mode anyway, so just encourage her to do it again."

"Above all, know this – if you turn against me or my immediate support staff, you will be the first casualty and the missing file will turn up. You keep your job as long as you are useful. No production means no job and, sure as Kansas tornadoes, no retirement. Is this clear?"

Joe knew she wasn't physically violent. If she had been, he might be in trouble now. The white in her eyes was again showing. The tears had stopped but this was definitely a significant emotional event for her. What was that smell? Perspiration beyond her usual ability to control?

She had done things like this before but never had she been forced to. Now, she had to and it was no longer the grasping, rapacious thing it had been. Now it was about survival.

After she left, the general laughed. "Joe, the longer I work with you, the more surprises I get. I wish I had known you when you were a sergeant. I could have used your talents."

Joe considered a laugh. The disgust he felt overpowered a wry sense of humor. He drew a deep breath and let it out at once, pooching his lips. He signed on for this but the duty was disgusting, even to him. He wasn't a quitter, so that escape wasn't even considered.

"I don't know." The general tried to read his emotions but there was nothing there, just the usual poker face.

Chapter Twenty-One

The boa constrictor is dangerous but only to its prey and if it is hungry. Leave it alone and it will leave you alone – maybe.

"It's you or me so you have to go." She was on Joe's list and knew it. Josephine had been instrumental in Joe's removal years earlier. Now, as Joe was walking down a seldom-traveled hallway in the basement, she was just there.

Startled, he asked, "Where did you come from?"

She pulled her hand out of her purse and aimed a gun right at Joe. Though it was dark, Joe recognized it immediately. He knew a lot about firearms and this one had been in the news a lot lately.

The Glock 380 was one the gun control crowd had been after almost as much as the AR-15. "It has no purpose except to commit crimes. Too easily hidden," they said. "It might even get past metal detectors," they argued.

"How did you get that in here," Joe demanded.

Ignoring his question, she just said, "You're a threat to me and my family – my friends too."

They were only five feet apart now. Even with her shaking hand, there was virtually no way she could miss.

"With any luck, I might even get away with it. You've been so cheap; there are no cameras down here. Security is at the front entrance. You're all alone. Any last words? Do you want to pray? Maybe you'd like to leave a message to your family on your cell? I would say friends, except someone like you has none." No laughing, she was serious.

That comment hurt most of all.

"Someone will hear the shots. You'll be caught."

"Thanks for reminding me." She pulled the silencer from her purse and attached it. She'd been practicing.

"You do know that a silencer won't really stop the noise. It just muffles it a little bit. It'll still be heard. It's not like on TV."

"I'm not stupid! It'll do well enough for my purpose."

"Now, don't get excited. So why do you want to shoot me?"

"I already told you. I don't want to be fired."

"I haven't fired anyone."

"No, you just make them resign or retire."

"So? They still keep the benefits they've earned."

"Like I said, I need the job. My children need my help. This job is all I have except for them."

"Oh yeah. As I remember, you have a son and a daughter. One is going to be an actor and the other is a singer."

"Yes. They're very talented."

"But that was ten years ago. Are they still going to be? When are they going to stop going to be and start being?"

"I know what you're trying to do. But my kids are my life and this job is the rest of it. I can't just retire and I sure can't support my kids on a retirement pension."

"So now you're going to support them...how long? Till you're eighty? Maybe till you're ninety? You've already failed them. A parent teaches their children to be self-sufficient. You're no parent. You just enable them to be less than they could be. How will they feel when they find out what you did today? Hmm? Will they respect you? If they find out you killed someone in order to support their failed lifestyle, what then?"

The tears were falling; Joe had gotten through.

"Okay, just stop it!" she said wiping the tears. I've made up my mind. They'll never find out. Nobody will."

This was going to hurt. The other times he'd been shot were minor; just flesh wounds. From five feet away, even a small '380' would do a lot of damage. She was focused on him. He needed a break, a small distraction.

"You're wrong about another thing," Joe said. "I'm not alone. Security patrols this hallway. There's one of them behind you."

"Wow, that's desperation!" she said. "One of the oldest lines ever."

"Sergeant, shoot!" Joe shouted, looking behind her. "Now! Before she does."

Boom! A shot rang out. It was loud and surprised both of them.

"You're done for," he said. "Look at your blood on the floor."

"Startled, Josephine looked down.

Joe leaped forward instantly and grabbed her wrists, pointed the gun upward, and wrenched the pistol from her grip, knocking her to the ground as he did so.

"Alright," he said, "let's go to security. You know the way."

Around the next corner, he ran into three security guards and they were laughing.

When they saw Joe, they became serious.

"Uh, sorry. Sir, we have to make an incident report."

"What about?"

"A firearm incident. It was an accident but Bob here fired his weapon."

"So that's where the sound came from," Joe said.

Bob had that scared look. He knew he was about to be fired.

"Well, I guess I didn't sleep well before I came on duty. Anyway, I was about to go off duty so I had to clear my weapon. I removed the magazine and aimed the weapon here in that sand barrel and squeezed the trigger."

"Ah, I see. You forgot about the chambered round."

The three security guards stared at Joe in amazement.

Don't worry though. Stuff happens." Joe added. "By the way, you might be interested to know your accident saved my life. Jim, you're the supervisor. Check it out and see if you can get Bob an award."

"Huh?"

"That mistake distracted Josephine here. She was going to shoot me."

"What?"

Pulling the pistol from his belt where he had tucked it, Joe handed it to Jim.

"You should find my prints on it – and hers too. If the bullets have her prints on them, that should validate my story. Oh. I almost forgot. Find out how she got that thing in here."

"By the way, Josephine – you're fired."

"So what? You were going to fire me anyway."

"Not without proof of something illegal. You just gave that to me."

"You mean my attempt to kill you was for nothing?"

"Yes. Yes, I do."

Chapter Twenty-Two

The sucker footed bat, like all of its cousins, can be beneficial – and dangerous. Although it eats a large amount of insects, it can also carry diseases. It's still a swamp critter, so be careful with it.

In spite of the near-shooting, things were going well. Joe was in a rare, good mood. As he considered his good fortune at escaping Josephine when she had him cold, he realized someone was watching out for him. A guardian angel...someone further up the spiritual chain?

I feel like celebrating. "Well general, things have been going well, haven't they? We've been able to remove ten percent of the workforce that was just taking up space."

They were always on a first name basis – Joe and the general. It had only been three months and Joe was practically dancing. Spring had arrived and the birds were singing. A perfect 75 degrees and clear skies said that life is great.

"Maybe too well," the general reminded him. "When the attack is going too well, it often signals an ambush." Joe had forgotten that adage but it was appropriate.

"I was ready for a parade and here you are raining on it."

"I wouldn't be much good to you if I didn't point it out," the general answered. His arms crossed, he and Joe locked gazes.

Finally, Joe nodded. "Okay, so what do you think is going to happen? Where is the ambush coming from?"

"If I knew that, I could probably stop it. Maybe I could even create a counter ambush. But it's coming. As sure as your good looks, it's coming."

"So, in other words, maybe not?"

The general just smiled as the tension ratcheted up again. But they couldn't just stop to circle the wagons. They were in enemy-occupied territory and knew it all too well. It was best to proceed and just wait to see where the attack might come from. Planning for the unknowable was useless anyway.

It was time to move on from the unknowable to what they could actually do something about.

"Okay general, so what's on the schedule for today? Are we going to encourage anybody to pursue their happiness elsewhere?"

"Here's a copy of the agenda. You have meetings with the ten workers indicated. You'll note that we've gone through the substandard performance evaluations and translated those employees' status."

"You mean fired them; I still insist that we speak plainly in this office. Outside, use all the PC language you like." The general just gave him that same look. He knew better than Joe what the media could do to them. Top smiled but he was plain speaking, just like Joe. "So, what is the group today about? Why are they leaving?"

"It's the Avatar. She has statements here with dates, times, places, and witnesses."

"She came through, huh?"

"Yes."

"So...what did the soon-to-be-departed do?"

"They used very explicit language in their opinion of our mission, of you, and of our president. Most notably, they said they would never support his 'radical' agenda."

"Well, we certainly don't need that kind of trouble, but is it enough?"

"Yes. I ran it by one of those lawyers you had me hire. They all signed an oath of office when they took their jobs and agreed to support and defend the Constitution. Part of the Constitution puts the president at the top. They have to do what he says. Also, they all have security clearances. If we report this, they will lose the clearance and be subject to termination anyway."

"Are we reporting this?"

"Why, yes we are." Sam had chimed in and he handled the routine administrative stuff. His Cuban accent added extra panache to the situation.

"Great. Let's get this done then." Joe spoke loudly but somehow seemed less sincere that he used to. The enthusiasm was waning. The viciousness of the critters had been on the decline. It was starting to feel more speculative.

Then, there was that dampening the general had provided. The threats were real, and Joe knew he was on thin ice, surrounded by enemies he didn't know.

The speech to each worker was the same as Joe had used many times before. The results were also the same. Sally Jacob had yelled at Joe. "You can't do this! I have the right to free speech. You can't shut me up! That Prima Dona has no place in the government. He's not *my* president!"

"Have you heard of the Hatch Act? Hmm? Well, that look on your face says that you have. As you know, you can say what you want outside these walls, but it stops when you come in here. Vote for whomever you like, but you don't get to come in here and talk bad about the boss."

"So, what's it going to be? Fired or resign?" Her response was clear and colorful and not to be repeated. She also knew the odds of her succeeding in an appeal were low. She took the resignation. At least she could claim that leaving was her idea. Getting fired meant lower chances of another job.

With the others it was the same. Crying. Anger. Some screamed. The language was just like Sally had used. But disloyalty couldn't be tolerated either. People had taken the job and worked for the president and those appointed by him.

Joe thought of that old western novel again and the phrase "riding for the brand" came to mind. Even when he hated the direction the work was taking, he had always done as directed and kept his tongue. The old soldier had difficulty with those who would not comply with lawful orders and instructions – he had done it so why couldn't they?

"General, have you also reviewed the social media for the comments that our people might be posting there?"

"Yes. Sam is a crackerjack user. He knows computers and all the social media sites. He's working on that and should have a list of the naughty and the nice for us in a week or so. Just in time for Christmas terminations."

Joe had known Sam for a long time. His ability on the computer was one of the big reasons why he had recruited him. Sam was even better than the general had bragged about. Social media was an outlet for the workers. It was also very visible. Sam had become friends with many on the various platforms.

One worker had stated "This 'Nutcase in Chief' thinks he

can work me to death! Well, I've been doing this job for fifteen years and that's been good enough up to now. I decided two months ago to take an extra month on everything I do. What can he do about it? Nothing! I was here before those deplorables elected him, and I'll still be here when he's done. Two years and counting till he's gone!" Like him, many were holding out hope for the next election.

When Sam read that to the office group, the laughter continued for an inappropriately long time. Then Top added, "I think maybe there is something that can be done. Joe, let me handle that one. I need a little R & R and that would be the ticket." The social media was a goldmine for potentials to remove. It was there in print, shouting to the world that they were actively sabotaging the president's agenda.

Joe just shook his head. "Some of these people make this far too easy. Not even sporting. I need a challenge – but I do appreciate the levity they provide us with. By the way, Sam have you also looked for any blogs that might be out there?"

"Wow, I forgot about that. I'll get right on it."

"Hey, Joe. Check this out." Sam had been on another website.

"You're not online gambling are you? I really don't have time to look at those funny websites you keep finding."

"No, that's not it at all. You really need to see this. See this person?"

"I'm looking. So what?"

"Well, he may not look familiar to you but he works for you."

"Huh? What's this website?"

"It's felonies. This guy has one. I checked with Noni in personnel. It wasn't on his application. Guess what else?"

"Go on."

"Well, he's also one of those who are only average in work ... and it gets better. He's also in the group that Lorna told us about. He's working against you and against the changes."

"So, what are you saying?" Joe was a bit slow that morning, probably the lack of sleep last night. Losing sleep was starting to become a problem.

"This is the cause to terminate. Bottom line is that he lied on his application."

"Ah, I see now. How in the world did this happen? Hasn't GSA been checking this stuff while doing the security clearance and background checks?"

"Apparently not, or at least, not 100 percent."

"Okay, get with Top and make it happen."

"Anything else?"

"Yes, I also found a website of sexual offenders. We can run all these names and cross reference with our work force. Apparently, GSA hasn't checked out its past hires very well."

"We're doing that now, aren't we?"

"Oh yeah. That was one of the first things the general put us on."

"Great. So cross reference and see who we need to get rid of. This is all we need! Great work Sam! I'm going to have to get you a box of donuts to celebrate."

"I like cassavas from the Cuban restaurant on Havana Street."

Chapter Twenty-Three

The tropical fire ant of the swamp is significant because it is so numerous. By itself, it would be of little importance. A bite from one can lead to painful swelling. Many bites can kill. The nest of ants is also very hard to eradicate.

Joe was especially hard on supervisors. He knew that responsibility had to stop somewhere. "If somebody is not doing their job, it's because nobody is requiring it of them. It's one thing to give lower bonuses to the lower performing ones. But if they believe they can skate by while doing the minimum, many will do just that. I want to get rid of the supervisors who aren't doing their job. If we get rid of bad supervisors, we can get some good ones and they will ensure the people are good too. Are we all clear on that?"

The staff meeting had started off with donuts, cassavas and a few laughs. The mood was changing. All agreed they needed to get rid of bad performers, but how were they going to identify them and force them to leave. If supervisors covered for them, it would be next to impossible to identify them. Top said as much. The general just smiled which said the same thing. "Go around the parking lot and find out who voted for whom."

"But Joe, you can't fire for political reasons. That's illegal. It violates the Hatch Act and I don't even need to ask the lawyer about that." The general was on the same page, but keeping Joe out of harm's way was becoming a more than a full-time job.

"That's very true but we can identify some potential critters. Here's how we'll do it. After we check out the parking lot and identify those people and see if they voted against our man, dig deeper. Carlos, how's that special project coming?"

"Great. Noni and I really hit it off. We've been meeting every week for pastries. Sometimes she buys and sometimes I do."

"And?"

"She has given me information on those employees who were terminated, failed probation, or failed their internship."

"Have you done the analysis?"

"Yes."

"And?" It was getting tiresome for Joe to have to drag it out of Carlos.

"There are definitely some trends. For example, Kathi Soon has failed ten interns over the past five years. All were males. Jackie Weber failed five during the same time and all but one were males. She also recommended termination on two probationary employees. Again, all males. One was a Muslim."

"Is that significant? Come on, this is getting old. Spit it out before I have you doing pushups."

Carlos had always hated the pushup routine so the threat was significant. "I followed up with each terminated employee. The Muslim too. I got similar stories from each and about half of them provided signed statements. Since they don't work here anymore, they weren't afraid but several didn't want to get involved. They've moved on with their lives and just want to forget the experience."

"Anyway, they said that they saw extra attention given to females in the same category, intern, probation, etc., but they couldn't get help when they asked. The typical answer went something like 'I'll see what I can do. But for now, don't worry. Just keep at it and you'll get the hang of it.' Of course, the extra help never came. The hang part probably meant they would be left hanging."

"Great!" Joe was getting excited. "By the way, were there any religion issues? What was the religion of those terminated?"

"Well, one was Jewish and two others were Christians who said they had some religious mementos in their cubicles. I asked them if religion was ever mentioned but they said it hadn't been. However, they also said that the supervisor had been to their work area so they undoubtedly knew.

One even said the supervisor walked him out to his car after work one day and seemed surprised by the fish symbol in the back window of his car. She asked him about it and when he told her, she just nodded and smiled.

Another said he saw someone out by his car when he was leaving work. He wasn't sure but thought the person was writing something on paper."

"Did he have anything on his car that would have been of interest?"

"Well, he's changed cars since then, but thought he had a political sticker on it."

"The Muslim fellow? Are you ever going to get back to him?"

"Oh, sure. He said that whenever he went to his supervisor, she always called another female supervisor into the meeting.

He thought that was strange but thought maybe it was just part of GSA culture."

"Okay. Now, I want you to get the statements, the personnel information, the terminated employees' files, and the files on the involved supervisors and their supervisors too. Take it to the lawyer team and ask them to review to see if grounds exist for removal. By the way, are any of the supervisors from the same political party as our president?"

"Only one."

"Well, refer her – it is a her isn't it?"

"Yes."

"Then refer her along with all the others. Swamp critters come in all sizes, shapes, and colors."

****

It was about a week later; Joe took the tour of the offices – unannounced. As he went through the old section he had worked in before, he saw the same old man. Sleeping at his desk, he didn't notice Joe's approach. "Why is this man asleep?" he asked.

The supervisor said, "Well you know him. He's been doing this for years. He'll wake up before long."

"Does he have a medical condition that causes this?"

"Yes, that's why we've ignored it."

"So why haven't you medically retired him?"

"Nobody wanted to take on the union."

"So, you've wasted taxpayer money. You've passed on part of what should be his workload to someone else. You've done nothing but plead lack of backbone?"

"You just don't understand."

"Don't I? I want his retirement or dismissal by the end of the day. If you don't have it, then bring your own."

As he walked out, he told the general. "Find out everyone who has supervised him and get their retirement, resignation, or termination as appropriate. That includes Sheila back there."

"But I thought you gave her a chance to fix the situation."

"No. She's had a chance for years. It's action time. But wait on her till tomorrow. Maybe she'll at least take care of Sleepy Bob. These are the kind of critters we came to remove."

The removal of Sleepy Bob ran up against a speed bump – the Union. The Union rep was as hostile to the new model as anyone could be. Sleepy Bob did wake up long enough to visit her and submit a grievance. This was just the opportunity Salli had been waiting for. She immediately sent a terse email to Joe.

"Dr. O'Flaherty, I have just received a grievance regarding an employee who is covered by Union representation. The union demands that you cease and desist in the firing of Robert Scanlon. He has a valid medical condition which causes him to lose consciousness during his tour of work. Under a long-standing agreement between the union and management, he has been allowed to continue his employment, accepting the occasional issues which his condition brings about."

Joe knew she could be a powerful ally or enemy. Which approach she took depended on him. *Maybe I can get her on my side. I don't really have anything against her.*

A conversation with the general resulted in the same conclusion. "Joe, you should try to reach an accommodation with her. When I commanded a Division, I was able to do that with another union official. We both wanted the same thing – to enhance the Army with good civilian workers. Why don't you take her to a nice restaurant? Talk to her about why this new approach we are taking will result in a much better, taxpayer-friendly organization. With a bit of luck, we may get her on our side."

Joe *did* take her to lunch. The Cowhand Bistro was more than its name implied. In an old factory building, it had known many lives. Originally constructed in the late 1800s to construct ore carts for the nearby goldmines, it had been used as a makeshift hospital during the flu epidemic of 1918. Since then, it had served as a furniture factory, a warehouse, and a recruiting depot during World War II.

Now, some enterprising entrepreneur had turned it into a theme restaurant. Each parking space had a horse hitching post in front of it. High wooden beams supported the walls and roof. Ten-foot brindle longhorns were above the bar. Cowhides were everywhere on the rough wood walls. The tables were converted from upside down tree stumps, cut into tables, and covered in clear varnish. The name also denied the high prices that Joe encountered – five-star prices reflected the menu items.

The waiter approached the table and said, "Howdy partner, what'll it be?" Joe examined his cowboy attire. Even the pair of six-shooters looked authentic. The food was good but the ambiance was what set it apart. It also doubled the cost of eating there.

Joe expected resistance from Salli since they were responsible to different people.

"This place is great," she said. "I seldom get out of the basement where I work."

"I'm so glad that you like it. I've been thinking almost the same thing."

"Oh?"

"Yes. You've been with us a long time. That small office down that dark hallway never sees the light of day. I definitely would like to see you more often. Maybe we can help the organization by meeting more often and tackling problems together. How would you like to get a new office on the top floor? I was just up there yesterday and the office is amazing. You can even see the snow-capped Rocky Mountains from there. I've got a new position opening up and it's yours for the taking."

"Does this have anything to do with Bob?"

"Well, I admit that we could use some help. Bob isn't well and needs to retire. You could help him and yourself too."

She saw right through him and was less than receptive. "Are you trying to buy me off with a window?"

"No, no. Not at all. I just think we could...we should work together more. I'm here to make this organization stronger. We need to get rid of those who are weighing it down and move toward a more sustainable basis."

"And you're going to do that by firing people who are union members? Have you forgotten who I represent? Joe...Dr. O'Flaherty, I also want this place to succeed but you can't do that by getting rid of the workers. You need us more than we need you. I care about the workers. Who do you care about?"

Joe was silent. He knew this was going nowhere. Her words stung more than he was willing to admit.

The food arrived and both ate in silence. As they left to go back to work, the door greeter gave them a colorful greeting. "I hope the chow was rib-sticking good. Now, don't go away mad, just get on your cayuse and light a shuck on out of here."

They were certainly going. Mad? Joe didn't feel mad. He didn't feel glad either. *This was a really bad idea. To have thought that we could work together – the swamp and the swamp drainer are never going to work together.*

It was time for a new, old approach. The carrot hadn't worked so… A review of Salli's work showed that she was working ten hours a week on government work and thirty hours a week on union business. He also found that some of that "union business" was campaigning for the losing presidential candidate – a clear Hatch Act violation.

The last Union agreement authorized as much as twenty hours a week on government time for union business but for the past eight years she had only worked ten hours a week on government business. Supervisors just let it go out of fear. They would have been happy to not send her any government work to do.

Because of the new evidence, he had the new lawyer bring her in and charge her with fraud. There was no doubt where this came from but she also had little choice.

She caught Joe in the hallway that same day. "So, this is how you play, huh? I heard the rumors, but I knew they just couldn't be true. There must be some good in you. Boy was I wrong. You've gotten a lot of people to leave and you fill their positions with lackeys that support what you and your friends want!"

"Didn't you do the same?"

Her mouth just hung open as she stared in disbelief.

There was going to be no talking to him. He had no conscience, no values that she could see. He was just a hired gun, here to fire everybody and make this a ghost town like some old western movie. She also knew that she was out of options. She was getting too old to go to prison. The union couldn't protect her.

The charges were true, she knew all too well. It was time to cut her losses and get out while she could. She contacted the general and told him she was ready to retire if the government would drop the charges. An agreement was made. obviously, not on paper.

The speed bump was gone. Joe helped a new candidate for the union president office get elected. The newer employees who were there to work helped with that. The new union president and Joe often talked things through. Aware of the danger, he was far more cooperative. He also enjoyed the view from his window.

Chapter Twenty-Four

The common squirrel is a swamp resident and both food and feeder. Other critters seem more vicious, but the squirrel is nothing if not resilient. If anything good grows in the swamp, you can be sure the squirrel will find it.

"The union battle is over and peace reigns once more." Joe kept saying that to himself. If he said it often enough, it might, in time, be true. He kept saying it, but knew in his heart that it wasn't so.

Needing a diversion, he walked around in the yard at home and noticed the lawn needed to be mowed. Riding around the large yard on his mower, he passed a dwarf peach tree and noticed a lot of green peaches lying on the ground. Some were partially eaten. Stopping to take a look at them, he saw green peach flakes flying through the air. Looking up, he saw a squirrel sitting on the overhead power line with a green peach. It seemed to be laughing at him. It felt like the scene Bill Murray had with a gopher in *Caddyshack*.

Inexperienced with squirrels, since there weren't a lot of them when he grew up in Lamar, he asked Dave for advice. Dave knew almost everything worth knowing. Meeting at the coffee shop, Dave sympathized with him.

"Well, you're in town so you can't shoot them. They're very

crafty. You may just have to put up with them unless you have a dog in your back yard to chase them off."

"In other words, nothing. I'm stuck."

"That's pretty much it, short of a God-given miracle."

A few nights later, Joe again considered the problem and wondered what he could do when he heard a loud bang. The power immediately flickered and went off. Joe glanced outside the window and saw the squirrel flying through the air. He had found the bare spot in the power line and his peach-flaking days were over.

"Yeah!" Joe said, raising a fist in salute. He had gotten his miracle. "Thank you, God!" Of course, there were more squirrels so he built nets around the trees since he only had a few.

I wish I could do that at GSA to keep the two-legged critters out. Hmm. Why can't I? This epiphany, similar to his earlier one that had gotten rid of bad suppliers, seemed to be God-given.

The more he thought about it, the more he realized it was the only way he would have any lasting effect on the swamp. Oh sure, he could drain it now, but the critters would be back as soon as he left.

The nets were the next project. Policies, rules, and internal memos that would keep the critters out. The only way to transform the swamp was to level it out and plant some nice green grass. Get rid of the trees, bogs, and other hiding places, and the critters would have nothing to come back to.

The next day, Joe was reenergized. Arriving at work an hour early, he shut the door and started making notes and outlining a plan. Like a net, it needed intersecting lines that would keep the critters away. By the time the rest of the group had arrived, he was ready. His outline had several plans.

"Folks, it's time to lock our accomplishments in concrete. We've been successful so far but we won't be here forever. I want a plan that eliminates this place as a swamp. I want to make it look like a desert to swamp critters. Just like a golf course, we need to get rid of hiding places and provide a level playing field for all who contribute."

"Joe, don't you think we all want that?" The general was unsure where Joe was going with this.

"Sure, so let's make it happen."

"But if it could be done, don't you think it would have been done before now?"

"No. No, I don't. When the swamp controls the organization, they have no reason to plant grass. Here's how we'll do it. Now, keep in mind, this is not just for our workers but also our processes."

"We want to speed up our slow hiring and firing processes. Get good people in and get the bad ones out. Right now, it takes months to hire a new employee. Get that down to three weeks."

"We also need to identify processes to get rid of marginal employees. We need to make it fast, identify all who aren't contributing, and leave no place for them to hide."

"Next, we want to eliminate expenses for trips elsewhere. I've talked about this before. Now, we cut it into stone."

"But we have to have the training. Law and regulations require it. People have to travel." The general had on his *save-joe* waders and the stream was starting to flow fast.

"We'll have the training but we'll have it here. We don't

want to pay for flights, expensive hotels, and expensive meal rates in D.C. We can save on all that if we just conduct the class here."

"We can get the trainers to come here and conduct the training. Also, let's look into getting some of our people qualified to conduct the training themselves. If we can get the training online or get it redesigned to be online, let's do that."

"General, you're in charge of this part of the change. I want to save money and I want you to squeeze every penny until Lincoln screams Jefferson Davis."

"Next, we're going to eliminate travel to trade shows. We'll sponsor them here, in this building. Get the sales people to come to us if they want to show us what they have. They'll do anything to make a dollar. This city has a lot to offer so we will use it to attract sales people."

"Now, there's the issue of contract set-asides. Any time we set something aside for a particular group, they hike their price and we pay more. I want to do something about that. No more set-asides. We can give the groups a small advantage but I emphasize small. When we pay too much, we are stealing from the taxpayer. I'm a veteran but even veterans are taking advantage of us. Many companies use the set-aside and do little work other than just putting their names on the contract. These pass-throughs are just wasting money and acting as a form of small business welfare."

"Joe, for a lot of that, you simply don't have authority. Nobody here is going to violate the law to make you happy."

"I figured that. Remember the president's pen?"

"Yes?"

"Well, we write it up so that he issues an executive order. If anybody complains, let the lawyers keep them in court for the next ten years."

"I've also talked before about leadership being a top priority. Now, we make it permanent. As an example, employee appearance, motivation, performance, and contribution of cost-saving ideas will be a focus of all supervisors. If they aren't doing their job, neither will the workers."

"General, I want you to write this up. Design the net to get the best people and keep the critters out. Ensure we are going after any contractors who rip us off. Save money by avoiding travel and other unnecessary expenses. Look at our profit structure and keep us on a pay-our-own-way basis – permanently."

"I want you to have the meetings with department heads to identify other measures that get us from here to there. Use any resources you need including those in this office."

"Get with Terri. She's got a lot of ideas. We had lunch yesterday and she unloaded them on me till we ran out of lunchtime. I also expect ideas from everybody here, in this room. When you have the plan, we can meet and talk. I want Terri in on that meeting. Don't take no from her. She'll say she's busy. She's always busy. Tell her to make time."

"Those ideas that need presidential help, we can forward to him. Also, we may want to share these with the other regional offices."

As they left the office, they were dragging. Joe had worn them out in only one hour. When Top passed by the coffee pot, he noticed it was empty. *I wonder? Who emptied it? Joe was in early. Is that why he's so wired?*

"General, did he say when he wants this?"

"Not in so many words ... which means we have one month.

If we drag it out past that, he'll be looking over our shoulders. I don't want that." The general was already calculating the overtime he would be working.

Chapter Twenty-Five

The grootslang is as old as the world from which it sprang. With the body of an elephant, the tail of a snake, the strength, wiliness, and intelligence of both, it is ruthless. It lures its victims into its hole with a nearly bottomless pit. It can, however, be bought off with enough diamonds. No swamp should be without one.

"Joe, it's the boss." Joe had been on the phone many times with the president's aide but today, he wanted something new.

"Huh?"

"The president. He wants to talk with you. Just say yes and agree with him and give him what he asks for. That's what we do up here. It saves time and aggravation." Somewhere between Patton and the Godfather – well, today he was more like Patton.

"Joe, do you remember that deal we made?"

"Which one? The one where you were going to adopt me?"

"No." He also didn't laugh. "I'm having a bunch of you directors get together in Las Vegas next week and compare notes. I told you I would want an overall solution to GSA issues. I'm having you meet with a lot of other agencies too."

"I want that overall approach to make government buying more efficient. I heard you developed a critter net down there so now is a great time to do this." Now the Godfather part was showing.

"Oh, that deal. Okay. I'm with you now. Sure. I can do that. It sounds like fun." To old soldiers like Joe, *fun* was synonymous with *interesting*.

"I hope not. I'm not having you guys go there for fun. This isn't the old GSA but the new, improved version. There won't be any clowns or fancy dinners. Get me the goods. Get me a plan. You're the old sergeant and they may need leadership. Whip them into shape and get it done."

Joe hadn't had to agree or say yes. He just listened and received his orders. It was just like being in the Army – salute and move out. Vegas wasn't bad, at least at night. There were shows, food, and far too many distractions. The trip also gave him a chance to visit with cousins he hadn't seen since they were kids.

Diona went too, so she had to do some shopping. The trip wasn't free. While the government paid for the lodging at the cheapest *Motel 7 and a half* they could find, Diona spent her share of Joe's big salary in clothing. "Well, I have to do something during the day while you and the other bigshots are conventioning."

She knew it wasn't really a verb but she had always made up her own words. There was no reason she was going to change now.

****

It was an old custom – an Army custom. Joe had just gotten back from that long trip to Washington. Now, he would brainstorm on other ways to drain the swamp, permanently if possible.

He had offered many ways to fix the swamp at that conference. The ideas flowed and nobody's imagination was more fertile than Joe's. "What else?" the fatigued chairwoman asked as he offered his tenth proposal.

Now, he was back at the office. It was time to visit with the staff and make sure everything was in order.

"Good morning, Dr. O'Flaherty." The secretary was smiling her usual smile.

"I wonder if she really means that," Joe wondered. She had been here many years and seen a lot of people come and go.

After he dropped the tote shoulder bag on his desk, he came out and greeted everybody in the office. "Sam, how's it going?" "General, I see you're your usual uplifting self." "Carlos, how's the family? Have they got the house and the shop fixed back home?"

As he made the rounds, he walked around the headquarters suite. Old sergeants made sure the work areas were neat or at least relatively so in spite of the work going on. Trash had been picked up. The windows had been cleaned the week before. Everything looked right. Dress right dress, they called it in the Army. Like every day before, he made the circuit around the office, just checking things out.

Then he saw the box on the secretary's desk. "Lidia, what's that?"

"Oh, I almost forgot. It came just a few minutes ago."

"What is it? Who's it from?"

"Well, the box says it's from one of those online cake companies. The address says it's from Mom. Joe, it's your birthday isn't it?"

Sam joined the banter – "You always said that your Mom never forgot your birthday. I expect a piece."

Joe continued to stare at Lidia, but the smile was long gone. "Did you say it's from Mom?"

"Yes. Happy Birthday."

"Not quite."

"Okay, so it's early. We all want a piece."

Joe grew serious, his face was white. "Get out of here."

"What? But Joe, I'm sorry." She had never seen him this unpleasant.

"No, get out of here – now. Get all the way out – all of you."

"What's going on?"

"Just get out now." He whispered to the general, "Evacuate the building but do it quietly. Everybody just leave here without saying anything." Now he had the entire crew looking scared. They knew better than to argue.

The general just said, "Come on. I've got some party stuff in my car. I need help."

"Should I call anyone?" the secretary asked.

"No, and don't touch the phone."

As it started to ring, she moved to answer it.

"No! Get out now. Leave that phone alone."

As they approached the security desk, Joe told the sergeant, "Order an evacuation. Call the police. Tell them to bring the bomb-busters with them. I might be wrong but I need to be sure."

The sergeant immediately picked up the telephone and called 911.

As they reached the parking lot, Sam asked, "I don't understand. How did you know?"

"I forgot to mention it because it was a very personal thing. Mom passed away two years ago. I still keep her picture on my desk because it makes me feel like she's not really gone. Someone must have seen that picture. We've always figured we have spies ... but this!"

The first police unit was there in two minutes. The bomb squad took a little longer. Ten minutes into the ordeal, they finally arrived. All suited up like astronauts, they looked like they were headed for the space shuttle instead of a small cake bomb. The lieutenant found Joe easily enough. All the suits were gathered around him. The rest of the workers were in their assembly areas, wearing business casual, and neckties were as scarce as lie detectors at a political convention.

"Are you in charge?" the lieutenant asked.

"Yes, I guess I am unless the security folks want to be."

The lieutenant missed the humor and just stared for a moment. "Well, alright then. What's the problem?"

"There might be a bomb. That's why we called. I hear that's pretty much what you do."

"Yes, that's what we do." Humorless, he was already at odds with Joe. Quickly, Joe gave him a rundown on what had happened and the layout of the building.

The lieutenant pulled out a radio. "Get the 2F unit."

As the robot rolled up to the lieutenant, the officer with the controls introduced him. "Meet Fat Freddy." This officer was wearing sergeant's stripes and had the humor that his boss lacked.

"So why do you call him Fat Freddy?" Joe asked.

"He eats everything he can. Always happy to eat something with a kick. See that big space in the middle?"

"Yes."

"That's a door that he opens and sticks the explosive in with his mechanical arms. He can hold the equivalent of one pound of dynamite."

"Wow. That hardly seems possible."

"Yes, but true. He's built like a tank."

"So, where does the pressure go? I mean, it has to go somewhere."

"That's a great question. Most don't ask about it. You must have some military background."

"If you only knew," Joe said.

"Well, Freddy is built with a tungsten-steel alloy. He's got redundant metal plates inside that will move if enough pressure is exerted. That's another reason he's so fat. Then, he slowly lets the pressure out. It sounds like, well, maybe you better use your imagination."

"I see."

"Well, we better have at it. Is everyone out?"

The security sergeant nodded.

"Do you know where you're going and what you're looking for?"

"Affirmative. We'll see you soon. Say bye Freddy."

"Later dude."

Joe wondered who had programmed the robot. He could almost see the young man with long hair, unshaven, unwashed, and a no-collar humor.

It had been a long time. Maybe twenty minutes but it seemed like hours. Joe watched the window where his office suite was. He expected the bomb to go off. Windows would be blown out. Paper scraps raining down, smoke, and fire; he expected it all while he hoped for nothing to happen.

Finally, Sam said, "Hey Joe, I think we're forgetting something. Maybe we should also pray. Hmm? We don't want anyone to get hurt."

"You bet. You lead us – but do it in English." Sam motioned the headquarters group to get in a small circle and he said the words.

As soon as he was done, the security sergeant said, "They're coming out." The lieutenant and the sergeant were just behind Fat Freddy.

No explosion. It was very anti-climactic. It felt like a letdown and yet, nobody really wanted an explosion. The lieutenant was all business. The sergeant was all smiles. Giving the thumbs up sign, he waved.

Ten feet outside the building on the sloped ramp from the doorway, they heard it. It sounded very muffled with a bit of a whistle. Fat Freddy had eaten the cake box and found it to be spicy. Then, Joe heard the sounds that the sergeant had warned him about. First was the rumble that sounded more like a belch.

"How fitting," Joe said.

Then another sound occurred. Everyone was silent. Then, laughter rang out as pent-up tension was released.

"All clear?" Joe asked the lieutenant.

"Yes. All clear. Your cake was all we found. You made the right call. If you like we can go through with the electronics and the dogs just to make sure."

"No, I think it's alright. That box looked suspicious so we had to make sure."

"Good thing you did. We'll need about thirty minutes with you to write up the report.

Just then, another patrol car pulled up. The deputy chief of police had arrived. Wearing his dress uniform with two stars on it, he found Joe almost immediately. Waddling up, it was clear that he hadn't had to take a physical fitness test recently. "Hi, you must be Dr. O'Flaherty."

"Yes, that's me," Joe replied.

"I'm Deputy Chief Frederick Solinski. The Bomb Disposal Unit is one of my charges. How did we do?"

"Great! Your guys took care of the problem and even left the building intact. Couldn't be better!"

"Good to hear."

As the deputy chief walked away, Joe glanced at the sergeant who just smiled. "Umm hmm," Joe said. An old sergeant too, Joe and the officer understood each other.

Chapter Twenty-Six

He was a wild dog, though he hadn't always been. He used to have a family. Now, even the other dogs and wolves and coyotes avoided him. No family, no home, and nothing to eat. However, he was still pursued as a potential meal.

"Get out of here! I mean it. I'll get the dogs after you." They were always so mean and yet, he couldn't care less. As he ambled down the alley, Brad ... was that it? It had been so long since anybody had used that name, he wasn't even sure that it was right. Pig, dog, puke, and a lot more colorful names than those. It was what he was called and he recognized those names as his.

Brad couldn't remember the last time he had eaten. It felt like years since he had been high. At first, he didn't care about food. Even now, clean from the drugs, he cared only a little about it.

How long had he been out here? Months, years? Who could tell? He had a lot of scraggly facial hair. Sometimes, when it got really long, he would look for something sharp to cut it with. Once, he had even stopped where some other 'homeless' people like him were warming by a fire. He thought he could use the fire to remove some of the beard. It hadn't worked out so well that time.

He was hoping for something from that grocery store back there. Usually, there was something still edible being tossed. A moldy orange, moldy bread, moldy cheese. All things moldy. Even that, he was being denied today. *Oh well, probably didn't need it anyway.* He justified this misery like he did everything else.

His life used to be a lot of black and white with the occasional gray. Now, he was color blind and everything was gray. If he could steal something from another like himself, that was fine. The shoes he wore, he had taken from another unfortunate who had fallen asleep with a bottle in a bag. "I needed them more than he did," he told himself.

As he passed by a parked car, he glanced inside and saw a pizza box. He hadn't had a pizza in a long time. He could kill for a pizza – literally. He needed it more than some fat, car-driving slob.

The doors were locked. He looked around for a rock or brick. Something to get that pizza. As he glanced toward the corner, he saw the man. He was big and was watching Brad. He knew what Brad knew and wasn't going to put up with it. He was almost running now. Brad ran too. Running pizza man cared more about his car than taking something off the indigent's hide, so he gave up the chase.

As Brad came out of the alley two blocks down the street, he saw the sign – 'Join the Army Team.' He smiled. For the first time in a long time, he smiled. He thought about it. *The Army. I bet they're eating well.*

He used to eat well. He had been a soldier – once. Now, he was an animal. He was worse than an animal because people cared about animals. Even animals had rights and feelings. He had none. Walking along, he thought about what he had become. He hadn't thought about it in a long time. Today, he thought about it.

When he started the drugs, he also changed. His mind had changed. Pot, hash, coke, horse, big O, bennies, acid. He had used it all. But that was when he had money. A long time ago he had money. The acid had changed him the most. It seemed to rewire his brain, and he had used it several times.

Taco Barn. The sign was full of color and inviting. *Looks good. I wish I had some money. Just enough for one taco. Something that hadn't come out of a dumpster. That would be ... what? He couldn't focus enough to know what he felt. I bet they're eating good in there. If I just had some money. A dollar – maybe two. They couldn't refuse me if I had money.*

Before he knew what was happening, he was crossing the street. A car almost ran him over. He didn't care. Life was worthless, especially his own. He didn't even notice the honking and yelling of the driver. *Maybe I'll just look. That couldn't hurt.* He felt drawn to the restaurant and didn't know why. Like a moth to a flame, it would probably turn out the same way.

****

"Joe, let's get out of here." Top had that look. Joe hadn't seen it in twenty years.

"Huh? What are you talking about?"

"Lunch. It's lunchtime. Most days you just have someone get you a sandwich from the cafeteria. Of course, some days you just skip it altogether. Did you think I hadn't noticed? How much weight have you lost since you came here?"

Joe just shrugged. "I'd love to but ..."

"Don't give me that garbage about too much work. It'll never get done and you know that. Just like the Army. I had to put my foot down there, too. Remember?"

Joe laughed, "So what do you have in mind?"

"How about Taco Barn? Just something simple and miles away from here."

"Well ..."

"I take that as a yes. Get your hat. I'm driving." Excuses were like blank rounds – limited range and no real effect. Joe was still in charge but Top ignored that whenever he wanted to.

Miles away was right. They were practically on the other side of the city before they pulled in. "They've got a new temporary special I've wanted to try. My wife won't come here with me so I had to kidnap you. I hate to eat alone."

Joe knew Top was inventing the motivation but that was something they could both play the ignorant game on, so he said, "My wife and I used to do that. We'd watch the commercials and go when something looked good. We haven't done that lately because of this job. Just one more thing I had to give up for the greater good." The new taco bombs were ready.

"Joe, I've wanted to talk with you about that. You've given up a lot – maybe too much. We both gave this country our best years. You know I've got your back but we should be able to enjoy the simpler life now. Leave our wars behind. It's someone else's turn to give blood."

"I know what you're saying but what if there is nobody else? It's like that old recruiting poster – *If Not You Then Who?* We've both seen what these swamp rats have done with the country we bled for. We need to take it back. Remember that enlistment oath line – 'I will support and defend the Constitution of the United States against all enemies, foreign and domestic?' This is that second part on steroids."

"For a moment, I thought you were going to quote something from the Bible."

"Alright then, how about this. There's nothing said in the Bible about retirement except death. We were put here to work."

"I know all that. I'm just saying don't kill yourself taking this hill. Pace yourself – and quit skipping lunch. Don't make me plant my boot – well, my shoe – on your backside." Joe laughed but Top was straight-faced. *He just might do it.*

The sunshine streaming in the window darkened and Joe noticed a man outside staring in. He saw them staring back so he slowly shuffled to the side door and came in.

Everyone was staring and the shift manager started to come over. The bum had to go. He was upsetting everyone. The stranger reached Joe and Top before the manager did.

"Please sir, can you help me?"

"Look, you can't be in here. Come with me." The manager wanted the stranger gone.

"Sir, please?" The eyes looked watery and his head was tilted toward the floor.

His appeal caught Joe where he lived. "It's okay. I want to hear what he has to say."

"That's all well and good but everyone in here is uncomfortable. He has to go."

"Look, I'll make you a deal. Give him one minute and then he'll leave. Won't you?" he said to the bum.

"Yes sir. I'll go."

"Well it's against my better judgment but I'll give you that one minute." He retreated behind the counter but kept a close eye on the man.

"Well, you're on the clock. One minute – don't waste it," Joe prodded.

As he began, Joe examined him – a jacket torn in numerous places, suede leather shoes badly stained with duct tape holding them together. An African-American, he hadn't shaved in weeks, his Rasta locks hung everywhere. The smell was even worse.

"Sir, I haven't eaten in three days. I used to be somebody but now I'm someone to avoid." His speech was far from the uneducated wino slurring Joe had expected and grabbed Joe's attention.

"I was even a soldier once. I had lots of medals but now ... Anyway, when I looked in the window and saw your Army veteran hat it reminded me of who I used to be. I know you're very busy and thanks for just listening to me. That's more than anyone else has done. I need help. I know that but I don't know what kind. I'm not even sure how I came to be this way. Can you help me? Maybe just your change from lunch?"

Joe glanced at Top. Top was looking down, so it was clearly Joe's play. *There but for the Grace of God go I*. Joe remembered the first time he had seen a beggar and Mom had chewed on him a long time for his uncharitable attitude. He glanced at the manager who was already coming over. The minute was up and he wanted the bum gone.

"Sir, I need to add to my order. Give us a number one combo for our guest."

"He can't stay."

"He *is* staying. Do you want the TV news guys doing a piece on this? Look, in thirty minutes we'll all be gone. It's already late and past the lunch-hour. Most of your customers have already gone back to work so how about giving him a break? This will be your good deed for the month. Oh, and please bring the plate and drink here. We don't want to offend the few customers who are still here."

"No, we don't," the manager said, obviously angry.

"Sit down," Joe directed the desperate man. "Tell me your story. Where are you from? Where did you serve? What happened after you got out? Just give me the short version. Give me your name too. I can't keep calling you 'You'."

"Alright. It's Brad. Brad Paeston. When I was in the Army, I did well. I had a lot of ribbons. I went where they sent me and was proud to do it. I met my wife there too."

"You're married? You have a wife?"

"Had. I loved the Army, but she didn't. She said if I wanted to keep her, I had to get out. It was the Army or her. Well, I made my choice. Nobody's fault but mine. I loved her and she loved me. Life was still good, for a while at least. Then I found out that she married the image, the soldier. The real me was, well, boring."

"I had a few years of college that I picked up in the Army, and I got a job with a paper supply company. Not exactly what I was doing in the Army, but it paid enough. Life seemed good."

"We even had a daughter, Rachel. She must be about seven now. How I loved that child. Every day when I came home, she met me at the door. Daddy! She would scream, and I picked her up and carried her around for the next half hour."

"My wife, Bethenny, well, maybe she was jealous of the attention I gave Rachel. Or maybe she just thought I was spoiling little Rachel. She would get angry often anyhow."

"Put her down," she would say. "Supper's ready. I've been working for hours on it. The least you can do is be ready when I call."

"That always put a damper on the evening. That went on for months. Then one day I came home. No Rachel. No Bethenny. Nobody at all. Just a note. Really brief, too, with no real explanation."

"We're done," she wrote. "That's all it said. I found out later she was living with her sister. I tried to call her. I tried to visit too. That time, her sister had the dog chase me off. Can you imagine? A large german shepherd. She didn't ask for money. She just got one of those 'quickie' divorces. She even produced a forged letter from me giving up all rights."

"I hadn't used drugs in the Army and seldom alcohol. That changed. I went to a bar one night. *Mickey's House of Spirits*, it was called, a neighborhood bar just down the street from where I lived. I became a regular, going there every afternoon and night, till they closed. I don't remember anymore how the drugs started. They just did. I lost the job, the house, the car, and myself too."

"How long has it been?" Joe asked Brad. "How long since all that started?"

"What year is it now?" Brad asked.

"2020."

"I guess it was about four years ago now."

"You've been living on the streets all that time?"

"Most of it, yeah."

"Are you ready for a change?"

"I only wish. Maybe it's too late for me."

"It's never too late."

"Come on. Look at me. I saw you hold your nose when I came over. I'm like the garbage this place throws out. Good for nothing except for some bum like me to pick through."

"It's never too late. You're only garbage if you choose to be. Remember your time in the Army? It wasn't always easy was it."

"Well, no. There were hard times. But I always knew I'd get through it. I had faith."

"And now?"

"Huh?"

"Do you have any faith left?"

"You mean like church and God and that stuff?"

"Yes, like that stuff."

"Well, I still believe but I don't think I have any value to Him. How could I? I don't even value myself."

"That's the real point isn't it? You need to get some self-respect back."

"Hah. That's years in the rear-view mirror."

"It doesn't have to be. Look, if you want to turn this thing around, I can help. I know someone who can help you and he's only a phone call away."

"Man, I'm trying to believe but it's hard. I've been this way so long."

"Just say yes. It's that easy. Say you want to get back your life and I can help you to make it happen. The mission. The Denver Rescue Mission has a program, but it's tough."

Brad couldn't speak. He stared at Joe as his eyes began to

water. The tears were coming fast now. He just nodded. "Please, he said. I'll do anything."

Joe picked up his cellphone and hit the contacts where he found Paul's number. Paul was always busy, so Joe was surprised when he answered the phone. "Hey Paul, this is Joe O'Flaherty."

"Hey Joe, how's it going? I've been meaning to call you. We're just getting ready for the Christmas collection. Only a few months away you know."

"That's great Paul and we can talk about that later. After the ten years my church has been supporting the mission, we're not going to drop the ball now. Paul, I need a favor."

"Sure, anything."

"I just met an Army veteran who's been living on the streets. He's ready for a change. Can you get him in your program?"

"Well, of course I'll have to interview him but we probably can."

"Great! Can you also pick him up?"

"Where?"

"We're at the Taco Barn down on Larimer Street."

"Sure. I can be there in twenty minutes."

"See you then."

Joe looked into Brad's eyes. They were cloudy, his face covered with tears. "Don't drop the ball," Joe warned him. "I went out on a limb but I believe you can do this."

"Oh, I will. I won't let you down."

"One more thing. Here's my card. When you are near completion with the program, you're going to need a job. Call me a few months out. I mean it. Call me. Top here will help me to get you a job. You've got college and are a veteran so we can work with that."

"I...I don't know what to say. I just came in here hoping for a dollar to get a taco. You've given me a life."

"No, I haven't. You'll have to work for this. You took the first step when you came in here and admitted you needed help. Everybody needs help sometime. I may need your help one day."

"Yeah, right."

"No, I mean it. One day, I may ask for a favor. If I don't, just pay it forward and help someone else."

Paul was as good as his word. Nineteen minutes later he pulled up with the white van from the mission. He was of obvious Asian descent, Japanese-American, and he related to all ethnic groups easily. Since he had experienced hard times himself, he related well to those like Brad who need help.

Joe knew that Paul worked far too many hours, but it was his calling and he wouldn't cut back on his time on the job.

"Paul, when he gets near the end of the program, maybe two or three months out, call me. I will try to get him a job so he can really succeed in changing his life. By the way, what's on the menu for supper tonight?"

"Tacos. Why do you ask?"

"No reason," Joe said grinning.

As they walked out, Joe said "You were right, Top, I did need to get out of the office."

Top just shook his head. "This wasn't exactly what I had in mind. But I guess you were right when you said the Bible doesn't provide for retirement. Maybe I'll have to go to that church you keep inviting me to."

Chapter Twenty-Seven

The star-nosed mole was useful, even if it was also a swamp critter. Possessing a star-shaped nose with 22 feelers around the nose, it can't smell but can use the nose to touch and feel its way around. It eats fish and other creatures with backbones. It is also nearly blind. In the same way that the mole uses its star, other critters can help by consistently recommending the wrong action.

The past three years had been long ones. The organization was now on a pay-as-you-go basis. It generated all of its operating funds. Many of the critters were gone. Work production was up. Government customers were happy with the service. Contractors weren't quite as happy since their profits were down, driven by Joe's new approach, but it seemed like a good trade-off.

Joe should have been happy. He felt tired. He also felt apathetic. It had gotten old, real old. But firing people didn't bother him as much as it used to. He was even passing that job off to others in a lot of cases.

"Joe, I'm starting to worry about you." The general wasn't smiling.

"What do you mean?" This was the same old conversation again. Today, it seemed more intense. Joe wanted to avoid it, but the general was blocking his retreat. It briefly reminded him how his grandson did the same thing, in a better time, to keep Grandma and Grandpa from going home.

"I know you don't enjoy firing people. But you also don't seem to hate it like you used to. I don't want you to lose your humanity. You also seem down...maybe even depressed. That's what's got me really concerned."

Joe just shrugged. He knew what the general meant, but he had no response. He had been thinking about it too. The rest of the day dragged on. Joe stared at the computer screen, his mind trying to focus but failing. Glancing at the clock, he realized it was time to go home and he had accomplished almost nothing. Where did the day go? Grabbing his hat and coat, he realized everybody else was gone. It was as if he had zoned out for most of the day. A wasted day. Was that what depression was like?

That night, he caught his wife staring at him. She noticed that something had changed, even if Joe might deny it. "How's the job going?" Dinner was Joe's favorites – tamales, red rice and refried beans with cheese generously applied. Even apple pie. Of course, it was ala mode. Joe was unenthusiastic.

"Oh, alright I guess."

"Umm hmm. Joe, you might not say this to those people you work with. You might even deny it to yourself. But I see a change. You don't talk. You don't laugh. When was the last time you hugged me or kissed me? You aren't the only one paying the price for your service. I'm paying it too."

"I don't know. I guess I just have things on my mind."

"Like the weight of the world? No job is worth it. You're depressed. I can see it even if you can't. You need to talk to someone. I don't want to hurt your feelings but maybe you also need to leave the job. Haven't you done enough? You sacrificed yourself as a soldier, then as a civil servant. Now, it's worse than all of those others put together."

That night, it *was* worse than ever. He was driving the car – a fully restored red 1967 Chevy Impala SS that had belonged to Dad. Suddenly a crowd appeared and lifted the car up off the pavement. They began to pass it back and forth...and Joe was still inside.

"Let me down! Let me down! You can't do this to me. I'll get you! I'll get you all!"

A strong hand reached through the open window and grabbed Joe by the arm, pulling him out. Suddenly, he was awake and Diona had his arm. The dream had seemed so real. He realized both his arms had been flailing in the air and Diona was scared. Not just for Joe but also for herself, also.

****

As Joe and the general worked through the organization, morale dropped among some workers but rose among others. The ones who appreciated the efforts were those who had been working hard, yet saw the promotions go to those who played the politics game well.

It was undeniably a discreet witch hunt, ferreting out those who were not really performing in the work but had managed to stay hidden and rise when nobody was looking. Critters like these were plentiful. It would take ferrets, anteaters, and others who understood the bottom-feeder psychology. If they were not former critters themselves, they at least had to understand those who were.

Three years had passed by and the organization was looking and performing differently. Prices had dropped for its products, while it was now generating all of its costs. Bonuses were fewer, but pride was taking hold.

Joe also had to replace those who "resigned." He made sure that at least one of the members of his staff was on each selection board. He also had Lorna on the interview panel as well. One day, she asked Joe about it. "I've been on twenty panels so far and I noticed that none of those I voted for were selected."

"Have you also noticed that you almost always voted differently from the other panel members?"

"Well, yes, but I've been doing this for years. I know what I'm doing."

"Maybe you're still missing the point. I came to drain the swamp. Not to restock it with new critters. But your service has been useful."

"How? I mean if I voted differently than the others on the panels and none of my preferred hires were actually hired, how did I help?"

Joe had to smile. "Each time you voted and ranked the applicants, I took your rankings and reversed the order. Knowing who you would hire told me who I should not hire."

The very next morning Joe was on his way to work when he saw the car. A tan Lexus that had seen better days was following him. On a high-speed freeway, the car was no more than twenty feet behind him.

As Joe signaled his left turn, suddenly the car shot around him – on the left. Joe braked suddenly, swerving, momentarily losing control and resting on the shoulder of the road. The reckless driver continued on his way, unimpressed by what he had done.

Joe was mad. He was scared, which made him real mad. He

got back on the highway and followed the Lexus. Finding his cellphone, he started to dial 911 to report the incident. Then he noticed the driver was approaching the same place where Joe worked. Curious, Joe followed him. The driver parked in the GSA parking lot and Joe parked two spaces from him.

As the driver got out, Joe said "Do you realize what you did back there? You ran me off the road. You almost killed me. What were you thinking?"

The driver, a young African-American man of about thirty just glanced at him and said "Get out of my way old man! You shouldn't be on the road." He rushed past Joe and on into the building.

Joe took down the license plate number. 518 HRC. When he got in the office, he gave it to Top. "Can we track this plate number down? I think he works in this building. He almost killed me this morning and then had the nerve to say it was my fault."

"Sure. You know I love to go after guys like that. I've been talking to Lieutenant Jack on the Federal Police force. He's an old soldier. Actually, we were stationed together in Germany years ago."

That afternoon, Top had the information. Lieutenant Jack had contacts on the local police force and ran the number 'unofficially.' "The race car driver *does* work here. He's a fairly new intern and works under Eldana. Would you like for me to handle this?"

"No. I will handle this one myself. I need some R & R."

Top watched Joe walk away, his fast pace matching his mood. *I guess that's how I trained him so ...*

As Joe entered the section, he asked where the man worked

and had the cubicle pointed out to him. Joe made sure to walk by the cubicle. "We meet again," he said.

The intern looked at him. After a moment, he recognized Joe as the old man he had run off the road. His eyes widened. "Ah, ah...do you work here?"

"Yes, I do." Joe's smile was huge.

Eldana was expecting Joe and greeted him as he walked into her office. "Hey boss, great to see you!" The intern's cubicle was in earshot of Eldana and Joe smiled, realizing that the intern had heard the greeting. Joe closed the door and sat in the armchair.

"Eldana, you have an intern named Jacob Glantz."

"Yes."

"How's his work?"

"Well, it's spotty. He's new at this but we're trying to get him over the hump. Extra coaching, that kind of thing."

"Don't."

"Huh?" Joe laid it out for her and spared no detail. "Wow!" was all Eldana could say.

"The bottom line is that I want him gone. He's a weak performer so you have cause to do this. Besides being a total jerk, his conduct doesn't seem like the non-swamp quality that we are trying to migrate to. Someday, he's likely to kill someone on the road and we don't want that connected with this agency. Remember when I promoted you, I told you I might need something from time to time?"

"Yes."

"Well, this is it." As Joe left, he detoured past Jacob's desk again. He just smiled. Jacob was without words, so different now from his earlier reaction in the parking lot.

"Jacob, I need for you to go see Noni in Human Resources." Eldana hated stuff like this but also knew Joe's logic was sound.

"Okay. Is there something I need to know?"

"Yes, you'll hear it soon enough. Your employment here is being terminated."

"But why? I'm really trying and I really need this job." He even played the race card. "You and me, we got something in common. Come on sister, give me another chance."

"Don't use that *sister* stuff on me. Officially, you're being terminated because of your weak performance. We have the right to do that during your new employee probation period."

"You said officially."

"Yes."

"What about unofficially?"

"Unofficially, it's for doing something stupid. Do you need me to explain that?"

"No, I guess I know where this is coming from."

Chapter Twenty-Eight

The bunyip was a strange creature, even strange for the swamp. The head of an emu, its body and legs resembled the alligator. In the water it swims frog-like, but on land, it walks upright. It's best known for preying on women and children, either gobbling up the smaller ones or hugging them to death first. It couldn't really exist, could it?

"I want to go out and have a visit with those guys in Denver at GSA." The president had just finished getting another briefing and his chief of staff was glowing – almost an I-told-you-so moment. "That sergeant we sent out there, what's his name?"

"O'Flaherty. Joe O'Flaherty."

"Yes, that's him. This is great. Super. Yuge. I want to give him something. How about a medal? Don't we have some of those for civilians?"

"Well, the President's Award for Distinguished Federal Civilian Service might be appropriate. It could encourage Dr. O'Flaherty and demonstrate your support for him to his employees and the citizens of Colorado."

"I like it. Do it. Make it soon. Oh, and find me a great restaurant with great security. You know what I like. I don't need to experiment with what's fashionable. I just want to be seen by the media. Make it a very ethnic place."

Many critters had suffered under the new regime. "You all know why we're here. It's just a miracle that we're still working."

"Yeah. But what's the point. Even the cake didn't work. I tell you man, that guy has a guardian angel. He's bullet-proof." B.J. had escaped Joe's notice so far. He was hoping to outlast Joe.

"Yes, I know that our previous attempts failed. But we also know our time is short. We finally have a plan – and an opportunity. My contact tells me that the president is coming here. It's a secret but we can count on it."

"What for? Why's he got to come here?"

She laughed. "The Director is getting an award. For all the damage he's caused, he's getting a medal. How do you like that?"

"What's that got to do with anything?" The woman couldn't see any advantage in a presidential visit.

"It means we can embarrass the director and the president at the same time. Better still, we can give the president something he can't ignore."

"So ... what are we going to do?" A swamp critter, her ignorance of strategy showed. In the back "Oedipus" stood up.

The speaker identified him. "Some of us know Mr. Kim but from now on, we'll only refer to him as Oedipus. At work, we can use his name but never, and I mean never, use his code name out there. It's only to be used in strict confidence as we organize this restoration."

Coming forward, Oedipus said "I have military training and I have a plan. Some of you know that I have my own issues too with our director and my time is as short as yours. Here's how it will work. Much will depend on Brandi. She's one of our newer employees."

"Joe doesn't know her, but she has a great resume – however, the real her is a secret. We helped get her on board just for this effort. We're counting on her physical qualifications to be our major weapon. I'm told she's also got some acting classes."

"I don't need to tell you that we'll only get one shot at this. If we fail, we may all be fired and even go to prison. Joe is going to be caught in a compromising situation. He will be showing his true colors as he demands favors from a female employee."

"That's not possible. Haven't you heard – he has a rule that keeps that from happening."

"Yes, yes, we all know. However, there are some situations that can't be helped." Slowly, he laid it out for the group. It seemed foolproof.

****

"Hey Joe. Guess what? You'll never guess. Guess anyway. Come on, guess!" Sam was finally out of breath but the excitement showed.

"Sorry but I'm going to have to pass. So, I guess you're right – I'll never guess."

"The president is coming. Here. Right here. Wow, imagine that. I'll be as close to him as I am to you. I can't wait. I voted for him. Do you think he knows I voted for him? Maybe I can find my campaign button and hat. If I wear that, he'll have to notice me. Do you think he'll notice me?"

"Calm down. Why is he coming here and how do you know he's coming?"

"I just got it from a Secret Service guy. He needed a contact with our security here in the building. Wait ... wait a moment. Okay, here's the email from the aide. Yes, it's true. He's coming."

"*Why* is he coming?"

"Oh yeah, he wants to give you an award. They won't say what it is, but it's all about you. We have to prepare. Do we have any red carpet in the building? What about snacks? What does he like? Will his wife be coming? How about his daughter? They're both awesome! The building needs a good cleaning. I'll get with housekeeping. Need to get the floors waxed – but not too slippery. Wouldn't want him to fall." Joe flashed back to his own accident, here on the very same floors.

"Oh, for ... I don't want an award. I already have a closet full of them from my Army time. Get with the aide. Let's see if we can get this canceled."

"Not on your life! I'm going to put my foot down now and right on top of yours where it will hurt." The general was more than irritated – he was fighting mad and got right up nose to nose with Joe.

"Joe, this is for you but it isn't just about you. It's about all of us. Look around this room. All these people have gone through a lot, right beside you. In the Army, you would've given credit to your unit for any success, wouldn't you?"

"Well, yes. But this ..."

"Is the very same thing. Look, he's coming because of our great successes. We've cleaned most of this swamp. A few critters remain but look at the bottom line. We're now generating our complete budget. The changes you recommended to the GSA director on that trip to D.C – it's doing the same thing across the whole agency."

"This recognition isn't just about you. It's about all of us. If you turn this down, you're telling us that our work hasn't mattered. Why not just slap us and be done with it? It's really the same thing."

"I'm sorry. Thanks for putting me in my place. Of course, you're right. I really appreciate the hard work and sacrifices you've all gone through. You've been in the same bad place as me. Reviled, ignored, and talked about. You've shared in my misery so you deserve as much credit as me and more."

"Okay, Sam, bring it on. Make the arrangements and pull out all the stops. If we're going to do this, let's do it right and better than it's ever been done. But, I want all of you in the front row seats. If I have to do this, you do too."

The laughter lasted a good five minutes and a huge cloud was lifted. Reenergized, the group now had a new mission and purpose.

"How long do we have before his visit?"

"Two weeks."

The day of the visit, everybody was running around, making sure of all last-minute arrangements. Sam hadn't been able to find a red carpet. "I found one that's yellow. I'm sorry boss."

"Yellow? Really? Don't you know? That's his favorite color. He has that in the Oval Office. Get it! You outdid yourself this time."

About that time, Felix called. "Hey, Joe. I know you love cinnamon rolls and we have some made fresh. You should come down and have one."

"Now? I'm pretty busy."

"Yes, I think now would be perfect. I would sure like to talk with you." So strange. Felix had never asked Joe to come to the cafeteria. He seemed to just wait for Joe's visits.

"Well, sure. It's snack time and I could use a break."

Carlos had already coordinated with the cafeteria for the snacks. The potato chips and diet coke were there – cookies for the rest of the visitors. The ceremony would be held in the huge Opus Auditorium. Skylights in the ceiling let in natural light which the many plants, lining the sides of the room, gladly received.

The storage cabinets in the back of the room held essential conference room supplies but were almost invisible. Their wood paneling matched that of the wall covering. The seats were arranged in a semi-circle, elevating towards the rear of the room.

In a pinch, the room could seat 700 people. It was also located next door to Joe's executive suite so he and the president would enter from there, through an ante-room into the auditorium. Equipped with near theatrical-quality sound and lighting fixtures, few places in the state could boast such a facility.

GSA had spared no expense in creating the auditorium under the previous administration. Even the chandeliers in the ceiling boasted an extravagance that the president had seldom seen.

"Joe, did you do this?"

"No, Mr. President. It was done under your predecessor. However, since the money was already spent, I saw no reason not to put it to full use."

"You're right of course. I might need to schedule some meetings out here just to make use of it."

As they entered the stage, "Hail to the Chief" sounded

throughout the room. All of the employees rose to their feet. All was as it should be, and Joe had one of the proudest moments of his life. His staff had really pulled it off.

"Please take your seats," the general said.

"Thank you. Thank you everybody. It's so wonderful to be here in the mountain state and with so many great Americans." The usual speech and usual language showed the president at his finest. Even the leggy aide was there, all part of the show.

"You have all done great work, and I'm here to recognize all of you and your accomplishments. However, your director has to represent you since I only brought one award today." The laughter was genuine.

"Dr. O'Flaherty, come on up here. I've got something to say to you." Standing three feet to the left of the president, Joe assumed an old military posture, erect, feet spread shoulder-width apart with hands interlocked behind his back, and staring dispassionately at the president.

"Your prices have gone down and the soldiers, sailors, marines, and airmen of your country thank you. You have increased your profits so your entire budget is paid out of those profits and the taxpayers thank you. Most of all, you have a new pride in yourselves and we share that pride in you."

Then he nodded to the aide who read the words. "In recognition of his distinguished performance as ..."

Joe zoned out as he waited out the reading of the award. Finally, "the President's Award for Distinguished Federal Civilian Service is awarded to Dr. Joseph P. O'Flaherty."

The lanyard with the medal dangling from his neck was placed there by the president and he tendered a long firm handshake. "Joe, if you would like to share a few words, make them good ones." The laughter that followed was both for the president's comment and for Joe's obvious discomfort.

Smiling big in spite of his attempt at self-control, Joe took the podium. "I would like to thank everyone for their support as we have transformed this agency from..."

Suddenly, a loud noise erupted at the back of the room. A cabinet door popped open and out jumped a ball of fur. Snorting and growling, it charged forward. An overfed raccoon with its tail in the air, charging one way and then another as it looked for an escape, its confusion only increased with the screaming of the employees.

Then it charged the Secret Service agent standing by the door. Two agents tried to catch it, only succeeding in driving it forward, right toward the stage where Joe and the president were.

Two more Secret Service agents sprang into action, jumping in front of the president and forcing him back into Joe's office.

"Calm down! Calm down!" Joe attempted to regain control as the raccoon came within three feet of him and paused, staring first at Brandi and then at Joe, and growling.

Top grabbed the edge of the yellow carpet and threw it over the scared animal. He then rolled it up, trapping the raccoon inside. At the same time, Brandi who had been seated in the aisle near the front, screamed and fell onto the floor.

"Oh, for Pete's sake, what else," Joe said.

Carlos was immediately beside her. "Dr. O'Flaherty, I think she's unconscious. She may have bumped her head when she passed out."

"Alright, call an ambulance – and call animal control too.

Everybody else – I'm sorry for what has happened. We'll be looking into it. Please just go back to work."

"What about her?" Carlos asked.

"Well, we can't leave her here. A couple of you pick her up, carefully, and carry her into my office. Yes, that's right. Lay her down on the sofa. Grab that pillow. Here, use my jacket as a cover."

The ambulance was being delayed so Joe ensured the president was being entertained in the ante-room with the snacks. When the others had left, he sat down at his desk, checking the email and glancing at Brandi.

"Oh, my head," she mumbled.

"Are you awake now? How do you feel?"

"How did I get here? Oh ... that horrible animal. What was it?"

"A raccoon. He was just scared. Probably more scared of us than you were of him. Do you think you can sit up now?"

"Yes. Yes, I'm sure I can." She sat and rubbed the back of her head, covered with shoulder-length strawberry blonde hair. "Wow, I've never had anything like that happen before." Slowly she stood up and smiled at Joe. "Is everybody gone?"

"They're at the reception. We've got an ambulance coming and we need to get you checked out before you return to work."

"Oh, is that really necessary?" she asked, glancing around the room. The back door leading to the auditorium was closed but the front door was open.

"Yes," Joe said. "We want to make sure you're really alright. That looked like a serious fall you had."

"Oh, but look," she said. "I can walk just fine." To prove

it, she walked to the front door. Glancing into the hallway, she reached for the door handle and pulled the door shut. "I've wanted to get with you ever since I started here." She smiled with slightly parted lips and started walking toward Joe.

"I think you might have a wrong idea. I'm married and I intend to stay that way."

"Nobody will know," she said.

Joe put up both hands. "You really need to stop right there. I meant what I said."

Realizing time was short, the actress in her came out. "No, no! Stop!" She screamed as she grabbed the top of her blouse and tore the top button off. She pulled the skirt down slightly and ruffled her hair. Backing to the door, she jerked it open. Several employees were passing just then and watched the unfolding drama.

"Help me!" she yelled at them, tears starting to stream down her face.

Unsure what to do, they just stood there. "Uh, is there anything wrong?" Bill Myers asked.

"Is anything wrong? He attacked me. I bumped my head and then he attacked me when we were alone. I'm engaged and I just want to be left alone. Please help me! Call somebody. Please don't leave me here with him!"

Bill glanced at Joe but was unsure what to do. He was in a bind and looking for a way out.

Everything is fine," Joe said. "In fact, if you would like, you may escort Brandi down to security. She probably has a story she would like to tell them."

"You better believe I do!" She wasn't sure what she expected but Joe's calm wasn't it.

"Of course, if you would like to come back in, I have a show I would like to share with you. What's your name?"

"Bill. Bill Myers sir."

"Well Bill – you are invited too. You and the two ladies with you. In fact, I insist on your attendance. Please come in and have a seat on the sofa. Brandi, are you coming in too or is it just the four of us?"

This wasn't the way it was supposed to be. There was no fear. Joe was as calm as a person could be. He should be at least a little nervous. What did he mean by a show? Curiosity got the better of her and she came back into the office, sitting as far from Joe as she could.

Joe hit a button on his computer and the big screen that he used for briefings came alive. It was all there. Bill and the ladies were just staring. No words came out. They turned and looked at Brandi.

"That wasn't how it was. He must have had this made up before in case he got caught. I'll bet he's been watching me for weeks, just looking for an opportunity. It's all a lie. You know it is."

"Well, yes, I suppose it is a lie," Joe said. Bill was still speechless. "However, you are the one who told it. Brad, come on out."

Brad came out of the executive restroom, holding a soda cup with a straw in it. His time at the mission complete, Joe had hired him one month earlier.

"I thought that would never end. Do you know how hard the john is to sit on for a long time? And the air freshener – Dr. O'Flaherty, you need to get a better one in there. That stuff just smells so soapy."

"If you're done with that rant, tell the folks here what you heard."

Brad repeated the entire exchange, word for word.

"Bill, would you like to leave now?"

"Yes, sir. I think that would be great. Thanks for trusting me on this."

"Thank you for sitting through something that must've been very stressful for you."

Bill nodded and left, laughing all the way down the hall.

"Well Brandi, I'm sure we have a lot to talk about."

"So, what are you going to do – ask me to resign? Fire me? What can you do to me? I've got nothing to talk to you about."

"Actually, I think you need to prepare for living in federally-funded housing. You're going to prison. Top, come on in here."

"Yes, Joe?"

"Have that lawyer come by now. The one we talked with earlier. Also, have two security police come in to watch this critter."

"But, Joe – how did you know?"

"The cinnamon roll this morning ... it was really good."

"What's that got to do with ...?"

"Everything. Have you noticed? Felix never insists that I come to see him. When he did, I knew it was important. It's great to have friends in high places but also in the right places."

The meeting was right to the point. Bob Nielsen the attorney was either windy or brief, depending on the situation. Today was a brief day. After viewing the video, he just raised an eyebrow.

When Brad finished his statement, the attorney said, "Brandi, you're going down. Joe has all he needs to put you behind bars. Conspiracy, fraud, false statements – you'll be lucky to get out before that pretty strawberry blond hair turns white."

The day had started out so nicely. She was on the uphill path and even about to get out from under that threat. Now, she exploded in tears. Joe handed her a tissue but she asked for several more. The acting seemed to be over, so Joe was feeling pangs of guilt in letting her set him up. Still, she did it without his encouragement, so...

Then an idea occurred to him. Why hadn't he thought of it before? Did she have the ability to do this by herself? Joe didn't think so. She seemed to have a talent for acting but not one for strategy. That required someone else. It required intelligence. "Brandi, who was in this with you?"

"What? What makes you think there was someone else?"

"I don't think you have the ability to do something like this on your own. You've heard what the cost is probably going to be. However, if there is someone else behind this, you may even be able to walk away from this."

"No. No, I couldn't. I mean, I did it all. Lock me up."

"Now, I'm sure. Do you know what happens to someone like you in prison? Do you? For the next twenty years, you will always be looking over your shoulder. You will belong to someone else, someone larger, tougher, meaner, and nastier that you ever could be. We will offer you protection if you open up. Of course, the best protection is to put someone else behind bars where they can't touch you. Do you really want to go to prison to protect those who put you in this bind? Are they worth it to you?"

"Hardly that. Yes, there is someone else and I hate them more than you could imagine."

"So? Don't let them do this to you."

"You just don't know. There are at least two of them. Both are meaner than you could ever be. One of them is a witch, I'm sure of it. There's just no way she could do what she does, know what and who she knows, if she wasn't."

"I don't believe in witches or goblins or golems or anything like that. Now tell me and we can put this behind you. Get them before they can get you. Get off your backside and get on the offense. That's the only way you can overcome them."

"Okay." She said the word but it was less enthusiastic than she had been all day. "I'll do it," she whispered.

Brandi was supposed to meet her contact the next day. "How did you get caught up in this anyway?"

"I really don't know. I thought that thing was in my past. I just wanted to get a job and earn my way in the world."

"What was the thing?"

"Do you really need to know? No, scratch that. Okay here it is. I had some financial issues in college."

"And?"

"And ... I had a friend who made some extra money selling these pills. It's not what you think. They weren't the usual kind. These were called "wake up time." They weren't amphetamines but helped with alertness and removed the effects of too much party life and too many late hours cramming for tests. They had caffeine and I don't know what else."

"Anyway, she showed me how to make some extra money with them. Selling them. They weren't on the banned list. They weren't illegal. So, I thought it would be okay. Who could it hurt? It helped students make it through some tough classes – and tough social life too."

"So, what happened?"

"The pills were legal, but selling them on campus wasn't. A security camera caught me and then they set me up. I was charged and put on probation. My lawyer got the charges sealed since it was my first offense. I thought nobody knew about it."

"But somebody did."

"Yes. The witch has tentacles everywhere. I don't know how she does it."

"Sounds like an interesting person I would like to meet."

"No. She's not someone anybody in their right mind would want to meet."

"So where and when is the next meeting?"

"Tomorrow at eleven o'clock." It's at *Billy Joe's Mountain-top Biker Bar*."

"Biker Bar? Are you sure? Why there?"

"Why not?" Brandi replied. "It's out of the way. There's a place in the back with enough privacy. We're able to talk there and not be seen. The bikers leave us alone. If they ever try to get close, the witch just stares them down. Then there's DK. He backs her up if needed."

"What's the DK for?" Joe asked.

"I don't know. That's all I ever heard."

"Okay. Well here's what we want you to do. Just show up like normal. Meet with them. You'll be wearing a wire and we can hear all that is going on. Just tell them that it's all hush-hush for now, but that it worked just like they planned.

Tell them that you reported it. Get their reaction. Ask them if you're free now."

"Dr. O'Flaherty?"

"Yes?"

"You watch yourself," Brandi cautioned him. "She's got this thing about men in general and she especially hates you."

"But I don't even know her."

"Maybe. Maybe not. In any case, she hates you and she'll use magic or any other evil tool to get you. I know she's a witch. She has to be to do what she does. The rest of us – we're just tools to get to you. You're the one she wants."

The meeting would come off just as planned – at least for Joe. The witch would have another experience. Joe couldn't wait to meet her.

****

The bar was one of those places you drive by and never see. The fading paint on the exterior brick highlighted the old sign for *Mama Dora's Bakery* that had been there for years, going back to the 1930s.

Joe wondered what Mama Dora would think about the current clientele. He decided that she would probably come out from behind the counter and pray over them. She'd then tell them to get along home and behave themselves.

Joe arrived early and found a quiet booth near the back. He wanted to be able to hear the conversation. He had on a wide-brimmed cowboy hat. He seldom wore the old Stetson, but today he needed to not be seen. A large, well-worn coat with the collar turned up helped. A large soda and chili-cheese nachos completed the camouflage.

Brandi came in and glanced around. She didn't see Joe so

she seemed anxious. Taking a seat in her usual place, she was only two booths down from Joe. The wait was short. Two others came in and sat with her.

"Well, how did it go?" the man asked.

"Just like you said it would."

"Just a minute the old woman said. This place is usually quiet and empty. That guy back there."

"So what?" DK commented. "He's just an old cowboy. See how sweat-stained that hat is? See that gray, scraggly beard? Let him alone and he'll leave us alone."

"Alright," the woman said.

"You were about to say," DK prompted again.

"Well, I did what you said. He was nice to me but I started screaming and ran out the door. Several people were there. Joe seemed embarrassed so I just continued yelling and then crying. Two security guys came in and offered me a glass of water. They asked Joe if he would mind leaving the office so they could talk to me. He told them that it was his office. They insisted and he left. He seemed to be getting mad."

"After I told them my story, one of them called the Equal Opportunity woman and she came down. I told her too and she was very understanding. 'Don't worry,' she said. 'We'll get this resolved. There's no reason anyone should have to put up with that.'"

"Well, sounds like this was successful. DK, I had my doubts, but now I guess they were misplaced. After all these years. Finally, it's done."

"Ma'am, am I off the hook now? Can I go?" Brandi asked.

"Yes, I think you played your part beautifully. You should think about moving to Hollywood."

"Great! I'm so relieved."

"I bet."

"Can I ask you a question?"

"What is it?"

"Why do you have it in for him? Why did you want to get Joe?"

"That's none of your business."

Joe decided this was a good time to enter the conversation. He looked up from his nachos and said, "Maybe not, but I think it's *my* business."

"What?"

Joe stood and removed his hat. Then he smoothed down the ruffled beard. Walking over, the witch saw him." He saw her about the same time. It now made more sense.

"Hello Mara. Been a long time." DK, I presume, or should I call you Major Doug Kim? So, Mara, you were about to say why you had it in for me. Why now? It's been years since I worked under you and suffered your abuse, your lying about my job performance. You drove me out of my job. Did you just wake up one night and decide you had left something undone?" There it was again. It had been years but Joe remembered the hatred in her eyes. He was clearly hitting close to home.

"Well, at least we got you this time!"

"Actually, no. You didn't. This was a setup. Just like you set me up, I returned the favor. We put a wire on Brandi and have it all on tape."

"You did this to us? Why you little ..."

"Easy now. She gets to walk. You don't. We've got some federal police outside. Conspiracy, fraud, the list goes on. But you still haven't told me Mara. Why now?"

"Ha. A lot you know. Do you remember the problems you had at GSA? How you couldn't get a promotion at the VA? Then there's Kim. Remember the fun you had with him?"

"Are you saying that you ... that all of that ... it was you?"

"Ah, the eyes suddenly clear up."

"But why? Why me now?"

"Simple enough – you were the one who got away."

"That's it? Just because you couldn't terrorize me like you did all the others? That's why you did all this? I still don't understand."

"That day, they made me change your evaluation. *Nobody* ever did that to me. I knew then I had to break you. What did you do? You left. But I wasn't done with you."

"So, it's all been about revenge? About getting me because you tried to cheat me on an evaluation and failed? All these years of failure and bouncing around to escape one bad situation after another. You were obsessed with me because you failed to break me. That was why all this happened?"

"Yes, I guess that's pretty much it, though you make it sound so small. Every night I wake up with you on my mind. I want a good night's sleep. Bringing you down would have given me that."

"Well, I do have to hand it to you. You were effective if also vicious. So how did you do it? What I mean is, how did you get so many people to do your bidding?"

"I have a lot of friends and even more people that I have information on. Like everyone else, I needed a hobby. You were mine."

"Wow! Do you know, you had Brandi here believing you are a witch?"

"Maybe I am. Who cares?"

Chapter Twenty-Nine

The duck peeked around the fallen log, always alert for danger. Seeing none, she emerged, her six babies close behind in single file. This place had been very dangerous. Now, the peril seemed a distant memory. Still, it didn't hurt for her to be careful. One never knew when the vicious critters might return.

The revolt had been put down and there was every reason to be confident of success and to be at peace. The swamp was cleaned out for the most part. Only useful critters remained. It was beginning to look more like a beautiful forest than a swamp. Work was getting done, GSA was paying its way for the first time in its history, and morale was high.

Now, the workers were the ones who had love of country at the top of their daily to-do list. The ones who greedily pursued filling their wallets before considering any patriotic thoughts were long gone.

"Joe, I didn't think you could do it. I never imagined." Terri's down-east accent was filling the office as it always did when she got excited. "I'm so proud of you and so proud to have seen it happen. You could have been a Marine." From her, that was high praise.

"But, what will you do now? You need a challenge and when the mission is accomplished, you are going to get restless.

I know you and I know you won't be happy just sitting around, drinking your tea, and letting things happen around you."

"You're probably right. Actually, I know you are. But I also haven't been released from my agreement to do this job until it's complete. You of all people know that the boss gets to tell us when it's done."

She just stared, then nodded her head. That little action told more than words ever could. She knew, and Joe knew, that a soldier without a mission is at odds with the world and likely to get into trouble. Even when Joe was in his office alone, the music playing told others his mood. People like Joe don't play *Danny Boy* for no reason.

****

The day was sunny, the birds were singing, and the smell of fresh-mowed grass filled the air. Joe knew this was the calm before the storm and only bad could come from it.

The old soldier knew that good weather brings bad things just as bad weather brings peace in the conflicts of man. Top used to say, "It never rains *on* the Army. It only rains *in* the Army."

Joe wasn't disappointed as Diona met him for breakfast before he left for the office. "Joe, I'm afraid I have some bad news."

"Oh, what's up?"

"It's back."

"It? What do you mean?"

"It's hard to say the word. The doctor called me yesterday about the lab tests. I'm not sure how to say it except, the cancer is back. The remission is over."

"Oh." The word was so short, so unfeeling, so inadequate.

What does someone say at this time? Her mother had it and passed far too young. Now, well what *does* one say? That confusion was even more irritating than the pain he knew they were both feeling.

"Aren't you going to say anything? I know you've had it rough lately, but really can't you at least say *something?*"

"*We've* had it rough. I'm sorry. I'm so sorry. All these years in the Army. My battle wound. Then all that stuff in the uncivil service. I think it's nearly over. But we're supposed to have some time for us too. This isn't right. It just isn't." He was holding her hand and she looked up, her eyes filling with tears. Joe had them too.

His mind was still on Diona when he arrived at the office. The drive was a blur and Joe wondered how he had gotten there. Still in a fog, he walked inside and ignored the greetings. Today, he hated the job more than ever. He was still thinking of Diona, when Carlos cornered him.

"Joe, do you remember Jake Smithers?"

"No, should I?"

"Yes. You fired him."

So many removed, they began to look like each other, even visiting Joe in his dreams.

"Describe him."

"Well, medium height far too well fed, and this little goatee that was gray on one side and black on the other."

"Oh yeah, kind of looked like a skunk. What about him?"

"He was one of those in the protest group this morning. I think that agreement he signed required silence on his part in order to not be prosecuted for what he did. Being in the protest group probably violates that."

"Yeah, he probably wouldn't be there without having said something. I guess he's not just handing out donuts and coffee. So, what do you recommend?"

"We should send him a letter from the attorney advising him that he's in breach of his agreement and to cease and desist or face legal action."

"Sounds good. While we're at it, go by and take some pictures of the group. If any others are out there that were fired and signed the same agreement, send them the same letter."

"Hey, I have an idea. Send a letter to all the terminated employees and remind them that if they or any family or friends are participating or otherwise disclosing the conditions of their separation, GSA will be filing legal action. I'll bet there's quite of few of them out there on their own family and friends plan. Maybe a letter will thin the herd somewhat."

A few months later, the protests had not stopped. Now, the president was taking heat for the swamp cleaning. "The media is hitting me pretty hard. Talk to me about those terminations," he phoned Joe. "Are they all necessary?"

Diona's condition, the protesters, and now a chewing-out by the boss. This was all getting to be more than Joe could handle. Worse of all, he lacked the desire to handle it.

"Well, you sent me here to drain the swamp, Mr. President ... These are definitely swamp critters I've been after. Each one either opposes you, your policies, or supports your opposition. They have wasted government money in one fashion or another and all are focused on themselves. Each one has been researched to find their culpability. They financially support your enemies. Their removal reduces the amount of financing available to those people."

"I told you when you sent me here that there would be a lot of pushback from the workers, and that I would need for you to have my back. You said you would. Mr. President. You don't really think any of these people voted for you, do you?"

"I'm out here in my hip boots, snaring, hooking and removing them from the swamp. We are draining the water, diverting it to the ocean, and reclaiming the land for the people of our country. As we reclaim the land, we restock it with productive livestock and environmentally friendly wildlife."

The president seemed satisfied. However, Joe remembered the adage, "When elephants stampede, it's the smaller animals that get crushed." Joe knew he was going to get trampled if he stayed long enough. But he also knew he couldn't leave till the job was done.

A month later, the president gave Joe a hint of what was coming when he asked Joe, "If you had to leave at some point, who would you nominate as your successor?"

"Well, I guess it would be Terri, my deputy. She was here before I got here so she's part of the old crew. However, she knows how to work a large group with the highest finesse but also would be prepared to crack the whip as necessary. She would be my recommendation to overcome political issues."

"Now, keep in mind, she is not going to reform the organization along your lines but would keep the swamp from overflowing its banks. Probably more to your point, she would reduce the complaints."

"That's good. That's really good!"

"Is there something I should know?" Joe asked hesitantly.

"No, no. I just like to have a backup plan. And a backup to

the backup. You have a good day and get out there and continue draining your part of the swamp!"

Like any good political appointee, Joe always had his resignation letter ready to submit upon the president's request. The president hadn't actually requested it, but then it was a two-way street. He had agreed to take on this job as an act of public service. If he was no longer to be free to do what was in the national interest, maybe it was time to go.

Joe told the general about the conversation. They both nodded, knowing what it really meant.

"Please let the others know, he told the general. No reason to surprise them with the news when it happens. We both know what's coming." The general was looking forward to returning to Pennsylvania where he could be closer to his children and some ancient roots.

Joe knew the end was coming and he just didn't care. It was as if he'd been sentenced to prison and his eligibility for parole was approaching. He could almost hear a judge.

"Dr. Joseph O'Flaherty, you've been accused of excessive patriotism and found guilty. There can be no excuse. You are hereby sentenced to three years in the slammer. Maybe four years, but this court will decide later how long we want to hold you. There will be no appeal, no recourse, and no public statements. So, pick up your rock hammer and report for duty."

It was that realization that took hold of him and reinvigorated him. The time to resign had not yet come – but it was coming. It was also time to tie up some loose ends.

****

Joe said, "Oh, and by the way, I'll also give you administrative leave for the rest of the day – just like you gave me once."

It was time to finish draining the swamp once again. Joe had called in the avatar. He felt no satisfaction. There was no sense of getting even or even of a wrong being righted. It was simply something that had to be done. The swamp had to be drained.

Being a hatchet man had never been his goal in life. Yet, here he was, using a hatchet to cut out a trail through the swamp to the pools that had to be drained.

"Please, forgive me, the Avatar pleaded. I've done what you asked and more. I'm really sorry for what I did in the past. I thought it was the right thing at the time. I didn't realize you would be hurt so much. I've always had a very high respect for you, Joe. I've even started going to Church lately. Can't you forgive me? Please?"

"Yes. I forgive you. After all, I have a lot to be forgiven for too."

"Oh! Thank you! Thank you so much!"

"I said I forgive you and I do. But I still want your resignation or retirement."

"What! But you said ..."

"Yes, I said I forgive you for what you did to me. But I never came here to get even. I came to drain the swamp."

"Thirteen years ago, you were handed a pearl and you threw it into the pigpen. I've seen nothing to indicate that you are changed from the swamp critter you've always been. For that reason, I need to see you gone from here. "At least you are qualified for retirement benefits and at the highest grade. That's more than you left me with."

"So, these last three years have been for nothing?"

"No, not at all. You received three more years pay at the undeserved high salary of $150,000 per year. You received three more years to bulk up your retirement pension."

"You're leaving with a pension after discriminating against better people than you, as well as facilitating fraud. You get the opportunity to finally do something worthwhile and leave GSA much better off with people who actually want to work, people who want to serve."

"But I've worked hard here. That episode was so long ago. You recovered and moved on. It really never hurt you."

"No, actually it broke me. I took a downgrade to leave GSA and never again asked for a supervisor position. It almost destroyed my marriage. You were accuser, judge, jury, and executioner. You did it all. No right of appeal. Not even a right to discuss it. I didn't even have the right to face my original accuser. You took a rumor, didn't validate it by asking me, and punished me."

"There are always two sides to an issue. But you hate Christians, don't you? Who is intolerant here? Is it me or is it you? I was never unfair to anybody. Even if I disagreed with them, I was professional about it."

"You took your hatred for those of us who believe and applied it to me, ignoring all that I had done for you before. I made you look good as a supervisor. I gave you opportunities to excel. I even mentored you when you were first starting out. I hope it's worth the loss of your humanity and your soul. Also, that thing about going to Church – I hope it's true, but I really don't buy it."

****

The last critter terminated was the human resources specialist who had been working with Joe on the swamp draining project. She had been involved also in Joe's removal many years before.

What she did was wrong but also only what she was told to do. Of course, she had also seemed to enjoy it. As she came in, Joe laid the forms before her. She was surprised to see her name on them.

"You know the drill. You can retire today or we can prosecute. I know you were only doing what you were told to do. However, you did do it. You violated the First Amendment of the Constitution, not to mention countless laws and executive directives that are still in force. I hope you will choose retirement over jail."

As tears welled up, she said "This just isn't right. I've served for over thirty years. I've helped you to do things that I didn't think were right. Now, it's my turn? What kind of person are you?"

Joe was beginning to wonder the same thing. However, the mission was still in force. "What's your decision?"

She bent over and signed each document. Straightening up, she just paused to stare at him for a long time. Joe stared back. Without a word, she turned around and walked out. Joe could see the shaking of her figure, more hunched over now, as she left.

The following Friday, Joe was watching the protesters. The president was calling for him again. After that last call, this was unlikely to be a pat on the back.

"Joe," the president said, I think you've completed the mission that I sent you there for. Maybe it's now time to hand it off to someone else?"

Joe didn't argue. He had been expecting this call. Truth

be told, he even prayed for it to come. "Mr. President, thank you for this final opportunity to serve. May God bless you and America!"

"Yes. Yes of course. Good luck to you Joe."

Opening the letter, he entered the current date and posted an electronic signature to the letter. Reviewing it one last time, he saw the words, "Effective immediately."

As he posted the document into the email, he paused and looked out the window of his top-floor office. The sun was shining with a few clouds meandering across the sky. It was a beautiful day.

When he had retired only a few years before, he planned to be a writer of children's books. After the past years, that lifestyle beckoned to him more than ever.

"What a nice day to take a dog for a walk," he thought aloud. Getting up from his chair, he greeted the general for the last time. "It's been great! Don't know if I'll see you again but maybe in Church, hmm?"

Now, the heavy rain had come – accompanied with large hail. The streets had emptied. Another prayer answered. The streets were empty. It would be an easy trip home with nobody wanting to talk to him. The end had come.

Sometimes those who enter the swamp do not find their way out. Joe had taken his compass with him. Without the general and Top, and the others, he knew he would have lost his way. For a time, he did, even with them.

Joe didn't feel defeated, though. Why should he? He hadn't been defeated at all. He had won an important victory over the swamp. Now he could do what he had set out to do twenty years earlier. He wanted the quiet life of a writer.

The swamp and the president had released their hold on him. The Army too. He was free! At last, Joe understood. We will never be rid of the swamp because *we are part of the swamp.*

The swamp had proven resilient. It wasn't that it could not be drained or overcome. Quite simply, it existed because of its inhabitants. The swamp had contained bureaucrats, self-interested employees, politicians, and hangers-on – all of them ego-driven critters.

However, the most resilient aspect of the swamp was not these, which were simply bumps in the road. The real critters were the rest of them. The people who demanded services, benefits, programs, good paying jobs, and so many other things, and cared so little about what was happening around them and in the government. They demanded these many things and so much more.

Even a strong political leader cannot indefinitely ignore their hue and cry. They demand reform and then when they get it, they don't really want it. The swamp could not be overcome because *we are the swamp.* As the saying goes, we usually get the kind of government we deserve.

Joe couldn't just leave. He felt free but he owed a lot to others. The people who had backed him deserved thanks at the very least. When they were assembled in his last hour on the job, he began: "Ah, gentlemen, I have a few words of parting." Joe almost unconsciously assumed a brogue that was thick and brought smiles to everyone, an affectation he had almost never used before.

"There's an old Irish proverb," Joe said, "A good friend is like a four-leaf clover, 'ard to find and lucky to 'ave." That's 'ow I feel now. I've just been fired and I couldna' be happier." The audience were all laughing. The stress had taken its toll on all of them but especially on Joe. He was the one who had been the principal focus of the hate generated by his enemies.

Joe continued, "We've known this was a comin'. It had to come sooner or later, and today is a fine day farr it. I love all of you and I don' know whether I'll ever see you again. I 'ope so but today my retirement begins again and anew."

"Terri will be taking over, at least farr the short term but maybe a wee bit longer too. If you want to leave, 'tis a good day to do it. If not, get with Terri and discuss your options. We've drained this particular swamp and returned it to the people. Be proud of what we've done." He gave a firm handshake and hug for each and he was done.

"Time to walk the dog," he said out loud to nobody in particular. Walking out the door, he glanced down the hallway and saw it. All of the employees were lined up. There were hundreds of people and they were clapping.

Tears were unavoidable now as Joe lost control of his feelings. The general had put the word out, and they weren't going to let Joe go without telling him how they felt. Turning to the general, he said, "You did this? But why? I just wanted to sneak out and be done."

"It doesn't work that way as you well know, Joe. It isn't fair to those who have supported you or our work. Now, it's time to pay them back for their loyalty and hard work. Get to it Sergeant!" The old general was smiling. Joe had been like a son and the pride he felt in him was overflowing.

Leaving the building for the last time, Joe felt like he had just dropped his forty-pound rucksack after a twenty-mile road march and collapsed on top of it. The bliss of a well-deserved rest clouded out all other pain.

He could now forget the strain of the past twenty years. Let someone else carry the burden.

The dog. He could now walk his dog, after he finally found one, and spend his days on peaceful walks in the park with his second-best friend. Of course, Diona would always be number one.

As Joe drove away, he heard a loud hissing sound. Imagination? Looking in his rearview mirror, he saw, or did he, a half dozen snakes slithering back into his old building. The swamp was returning to its old self.

There must be something better I can do with my time. Organized crime, counterfeiting, or even robbing a bank. At least he could feel cleaner. Hey, maybe even writing. The only other job that paid people to lie was politics. Joe might have to think on that. Now, though, it was time for quality time with Diona. After forty hard years, it was past time and more than earned.

CPSIA information can be obtained
at www.ICGtesting.com
Printed in the USA
LVHW030740210221
679521LV00001B/55